Lourdes: The Original File by a Skeptic Turned Believer

Lourdes:

The Original File by a Skeptic Turned Believer

J.B. Estrade

Translated from the French by
J.H. Le Breton Girdlestone M.A. OXON

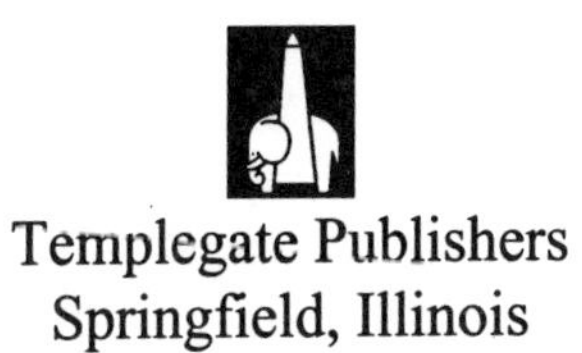

Templegate Publishers
Springfield, Illinois

First published in the United States of America by:

Templegate Publishers

302 East Adams Street

Post Office Box 5152

Springfield, Illinois 62705

217-522-3353

www.templegate.com

ISBN 0-87243-244-0

Library of Congress Catalog Card Number: 99-71180

Published originally in Ireland by

Clonmore & Reynolds

Manufactured in the United States of America

CONTENTS

FIRST PART

CONTENTS

SECOND PART

INTRODUCTION

ORIGIN OF MY BOOK.

AT the time of the Appearances I was living at Lourdes, employed in the Government office of "*contributions indirectes.*" * The first reports which came to me from the grotto left me utterly indifferent; I looked upon them as old women's tales, and took no interest whatever in them. Meanwhile the popular excitement went on growing from day to day, nay even from hour to hour; the inhabitants of Lourdes, especially the women, went in crowds to the rocks at Massabieille, and subsequently narrated their impressions with an almost delirious enthusiasm. The simple faith, the intense emotion of these good people filled me with pity, but nothing else; I laughed at them and ridiculed them, and without study or examination or any sort of enquiry into the matter I continued indifferent up to the time of the seventh Appearance.

On that day, never to be forgotten, the Immaculate Virgin, by methods hidden from me then, but recognised by me now in all their tenderness and care, drew me to her, took me by the hand and, like an anxious mother who puts her child again upon the right way, led me to the grotto. There I saw Bernadette in all the mysterious glory of her ecstasy. It was a scene of heaven, beyond all power of words to describe. Conquered by the evidence, I bent the knee and offered up to Her, Whose presence I felt, the first homage of my faith.

All my prejudices vanished instantly; not merely did my doubts all disappear, but from this moment a secret impulse drew me invincibly to the grotto. As soon as I had arrived there I mixed with the crowd, and showed my wonder and belief

* The "*contributions indirectes*" are the taxes levied by the French Government on such things as drinkables, salt, sugar, matches, tobacco, etc.

with the others. When the duties of my employment took me away from Lourdes—as happened from time to time—my beloved sister, who lived with me and who followed on her own account with devout attention the events of Massabieille, used to describe to me upon my return in the evening what she had seen and heard during the day, and we then recorded our joint observations. I wrote them down under their date in order to forget nothing, and thus it happened that at the end of the fifteen visits promised by Bernadette to the Lady of the grotto we had a little treasure of notes, not put into order but trustworthy and authentic, which we valued most highly.

The facts we ourselves witnessed did not however give us an entire knowledge of the marvellous events of Massabieille. Apart from the story of the young seer which I heard from her own lips at the office of the commissary of police, of which I shall speak later, I knew very little about the first Appearances, and the incompleteness of my notes troubled me much. An unexpected circumstance however happened which calmed my uneasiness and gave me the help I wanted. Bernadette after her ecstasies often came to my sister's house; she was our little friend, very intimate with us, and I was free to question her. We used to ask all possible information from her, the most exact and detailed—and the dear child used to tell us everything with the simple unreserve which was her most characteristic trait. Thus it is that I have gleaned, amongst a thousand other things, the touching details of her earlier interviews with the Queen of Heaven.

The special characteristic of my book then is that—except for some small details—it contains nothing but the *résumé* of Bernadette's own statements and the perfectly accurate account of what my sister and myself personally saw.

Doubtless in such important events there are some things which escape the most attentive observer. One cannot see and hear everything, and the historian is sometimes obliged to have recourse to the information of others. I have made enquiries all around me, and I have thoroughly sifted everything in order to separate the chaff from the wheat, and to avoid admitting into my story anything not absolutely true. And after making my selection I have retained scarcely anything but what I heard from my principal witness, Bernadette, and what I and my sister saw for ourselves.

* * * * *

During the whole period of the Appearances the town of Lourdes was a centre of religious joy and fervour. Then suddenly the horizon looked dark; a sort of dread gripped all hearts and one was conscious of the coming storm. And after a few days the storm broke out. The high officials of the State and the powers of hell seemed to enter into a conspiracy to drive away the Virgin from her lowly country dwelling on the banks of the Gave. The grotto was closed. During four long months I was the sad spectator of the sequestration placed upon that miraculous spot. The people of Lourdes were consternated. At length the storm ceased; in spite of threats, interdictions and lawsuits the barriers were taken away and the Queen of Heaven resumed possession of the humble throne she had chosen for Herself. And now to-day, more than ever, it is there that She, triumphant and glorious, receives the enthusiastic homage of the multitudes who crowd to her from all parts of the world.

I give later on in the course of my history details of the annoyance and measures of obstruction directed against the work of the grotto. I quote the name of the Government officials who planned and carried out this miserable undertaking. These officials, nearly all of whom I knew, were not hostile to religion. They were in the wrong I allow, but I believe that they were in good faith and had no intention of insulting the Mother of the Saviour. I merely narrate their acts; I do not attempt to pass judgment upon their intentions, which are known to God alone.

As to the machinations of the spirits of evil, I simply state them. It is the business of the theologians to judge them.

* * * * *

In noting down the incidents of all sorts which occurred beneath the rock of Massabieille I had no other end in view but that of satisfying personal inclination; I wished to have at hand a private and permanent memorial, a souvenir which would recall for me myself those sweet and gentle emotions which had flooded my soul and subdued it at the grotto. I had never dreamt of publishing one word of anything. Under what considerations, or rather under what influences, have I been induced to change my opinion ? I must tell the reader how it came about.

Since 1860, the year when I left Lourdes, scarcely a single summer has passed without my coming to the grotto to pray there to the holy Madonna and to revive the happy memories of the past. At every interview which I had with Father Sempé, the good superior of the missionaries, he pressed me to put into order my work upon the subject of the Appearances and to allow it to see the light. The pressure put upon me by the saintly man troubled me, for Father Sempé was the instrument of Providence, and I was always struck with the wisdom of his words and works, bearing as they did so visibly the impress of the Spirit of God. The house of Massabieille under his direction was all alive with love and harmony, with ardent zeal for the salvation of souls. The rule was observed there, not so much under the master's compulsion as under the influence and example of his striking goodness. Outside the house the works initiated by him were remarkable. The splendours with which he has adorned the hill of Massabieille would alone be sufficient to do honour to a man whose ambition was limited to earthly glories. The talisman wherewith Father Sempé obtained protection for his enterprises and success for his projects was the rosary. The rosary never left his hands, and when in public devotions he recited the invocations, the souls of all those present felt themselves lifted up to heavenly regions. " All for God " ; such was the motto of his life, and this motto was uttered by his lips at the very hour of his death.

By the side of Father Sempé, in the house of Massabieille, lived a man of charming personality, of profound learning, simple and modest as the humblest religious. His bright and pleasant face, his charm of manner and conversation, inspired sympathy and respect. This man, a layman, was none other than the learned doctor Baron de St. Maclou. Indignant at the bad faith of irreligious and hostile newspapers in regard to the miracles wrought by the power of the Virgin, he came to the grotto to make himself the Christian apologist. Appealing to the help and loyalty of his medical brethren he invited them all, no matter what opinion or belief they might hold, to study with him the marvels which took place in the waters of Massabieille. This appeal was heard, and the "*Bureau des constatations,*" established at this date and for this purpose, has gradually developed into an important centre for consultations. It is there that each year at the time of the pilgrimages *savants* of every kind are to be seen, notabilities belonging to heretical sects, sceptics obstinate until then in their unbelief, bowing their reason, abjuring their errors and returning to their old beliefs on coming into contact with the supernatural facts that take place beneath their eyes.

The reader will forgive me for having apparently wandered away from my subject in recording the virtues and the work of Father Sempé and Baron de St. Maclou, but I wish to record my deference and respect for these eminent men and the influence they rightly exercised upon me. Yet I resisted all their appeals. The good doctor, following the example of the venerable Father Superior of the grotto, urged me strongly to publish my souvenirs of the Massabieille Appearances. It cost me much to refuse, but I always answered him, and also Father Sempé, by saying that I felt myself unequal to the great dignity of the subject.

At length a moral authority, one who is in the very first rank of the French episcopate and whom I felt I could not disobey, scattered my scruples to the winds and conquered my obstinacy.

In 1888, at one of the yearly visits which I made to Lourdes, Father Sempé introduced me to Monseigneur Langénieux, Archbishop of Reims, who was at that moment with the Fathers in the Bishop's chalet. The illustrious prelate welcomed me very kindly and did me the honour of inviting me to his table. There were present the Archbishop and his secretary, Father Sempé and myself. At the beginning of the conversation the Archbishop turned to me and said, "It seems that you are one of the favoured witnesses who were present at the grotto Appearances?"

"Yes, monseigneur, unworthy though I am, the Virgin deigned to grant me that privilege."

"At the end of the meal I will ask you to tell us the impressions which you have retained of those great and glorious events."

"Willingly, monseigneur."

When the time came, I told the archbishop about some of the scenes which had most impressed me.

" The facts," he replied, " of which you have just told me are truly wonderful, but we want more than words ; we want your narrative to be printed and given to the world with your signature and supported by your accredited position as a witness."

" Monseigneur," I said, " allow me to observe in all humility that I should be afraid, in acceding to your desire, of tarnishing the story of the Virgin's work and injuring the faith of the pilgrims."

" How so ? "

" Because I have no literary skill, and to do what you ask of me I should need the competence of an experienced author."

"We do not ask you to write as an experienced author but only as an honest man ; that is all we want."

I could not but yield to the kindly but insistent demands of Monseigneur Langénieux, backed up as they were by Father Sempé, and I promised to carry out what was asked of me. Much as it has cost me, and conscious though I am of my incapacity, I am carrying it out to-day.

And now, gracious Virgin of the Grotto, I lay down my pen at your feet, only too happy to have been allowed to stammer out your praises and record your benefits. In offering you the homage of my humble work I renew my most fervent prayers to you, and especially that one which I addressed to you in narrating in this book your seventh Appearance, of which I was the privileged witness.

" Mother, my hair is white, and I am near the grave. I do not dare to look upon my iniquities, and more than ever do I feel the need of taking refuge under the cloak of thy mercy and thy pity. When at the last great hour I have to appear before thy Divine Son, vouchsafe to be my protectress and to remember that thou hast seen me on my knees and believing, beneath the sacred vault of thy grotto at Lourdes, in those holy happy days when thou didst reveal thyself to Bernadette, and through Bernadette to me."

J. B. ESTRADE.

FIRST PART.

CHAPTER I.

LOURDES.

THE little town of Lourdes, the name of which has become so popular, was scarcely known at the time of the Appearances. It is situated at the south-west of the department of the Hautes Pyrénées, at the entrance to the gorge which branches off to the several thermal stations of Cauterets, Saint Sauveur and Barèges. When the traveller from Tarbes stops at the station of Lourdes he suddenly catches sight of the little town of Mary on the south, situated in a verdant hollow, with the nearer mountains forming a picturesque background. An old citadel standing out on a precipitous rock protects the town at the west and makes, with the group of white houses spread out at its feet, a very striking feature in the picture and one full of contrasts. But the traveller, whether tourist or pilgrim, following the promptings of his inmost thought, seeks something else. And it is also on the west but a little further off that he soon discovers a spire, slender and graceful, which rises boldly up to heaven. This spire marks the grotto and basilica of our Lady of Lourdes.

If the traveller comes from Pau the scene is quite different. After having crossed a narrow gorge he enters a picturesque valley with the mountain of Jer and the grey walls of the old castle for a background ; on the right the valley is hemmed in by a clump of rocks, and on the left by green hills rising in tiers like an amphitheatre. In the centre of this picturesque valley, through which wind the blue waters of the Gave, stands out as white as mother-of-pearl the graceful basilica surmounted by its soaring spire ; at its feet are the great balustrades which surround the newly-built church of the Rosary. The eye looks upon a crowd of monasteries and convents on all sides, forming as it were a crown round the sanctuary of the Immaculate Virgin. Finally we come to the venerated grotto itself, the scene of so many miracles. If it is night, and especially the night of some great pilgrimage, it is lit up by a thousand torches, which give to the little valley the appearance of a scene from fairyland.

Lourdes, the former capital of the country of Lavedan, has a population of about 6,000 inhabitants. Although it is now but a simple *chef-lieu de canton*, it shares with Argelès the prerogatives of a *chef-lieu d'arrondissement*. It has neither the *sub-prefecture* nor the *recette particulière* of the treasury, but on the other hand it possesses a *tribunal de première instance* and contains the head offices of various public services. At the time of the Appearances, a platoon of infantry guarded the castle and two or three companies of cavalry occupied a district some hundred yards away from the town.

The people of Lourdes, like all southerners, are intelligent and lively. They speak French in their intercourse with strangers but among themselves they prefer patois, turning their phrases with great skill and expressing themselves with much wit. Nothing is more piquant than a humorous conversation between people of the locality.

Certain benefit societies which have always kept their old name of confraternity have existed at Lourdes from time immemorial. Each trade had formerly its own, and in 1858 eight were still in existence, being under the invocation respectively of Our Lady of Mount Carmel, Our Lady of Mount Serrat, Our Lady of Grace, St. Lucy, St. Anne, the Blessed Sacrament, the Ascension, St. John and St. James. Thanks to the healthy religious tone of these institutions, penetrated as they are by the Christian spirit, the inhabitants of the little town have never broken with the sound doctrines or practices of their belief. In their opinion these associations have no value or meaning except in so far as they are founded on the Christian faith and work on Christian lines. Strong in these principles which have made them happy up to the present, they close their ears to the theories of the so-called reformers of to-day and continue to live peaceably in the traditions of the past.

This does not mean however that Lourdes refuses to follow

the march of progress and civilisation, and, obstinately hostile to any sort of initiative, stubbornly settles herself down in the routine of the past. During the last fifty years the little town has developed marvellously. From the intellectual point of view she can hold her own with the most enlightened towns in the district. Long ebfore the legislators of to-day came into power, the municipal authorities of Lourdes had opened schools where every subject that could be of use to the working people was taught practically and thoroughly. All these schools, whether under the direction of lay teachers or of the religious orders, were equally endowed and supported, and in both kinds of school religious teaching had a large place. The parents' preferences created a wholesome and advantageous rivalry. Thanks moreover to the commune these schools were entirely free.

Without attempting to compare the former state of things with that of to-day, I ought to say that Lourdes was not without movement and life at the time previous to the Appearances. In the first place, there reigned the animation characteristic of all small garrison towns. Also the fairs and markets, reputed after those of Tarbes to be the best in the district, brought considerable crowds into Lourdes on certain days. During summer carriages coming from Pau, Tarbes and Bagneres de Bigorre set down men of business, tourists, and bathers who were on their way to the thermal stations at the end of the valley. At certain moments during the season the principal street which crosses the town resembled in its stir and noise the boulevard of a large city.

Round the castle of Lourdes centre historical and legendary stories of the greatest interest. As this is a matter outside my province I will only say briefly that the ancient citadel, founded many centuries ago, has seen floating from its towers the flags of the Romans, the Saracens and the English ; that feudal lords in their mutual hate and lust for power often fought beneath its ramparts ; that finally the Protestant hordes sought vainly to enter within its walls to kill and to destroy. In somewhat later times the castle became the fortified residence of the governor of the province, and more recently still it fell from its military glory and became a State prison. Descending to yet lower depths, the old citadel was used as barracks o1 even as a depot for provisions, and now it belongs to the town of Lourdes.

In spite of its comparative activity and ancient memories, the town of Lourdes seemed condemned to remain in obscurity, when an event quite out of the ordinary run of human things took place and brought it into notice. This great event of which I have to speak is known to-day from one end of the world to the other.

In 1854 Pope Pius IX., of glorious and pious memory, acting with the assistance of the Holy Spirit and in virtue of his infallible authority, consecrated solemnly, by elevating it to the certainty of a revealed dogma, the belief, that was already universal and many centuries old, in the Immaculate Conception of the most holy Virgin Mary, Mother of God. The Catholic world rejoiced and sent up to heaven a great and enthusiastic *Credo*. Touched by the proofs of love and tenderness which her children of earth had shown her, the Immaculate Virgin, as a beloved queen who delights in the homage of her subjects, condescended to come down into their midst, bringing with her as it were an echo from heaven and thus confirming the infallible pronouncement of the Vicar of Jesus Christ. This was in 1858. Taking the features of a young girl, features typical of simplicity and innocence, she left heaven to set her virgin foot upon a rock of Lourdes. There, clothed in the splendours of Mount Tabor and speaking to a humble and sickly peasant child, she said, after having raised her eyes to the eternal heights :—

"I AM THE IMMACULATE CONCEPTION."

CHAPTER II.

THE SOUBIROUS FAMILY.

On the extreme north of Lourdes, in the quarter known by name of Lapaca, there flows a large stream upon which stood formerly six or seven mills, situated at a little distance from each other. One of these mills, called "The Mill of Boly," had been held for many years on a long lease by the Castérot family of Lourdes. In 1841 the head of this family, Justin Castérot, died, leaving his widow with four daughters, Bernarde, Louise, Basile, Lucile, and a young son named Jean Marie. The eldest of the daughters, Bernarde, was already married to an honest artisan in the town. The duty of supporting the family thus naturally devolved upon the second, Louise, who was only sixteen. As a man was necessary to direct the mill of Boly, the mother had to think of marrying her daughter early. The young men who considered themselves worthy of Louise's notice were not slow in presenting themselves, and one of the most assiduous of the suitors was François Soubirous, a journeyman miller of Lourdes. François Soubirous was not at all well off, and the Castérot family, who were in a very comfortable position, might have looked higher in the matter of money. As however he was a miller by trade and as Louise preferred him to her other suitors the marriage was decided on and took place in the parish church on 9th January, 1843.

Under the management of the new miller the receipts of the mill of Boly soon decreased. Soubirous' somewhat ungracious manner did not attract customers, and moreover he was indolent and not so vigilant and careful in his work as he should have been. The flour he sent out was not always in a good condition, and very rarely did he deliver it to his customers at the time promised. Louise, his wife, was gentle, clean and tidy, but she was blinded by her affection and too young to fulfil all her domestic duties and did not notice or take account of the neglectfulness of her husband.

Thus husband and wife passed the first years of their married life, living in a sort of careless torpor and falling step by step to the lowest depths of misery. Whilst the receipts from the mill became smaller and smaller, the family burdens increased in inverse proportion. In a comparatively short space of time three children were born, and—as may be imagined—the parents' joy was tempered by much anxiety. In 1855 the little savings left by old Castérot at his death were entirely exhausted and the Soubirous found it impossible to pay the rent of the mill of Boly. Turned out of this mill, they rented an old tumble-down dwelling in the quarter where they lived, the Lapaca quarter, and hired themselves out to work for any one who would employ them for the day. So did times of trouble begin for the improvident couple.

Whilst the father and mother could go out and work with their hands they came back in the evening with at least a morsel of bread sufficient to feed the little family. When however outside work was wanting, or when for one reason or another the parents had to remain idle at home, it meant downright starvation for the unfortunate Soubirous. They were not even certain of a lodging; when pay day arrived the unfortunate family often found themselves without money and obliged to leave their place of abode. And thus we see them for three years, searching periodically for some dwelling-place, and sojourning for the time being in different quarters of the town.

At some moment when he was in even greater straits than usual Soubirous remembered that a relation of his wife, André Sajous, owned in the rue des Petits Fossés a building unlet and almost always closed. This building was no other than the former gaol of Lourdes, and in spite of the repulsion naturally excited by such dwelling-places Soubirous went to its owner to beg it of him. The latter, touched with compassion for the unfortunate family, granted his relative's request, and without asking any rent allowed them to settle into the old prison which was commonly known at Lourdes as "*le cachot.*" Soon afterwards, in 1858, from this dark and unhealthy dwelling-place every morning for a fortnight there sallied forth the eldest daughter of the Soubirous to go to the Massabieille grotto and receive there, face to face and heart to heart, the smiles and confidences and messages of the Queen of Heaven.

Up to the time when these events took place the former tenants of the Boly mill lived unnoticed. They were still very poor, but thanks to the free lodging given them by their relative Sajous they were not obliged to be continually looking for a new abode.

It has been said, and often with much truth, that misery makes the heart hard and causes family dissensions, but it was never so in the Soubirous household. The affection which husband and wife had for each other at the time of their marriage remained unbroken, and the six children given them by heaven only strengthened the bonds of conjugal union.

The Soubirous were by no means what is commonly called *dévots*, but they always performed the essential duties of their religion. In the time of their prosperity they had been as slack in their piety as in their daily work. But when the evil days came a happy reaction took place. They roused themselves from their former apathy and walked bravely in the path of resolutions which did them honour. On Sunday, husband and wife went regularly to the services in the parish church, leading their children by the hand or carrying those who could not walk. Every year at Easter, and sometimes oftener, they received with devotion the God of consolation and strength. Every night without fail, in spite of the fatigue of a long day's work and the scanty supper, family prayer was said in common. At the end of the ordinary prayers, say the neighbours, a child's pure voice was heard from within the *cachot*, saying the rosary devoutly. This voice, as may be guessed, was that of the favoured daughter who was destined to confer later so much glory upon the Soubirous family. But before passing on to this time we must introduce the reader to the Virgin's little protégée, whose name was to become known throughout the world.

CHAPTER III.

BERNADETTE.

Six children were born of the marriage of François Soubirous and Louise Castérot, the eldest of whom received the name of Bernadette, a name of happy omen, for it recalls that of a great saint devoted to the Virgin. This child came into the world on the 7th January, 1844, and was baptized on the next day at the parish church by Abbé Forgues, then curé of Lourdes. Anxiety and want had not yet entered the mill of Boly, and Bernadette's advent was welcomed with joy.

Six months after the young mother, in view of her approaching confinement, entrusted Bernadette to the care of a woman of the commune of Bartrès, Marie Aravant, who had just lost

Our tour guide said that Louise burned her breasts & could not nurse Bernadette. Marie Aravant was able to nurse her an infant boy. Bernadette was therefore taken to Bartrès where she remained fifteen months.

Bernadette was weak and feeble at her birth; in the first years of her life she was reared with difficulty, and without being actually laid up she yet was always ailing. At this time the first symptoms of a malady from which she was to suffer to the end of her life began to show themselves. A very severe form of asthma seized her in its iron grip, and when the fits of coughing took her she would be almost suffocated and fall into prolonged swoons. Her delicate constitution had need of continual care and good substantial food, but alas! the unfortunate Soubirous had difficulty in providing the barest necessities of existence.

The poor parents however neglected nothing within their power to protect and strengthen the health of their beloved child. Bernadette was clothed somewhat more warmly than her brothers and sisters; in place of the maize paste, the family's ordinary food, a little good bread was bought for her, and when their resources allowed of it a little wine was added, sweetened with a piece of sugar. This diet, insufficient though it was, might in some measure have strengthened the health of the little weakling, but the parents did not know that Bernadette was seldom allowed to profit by it.

Children are always jealous about privileges. The little Soubirous, too young to understand the reason which prompted their father and mother, looked with an eye of envy upon the special attentions of which Bernadette was the object. They were very fond of their eldest sister but when it was a question of better and more plentiful food affection was swallowed up by selfishness. The little upholders of equality were very careful to make no claims in the presence of their parents, but, so soon as the father and mother had left the house, they declared war upon Bernadette. When Bernadette consented to share the little store portioned out to her on account of her delicacy everything went well and happily; when, on the contrary, Bernadette attempted to resist, the others took up a determined attitude and passed at once from menace to violence. Bernadette so dearly loved her brothers and sisters that she never brought upon them punishment or even reprimand.

At the age of ten Bernadette was separated from her family for a second time. The winter of 1855 was particularly severe in the Pyrenees. For a long time no work could be done and the Soubirous household was one of those which suffered most keenly. Aunt Bernarde, always full of anxiety for her sister Louise whose poverty she knew so well, thought she could help her by taking Bernadette for the time being. The little girl remained with her godmother seven or eight months, and was treated there, not as a stranger, but with the same care and affection as the children of the house. When the coldest part of the winter was over Bernadette returned to her family in the street of the Petits Fossés.

Bernadette had not yet reached the end of her migrations and during the summer of 1857 she left her father's roof for the third time. Madame Aravant of Bartrès had never lost sight of the miller's daughter. Whenever she came to Lourdes she put at the bottom of her basket a bouquet of flowers, some fruit, a cake, a souvenir of some sort or other, destined to give pleasure to Bernadette. The child on her side was equally attached to the woman and several times in the year she used to go to Bartrès to see her.

It so happened that at this time the Aravants needed a young shepherdess to take a little flock of sheep and lambs to pasture. They asked for Bernadette. As may be imagined the Soubirous put no obstacle in the way of their daughter's departure ; it meant one mouth less to feed.

Many people at Bartrès still remember the little shepherdess of the Aravants. They love to talk of her, and all say how charming and bright and lovable she was. All who met her in the roads, driving before her her little flock, had some word of sympathy for her and the child would always reply intelligently and modestly. One day the parish priest met her as she was taking her sheep up to the high ground. He was so struck by the modest air and the intensely pure gaze of the child that he turned round several times to watch her as she went on her way. Speaking to the schoolmaster of the commune, Monsieur Barbet, who was walking with him, he said,

"That little shepherdess is exactly like what I have always imagined the children of La Salette to have been."

The good priest had no idea then that the comparison which he had just made was about to receive, and that so soon, a striking and solemn confirmation.

Bernadette had reached her fourteenth year and no one had yet spoken to her of her first communion. Her small size and her childish face deceived the clergy, and in the catechism she was always put in the back rows. Madame Aravant was the only person who reckoned the years and interested herself in the religious instruction of her little pupil. Every evening she took the child aside into the chimney corner and there instructed her in the first elements of Christian doctrine. As Bernadette could not read she had difficulty in retaining the instruction given her.

" She was thick-headed," said Madame Aravant many years after, smiling with affectionate remembrance. " It was useless for me to repeat my lessons; I always had to begin again. Sometimes I was overcome by impatience, and in temper I threw the book aside and said to her, 'Go along, you will never be anything but an ignorant fool.' "

The roughness of her mistress never made Bernadette bitter. She was shamefaced but never sulky. She often ended the embarrassment which followed the outbreak by throwing her arms round the woman's neck. The poor child consoled herself for her bad memory by having recourse to her little rosary, which she recited with perseverance and devotion.

Madame Aravant was too good a Christian and too conscious of her duties as mistress of the house not to be concerned about the state of things. She went to the curé of Bartrès to call his attention to the child of the miller of Lourdes.

The priest was of opinion that the child should no longer be forgotten and he would have taken upon himself the task of repairing the past neglect had not a project which he meditated been on the eve of its realisation. For some months the good priest had been seeking admission into the Benedictine order, and a letter recently received made him hope for a speedy fulfilment of his wishes. Fearing that the curé of Bartrès might be left vacant for some length of time after his departure he strongly urged Madame Aravant to send Bernadette back to her own family and to entrust her preparation for her first communion to the care of the Lourdes clergy. This advice was listened to, and in the early days of the year 1858 the little shepherdess of Bartrès once more took her way back to the town and returned to her father's roof in the road of the Petits Fossés.

The unseen hand which directed all these apparently unimportant events was leading Bernadette to the mysterious rock where such marvellous works were to be carried out.

CHAPTER IV.

THE GROTTO AND ITS SURROUNDINGS.

THESE privileged spots visited by the Queen of Heaven, though still the same in their general setting and conformation, have undergone in some respects certain necessary and truly marvellous transformations. To help therefore to the understanding of the following history, I will try by the aid of my recollection of the past to reconstruct the primitive appearance of Massabieille as it was at the time of the Appearances. In order to avoid confusion I will ask the reader to forget for the moment the present state of things and to carry himself back to the year 1858.

The grotto is situated to the west of Lourdes, beyond the Gave, seven or eight hundred metres from the town. To get there we will take the same road that Bernadette took.

And first of all on leaving the town at the end of the rue de Baons—(the present rue de la Grotte)—we pass under a square tower, an old and abandoned dependency of the ancient castle. After having passed this gate we descend by a steep and stony road to the banks of the Gave. A bridge of stone with the parapets near to each other, called Pont Vieux, built across the river above a gulf, leads to the opposite bank. On leaving the bridge we turn a little to the right and enter upon a narrow tortuous path called "*le chemin de la forêt.*" This path has on one side a quickset hedge of box and blackthorn, and on the other an irregular rocky façade. On the right, beyond the hedge, extends an immense field surrounded by poplars, the property of Monsieur de la Fitte of Lourdes. This vast mass of verdure opens out in a splendid sweep towards the north and then turns towards the west, to end in a point under the hill of Massabieille, almost opposite the grotto. On the right of the road above the slope rise several little square fields, crowned on the summit by the ruins of thick walls erected in times gone by.

When from Pont Vieux we have gone about two hundred metres in the direction of the forest, we see the rocky barrier on the left suddenly turn off to the south, and the little valley of Merlasse opening out. From this valley, arid and stony, a stream comes down which crosses the road and mingles its waters a few metres lower down with those of a canal belonging to the Gave. These united streams drive the mill and sawmill of Savy. On leaving these works, at the back of the buildings, they go through a clump of alder trees and poplars, pass to the east of the hill of Massabieille, turn round to the west and then empty themselves into the Gave just where Monsieur de la Fitte's field ends. There is no direct way of communication between the valley of Merlasse and the Grotto of the Appearances.

After having crossed the Merlasse footbridge we have to climb by an abrupt road, faintly made in the rock, to the point at the summit where the Basilica is to be built later on. We go round the hill to the west; then by a steep crag, over rocky ground, we descend to the banks of the Gave. We take several steps to the right along the rocks and find ourselves opposite the grotto.

The rock of the Appearances on the north side is cut vertically, presenting the effect of an imposing and gigantic wall. At the bottom of this rock is an excavation eight metres deep by twelve broad, resembling in its structure the chapel of a church. This cavity is the grotto. On the right and left of the arch which forms the entrance are blocks of marble, protecting as it were the dwelling-place visited by the Virgin. Above the excavations in the rock grow moss, ivy,—shrubs of every kind.

The front of the grotto is occupied by the waters of the Gave, into which flow at this place the waters of the canal of Savy. At the confluence of these two streams, at the end of Monsieur de la Fitte's field, rise three or four large blocks of stone partly submerged in the river which form a sort of barrier at the entrance of the excavations. The space from this barrier to the end of the grotto is about fifteen metres in length by at least twelve in breadth. The ground rises gradually to the height of a man except at the east where it is a little lower. Penetrating into the interior of the grotto, we see in the vault above our heads an opening shaped like a cylinder in the direction of a gallery above where daylight shines. This transverse gallery penetrates on one side into the interior of the rock and on the other passes into the open air by a sort of Gothic bay, partly intercepted by a granite block in the shape of a cube. Beneath this block an enormous bush takes root, shooting out its branches which fall to the ground in a cascade of verdure. Bernadette, in her picturesque patois, called this bush "*le rosier*," because the stems and branches of a wild rose tree formed its principal element. It is at the entrance of the Gothic bay of which I have spoken that the Virgin appeared, having behind her the block of granite which obstructs the passage and beneath her feet the first springs of the bush which bend to the ground.

No visible source flows within the grotto. A dampness, attributed to the rains, is merely seen on the surface of the exterior rocks on the left exposed to the west. At the bottom of these rocks a pool of water can still be seen, the origin of which will be explained later on.

Little clumps of dwarf plants grow here and there on the soil of the grotto. Especially to be noted are the *chrysosplenium oppositifolium* and the *cardimanea sylvatica.*

In a deserted out-of-the-way place and difficult to get at, the grotto is almost unknown. Some few shepherds, tending their flocks beside the Gave, take refuge there in times of storm and rain; fishermen are also occasionally compelled to interrupt now and again their peaceful occupation.

The basin of Massabieille has at all times been regarded as a retreat generously endowed by nature. When, from the summit of the little rocky hill known in the country as "*la montagne des Espélugues,*" one looks down upon the surrounding country, there lies before one first the splendid field of Monsieur de la Fitte with the silver girdle of the Gave shining through the foliage. Higher up beyond the river on a craggy hill one sees the castle of Lourdes, with its old castellated tower. On turning to the north one finds oneself in the presence of magnificent hills placed one upon another and climbing up, by stages, to the heights of the villages of Bartrès and Poneyferre. All these eminences, variegated by the fields and meadows and clumps of trees and brushwood which grow on their sides, present an animated appearance, numerous flocks wandering over them in all directions in search of pasture. On the west the valley of the Gave loses itself in the distant horizon. On the right and left stretch out the last mountains of Lourdes, succeeded by those of Peyrouse and Saint Pé, clothed with the drapery of their venerable forests. On the south the sight is ravished by the majestic curtain of the Pyrenean range.

CHAPTER V.

THE NEWS.

THE town of Lourdes was passing the winter of 1857-58 in its ordinary unruffled quiet when a strange piece of news, outside the common range of human things, stirred all minds and animated all conversations. At first this news was known only to a few persons and aroused no outbreak of excitement. A holy name was connected with it but at present for reasons of reverence this name was not declared.

It was reported that at Lourdes on Thursday, the 11th February, the little daughter of a former miller, by name Bernadette, had gone as is customary with the poor to pick up dry branches by the river side. When she had reached the hill of Massabieille she suddenly found herself in the presence of a lady marvellously beautiful, who held a rosary in her hand and smiled at her affectionately from above a bush hanging over the side of the rock.

So strange a story necessarily struck the popular imagination. Who could this Lady be, so marvellously beautiful, who showed herself in an inaccessible place and held in her hand a religious symbol? The people did not lose themselves in vain reasonings and conjectures ; with their natural intuition they pierced the veil which hid the mystery, and beneath all cloud and obscurity saw the radiant figure of the Mother of God ; they were not deceived.

At first however, as I have said, the matter was only discussed with reserve and reticence. The women might be seen in little groups of two or three, here and there, talking together in a low voice. No doubt the secrets confided in these little gatherings were betrayed a few moments later, giving place to others equally mysterious. Thus the news was passed from neighbour to neighbour and gained ground ; but it had not obtained public notoriety before it was known that the Appearances had been resumed and that little Bernadette went every morning to the grotto.

Some neighbours of the little seer began to frequent the scene of the wonder ; they returned from it almost beside themselves with enthusiasm. The next day and the day after the number of pilgrims increased, and all returned in the same transports of joy. The excitement became general. The Appearances were reputed miraculous, and soon every morning all the working people of Lourdes, both men and women, crowded *en masse* with an enthusiasm beyond description to the rocks of Massabieille.

Whilst the populace was profuse in its expressions of wonder and admiration with regard to the extraordinary events taking place at the grotto, a group of men, the only wise ones in their own conceit, held aloof and treated as mere fancies the stories which they heard. These men were the *savants* of the place. For them the question was settled *à priori*, and without any kind of examination or enquiry they denied that these visions had any supernatural character. The most favourable construction they would allow to be put upon them was that they were the hallucinations of a diseased imagination. At that time I lived amongst these men and I shared their ideas. The manner in which I received the news of the Appearances can best be described in an autobiographical note which I would have spared the reader had it not been necessary to the understanding of my story.

At the time which I am recalling I lived at Lourdes, where

I was the chief official in the bureau of the *contributions indirectes*. A dear sister, who has remained the companion of my life of wandering, was living with me there and made me the object of her devoted care. I was comparatively young at the time of which I speak, and anxiety for my salvation occupied a very secondary place in my thoughts. My sister, though younger than I, often discoursed earnestly to me and reminded me of the religious traditions of my family. Thanks to God I had not lost faith, but the faith was obscured by a cloud of prejudices which hid from me the true relationships of things. Thus, in regard to the question of miracles, I believed in the miracles of our Divine Lord recorded in the Gospels, but outside those miracles I regarded everything as phantoms, illusions, popular aberrations. Such being my state of mind one can easily imagine the reception I was likely to give to the budding legend of the grotto.

One day my sister, coming from out of doors, entered my office and said to me: "Have you heard the rumours which are going about? It is said that a little girl of the town has been favoured with an appearance of the Virgin in a grotto near the Gave."

"That's very pretty, even poetical," I answered my sister, scarcely thinking of what I was saying and continuing to write in my books.

My sister, seeing that I took no interest in the news, crossed the room and disappeared. The rest of the day we said nothing to each other about the visions of Massabieille.

The next day or the day after—it was early, for I was not yet out of bed—she opened the door of my room and said to me: "My dear, it seems that there are no more grounds for laughing at the news which I brought you yesterday. The appearance is confirmed, and Mademoiselle Millet, our neighbour, who has accompanied the seer to the grotto, declares positively that there is something supernatural in what takes place at Massabieille."

My sister was going to continue, but I turned myself round in bed and answered shortly, "Let me go to sleep."

There existed at Lourdes, at the time of the Appearances, a club where all the chief men of the town met—doctors, lawyers, magistrates, property owners and various Government officials. I have already alluded to this club. I again mention these men, whose views I shared, to say that many of them by the very fact of the visions were soon compelled to readjust their ideas. At the beginning of our discussions we were unanimous in rejecting the opinions accepted by the populace. Everything which we heard of the grotto seemed to us silly, childish and absurd and we shrugged our shoulders at it. An attentive observer might have noticed however one remarkable point. If the Massabieille affair was as futile as we seemed to suppose, why should we prolong our discussions about it? But it was useless for us to attempt to change the current of conversation; the theme of the grotto returned to our lips continually, and after having mentioned it once we felt the need of speaking of it again.

Discussing the affair so continually we only said the same things over and over again, and at last certain members of the club realised that we had nothing but suppositions to oppose to those who believed in the Appearances. Hoping to find better and more definite arguments they conceived the idea of each one going to the grotto, but independently, to take account of the mysteries of which it was the theatre. These men thought themselves strong enough to withstand any surprise, but when they arrived at Massabieille, seized by an unutterable emotion, they were cast to the ground like Saul on the road to Damascus.

Among the principal inhabitants of the town who openly declared themselves convinced should be named in the first place Monsieur de la Fitte, formerly "*intendant militaire*," Monsieur Pougat, president of the tribunal; Monsieur Dufo, barrister; Monsieur Dozous, doctor; Monsieur Lannes, proprietor of the tobacco warehouse; the captain commanding the fort; Monsieur Germain, formerly veterinary surgeon in the army. I might mention others, such as Monsieur Castillon, Monsieur Prat, Monsieur Moura, but the list would be too long. I also had to lay down my arms, and in my old age I am writing these lines in recognition of the marked favour bestowed upon me on the thrice happy day of my welcome defeat.

To sum up, I can give in a few words the general impressions at Lourdes with regard to the Appearances. All the common people from the first were convinced of the supernatural character of the facts of the grotto. In the upper class belief was not so prompt; men were divided between two opposite opinions. Those who were present at the ecstasies of Bernadette bowed themselves and believed, whilst those who scorned to go to the grotto were obstinate in their incredulity. The latter, about thirty in number, gave themselves up later on to a most bitter and systematic opposition; and this opposition only ceased when the Virgin by her miracles and benefits had made it impossible for them to fight any longer.

Now we will come to the subject which is the principal object of this book.

CHAPTER VI.

FIRST APPEARANCE (THURSDAY, 11TH FEBRUARY, 1858).

THE first Appearance, as I have already said, took place on the Thursday before Ash Wednesday, 11th February, 1858, at about half-past twelve or one o'clock in the afternoon; but I will let the little seer speak for herself. I have heard the following story ten times, twenty times, a hundred times, from her lips. I will try to reproduce it in its touching simplicity, translating word for word the patois of the Pyrenees, the only language Bernadette knew.

"The Thursday before Ash Wednesday it was cold and the weather was threatening. After our dinner my mother told us that there was no more wood in the house and she was vexed. My sister Toinette* and I, to please her, offered to go and pick up some dry branches by the riverside. My mother said, 'No,' because the weather was bad and we might be in danger of falling into the Gave. Jeanne Abadie, our neighbour and friend, who was looking after her little brother in our house and who wanted to come with us, took her brother back to his house

* Bernadette always called her sister Toinette, and the latter is registered under that name at the Mairie at Lourdes. Later on in the family, this name was changed to that of Marie. The new name is employed in this book.

and returned the next moment telling us that she had leave to come with us. My mother still hesitated, but seeing that there were three of us she let us go. We took first of all the road which leads to the cemetery, by the side of which wood is unloaded and where shavings can sometimes be found. That day we found nothing there. We came down by the side which leads near the Gave and having arrived at Pont Vieux we wondered if it would be best to go up or down the river. We decided to go down and taking the forest road we arrived at Merlasse. There we went into Monsieur de la Fitte's field by the mill of Savy. As soon as we had reached the end of this field, nearly opposite the grotto of Massabieille, we were stopped by the canal of the mill we had just passed. The current of this canal was not strong for the mill was not working, but the water was cold, and I for my part was afraid to go in. Jeanne Abadie and my sister, less timid than I, took their sabots in their hand and crossed the stream. However when they were on the other side they called out that it was cold and bent down to rub their feet and warm them. All this increased my fear, and I thought that if I went into the water I should get an attack of asthma. So I asked Jeanne Abadie, who was bigger and stronger than I, to take me on her shoulders.

" 'I should think not,' answered Jeanne ; 'you're a molly-coddle ; if you won't come, stay where you are.'

" After the others had picked up some pieces of wood under the grotto they disappeared along the Gave. When I was alone I threw some stones into the bed of the river to give me a foothold, but it was of no use. So I had to make up my mind to take off my sabots and cross the canal as Jeanne and my sister had done.

" I had just begun to take off my first stocking when suddenly I heard a great noise like the sound of a storm. I looked to the right, to the left, under the trees of the river, but nothing moved ; I thought I was mistaken. I went on taking off my shoes and stockings, when I heard a fresh noise like the first. Then I was frightened and stood straight up. I lost all power of speech and thought when, turning my head towards the grotto, I saw at one of the openings of the rock a bush, one only, moving as if it were very windy. Almost at the same time there came out of the interior of the grotto a golden-coloured cloud, and soon after a Lady, young and beautiful, exceedingly beautiful, the like of whom I had never seen, came and placed herself at the entrance of the opening above the bush. She looked at me immediately, smiled at me and signed to me to advance, as if she had been my mother. All fear had left me but I seemed to know no longer where I was. I rubbed my eyes, I shut them, I opened them; but the Lady was still there continuing to smile at me and making me understand that I was not mistaken. Without thinking of what I was doing I took my rosary in my hands and went on my knees. The Lady made with her head a sign of approval and herself took into her hands a rosary which hung on her right arm. When I attempted to begin the rosary and tried to lift my hand to my forehead my arm remained paralysed, and it was only after the Lady had signed herself that I could do the same. The Lady left me to pray all alone; she passed the beads of her rosary between her fingers but she said nothing; only at the end of each decade did she say the 'Gloria' with me.

"When the recitation of the rosary was finished the Lady returned to the interior of the rock and the golden cloud disappeared with her."

Usually the hearer stopped the little seer to ask her to give a detailed portrait of the mysterious Lady, and this is what she replied:

"She has the appearance of a young girl of sixteen or seventeen. She is dressed in a white robe, girdled at the waist with a blue ribbon which flows down all along her robe. She wears upon her head a veil which is also white; this veil gives just a glimpse of her hair and then falls down at the back below her waist. Her feet are bare but covered by the last folds of her robe except at the point where a yellow rose shines upon each of them. She holds on her right arm a rosary of white beads with a chain of gold shining like the two roses on her feet."

Bernadette then continued her story.

"As soon as the Lady had disappeared Jeanne Abadie and my sister returned to the grotto and found me on my knees in the same place where they had left me. They laughed at me, called me imbecile and bigot, and asked me if I would go back with them or not. I had now no difficulty in going into the stream, and I felt the water as warm as the water for washing plates and dishes.

" 'You had no reason to make such an outcry,' I said to Jeanne and Marie while drying my feet; 'the water of the canal is not so cold as you seem to make believe!'

" 'You are very fortunate not to find it so; we found it very cold.'

"We bound up in three faggots the branches and fragments of wood which my companions had brought; then we climbed the slope of Massabieille and took the forest road. Whilst we were going towards the town I asked Jeanne and Marie if they had noticed anything at the grotto.

" 'No,' they answered. 'Why do you ask us?'

" 'Oh, nothing,' I replied indifferently.

"However, before we got to the house, I told my sister Marie of the extraordinary things which had happened to me at the grotto, asking her to keep it secret.

"Throughout the whole day the image of the Lady remained in my mind. In the evening at the family prayer I was troubled and began to cry.

" 'What is the matter?' asked my mother.

"Marie hastened to answer for me and I was obliged to give the account of the wonder which had come to me that day.

" 'These are illusions,' answered my mother, 'you must drive these ideas out of your head and especially not go back again to Massabieille.'

"We went to bed but I could not sleep. The face of the Lady, so good and so gracious, returned incessantly to my memory, and it was useless to recall what my mother had said to me; I could not believe that I had been deceived."

Bernadette told the preceding story with such simplicity that those who listened, after having heard her, could not fail to come to the conclusion—this child has spoken the truth.

CHAPTER VII.

SECOND APPEARANCE (SUNDAY, 14TH FEBRUARY).

BERNADETTE had been seized by what might be called the "malady of heaven." Playful as she was by nature, she suddenly showed herself serious and grave. One single thought alone occupied her soul, that of the Lady.

On the day after the first Appearance the mother of the little seer noticed the sort of melancholy which seemed to have seized upon her daughter. Her mother's heart was distressed at it and with all the thoughtfulness inspired by tenderness she sought to divert and distract her child. She represented to her, as she had done on the previous night, that our eyes and ears are subject to error, and that in any case it is prudent to put away from us things of a doubtful nature. She recounted many facts and many stories to support her argument. In order to detach her daughter from the imaginary charms of the mysterious Lady she also added that the spirit of evil sometimes transforms himself into an angel of light, and that there was reason to fear that the event of Massabieille was of this nature.

Bernadette did not argue with her mother but she found it difficult to accept her reasonings. She could not persuade herself that all which she had seen and heard at the grotto—the gusts of wind, the swaying of the bush, the appearance of the Lady, the illumination of the rock—was but a succession of illusions. The child would have found it difficult to put into words her idea of the devil, but, however vague her image of him, she could not possibly believe that the spirit of darkness could change his grimacing face into that of the sweet and beautiful Lady who had appeared to her. And it seemed to her especially strange and contradictory that the devil should carry a rosary and that he should come to recite it piously at Massabieille.

Throughout Friday and Saturday, the 12th and 13th February, Bernadette, without asking express permission of her mother, let her see on several occasions the desire which she had to return to the grotto. The mother pretended not to understand, or if she spoke it was to combat her daughter's inclinations. Things continued thus until Sunday, 14th February.

During the afternoon of that day she heard in the depths of her soul a secret voice which urged her, sweetly yet strongly, to go to Massabieille. Held back by her timid nature the child did not dare to speak to her mother about this mysterious appeal. Feeling freer with her sister Marie she entrusted her secret to her and asked her to obtain the desired permission from her mother. Marie was not discouraged by a first refusal; without losing heart she appealed to her friend Jeanne Abadie to plead Bernadette's cause with her. Madame Soubirous still resisted; she remembered the bad effects of the first visit and she did not wish to increase her anxieties by allowing her child to be a prey to fresh dangers and emotions.

The Lady however called Bernadette to the grotto. Gently, without effort, she took away all obstacles and opened the road to her little protégée. Appealing to the maternal anxiety itself she brought Madame Soubirous to the point of wondering whether the step she opposed would not rather be the most efficacious means of freeing her child from the foolish ideas which possessed her. If, that is, the child saw nothing more at the grotto, might it not be taken for granted that she would herself be freed from her first impressions? The mother, although anxious, decided therefore to make the trial of a second visit. To the fresh appeals made by the two little children she replied, pretending impatience in order to disguise her change of opinion:

"Go along then, and don't bother me any more. And remember to be back here in time for vespers; if you're late, you know what to expect."

Outside the family circle Bernadette had never spoken to any one of the vision which she had had at the grotto. Her sister Marie had not been equally reserved. On the morning of the 14th February a dozen young girls of the quarter were in the secret and all had asked to be allowed to follow Bernadette, should she return to Massabieille. As soon as the mother's authorisation had been obtained Marie, faithful to the promises she had given, ran off to inform her friends, accompanied by Jeanne Abadie.

Meanwhile Bernadette dressed quickly and in imagination drew beforehand the picture of the joys which awaited her at the grotto. The picture attracted her and yet a troublesome cloud arose from time to time to darken the radiant view. The little seer remembered what her mother had said to her about the ruses of the evil one and although she felt within herself the invincible certainty that she had not been deceived she could not help a certain apprehension. By the advice of her young companions she fortified herself with a phial which she had filled from the holy water stoup of the church.

Thus armed against the artifices of the father of lies, she entered boldly upon the forest road, escorted by five or six young girls of her age whom Marie, her sister, had diligently collected. There were also others to come, but as their toilet preparations were not yet completed it was arranged that Jeanne Abadie should wait for them.

As soon as the first group arrived at Massabieille Bernadette fell on her knees on the right side of the grotto, opposite the bush above which the Lady had first appeared. She began to pray; then suddenly she cried out in a transport of joy:

"There she is! There she is!"

Marie Hillot, who held at that moment the bottle of holy water, passed it rapidly to Bernadette saying, "Quickly, throw water on her."

Bernadette obeyed and threw the contents of the phial in the direction of the bush.

"She is not angry," replied the seer joyfully. "On the contrary, she sanctions it with her head and is smiling at us all."

Immediately the young girls fell on their knees, arranging themselves in a semicircle on either side of Bernadette. A moment after she was lost in ecstasy. Her sweet and tranquil gaze remained fixed upon the recess, cold and empty for all but her, and she seemed intoxicated with the contemplation of heavenly beauty; her face, transfigured and radiant with happiness, had taken upon itself an indescribable expression; one might have said it was an angel in prayer.

In the presence of such a picture, so moving and so unexpected, the young girls were troubled, not knowing what to think. Several of them burst out crying and one of them exclaimed, "Oh, what if Bernadette were to die."

While they were kneeling there, anxious and doubting what to do, a fresh incident redoubled their alarms.

A stone falling from the top of the hill bounded off the rock and fell into the Gave. This was quite enough to madden with fear the young heads already over-excited. The friends of the seer fled from the grotto and, filled with terror, climbed up the rocky slope, uttering loud cries and calling for help. When they had reached the forest road they found Jeanne Abadie at the head of her little squadron of laggards clapping her hands and roaring with laughter. Everything was soon explained ; Jeanne, to revenge herself on the others for not having waited for her, had caused the panic.

When the terror had been allayed and peace been made the young girls who had come from below explained to the others the extraordinary state in which they had left Bernadette. They all came down hurriedly to help their friend. They found the seer kneeling in the same place in the delight of her ecstasy. They came up to her and called her affectionately by her name, but Bernadette was insensible to the voice of her companions. As if she had ceased to belong to this world, her gaze remained fixed upon the invisible object which captivated it. The young girls, not knowing if the little seer was dead or about to die, were moaning and weeping, when suddenly they saw the mother and sister of Nicolau, the miller of Savy, coming down. The two women had heard the children's cries of distress and had hurried to their assistance. Seeing Bernadette in ecstasy they remained stupefied and hung back, restrained as it were by a holy reverence. They came up to her timidly and tried by the exercise of gentle pressure to bring her back to every-day life. It was all wasted effort ; Bernadette heard and saw nothing but her beloved vision.

But it was necessary to take the seer away from the powerful charm which held her captive in so marvellous a manner. Without further delay the mother of Nicolau left Massabieille and went to fetch her son from the mill of Savy. The young miller, then twenty-eight years of age, ran to the grotto with a sarcastic smile upon his lips, expecting to witness some childish prank.

When he came up to Bernadette he fell back with surprise and crossed his arms.

"Never have I seen a more marvellous sight," says even now the former miller of Savy. "It was useless for me to argue with myself; I felt I was not worthy to touch the child."

However, urged by his mother, young Nicolau carefully took Bernadette by the arms and tried to make her walk. Upheld by the miller and his mother, the seer at length reached the mill of Savy.

But during the journey to the mill she seemed to follow with her gaze a mysterious being who kept in front of her and a little above her. In vain did young Nicolau, to break the charm, put his hand upon her eyes and compel her to lower her head; Bernadette continually returned to her first position, absorbed in contemplation. Only on arriving at the mill did Bernadette regain possession of herself, the dull and dingy picture of everyday life appearing once more to her sad and sorrowful eyes.

When asked about the cause of her ecstasy Bernadette told the story of the day's vision, which had merely been the repetition of that of the previous Thursday.

Bernadette's companions, after having followed her to the mill of Savy, separated from her and returned to the town, utterly astounded by what they had seen at Massabieille. On returning to her house Bernadette's sister broke out sobbing, and suffocated by her emotion she could not tell her mother the reason of her tears.

The mother, beside herself and thinking some misfortune had happened, hastened to the grotto road. By a fortunate coincidence she met two or three women in succession, who assured her that Bernadette was resting at the mill of Savy and that no harm had happened to her. But Madame Soubirous, remembering Bernadette's stubbornness in wishing to return to the grotto, gave way to a movement of anger against her obstinate child. She went into the mill with a switch in her hand and going straight to the little girl said to her:

"So you want to make us the laughing-stock of all who know us. I'll give it to you with your hypocritical airs and your stories of the Lady!" and she was just about to strike her, when old Madame Nicolau withheld her hand.

"What are you doing?" she cried. "What has your child done to be treated like this? It is an angel, and an angel from Heaven that you have in her, do you hear? I shall never, never forget what she was at the grotto!"

Madame Soubirous, worn out with emotion, fell into a seat and burst into tears. A few moments after, comforted by what the Nicolau family said to her, she once more took the road to the town, leading with her Bernadette, who from time to time cast behind her a secret glance.

Young Nicolau, to-day an elderly man, himself confirmed to me thirty years later the details which I give about the second Appearance.

CHAPTER VIII.

THIRD APPEARANCE (THURSDAY, 18TH FEBRUARY).

THE young girls who had separated from Bernadette at the mill of Savy returned to Lourdes, telling on the way the story of the extraordinary things they had seen. That evening, the next day, and during the days which followed, at home and among their friends and neighbours, they continued to talk with animated interest of the picture which had struck them at the grotto.

"Bernadette in ecstasy," they said, "was no longer like herself; she became like, but much more beautiful than, the adoring angels which are on the altars."

The world in general laughed at the excited prattle of these children and sent them away as silly little people.

This was not the case with one of the "*enfants de Marie*" of Lourdes, Antoinette Peyret. Much impressed by what she had heard, she embraced some pretext or other to go to the Soubirous' house and ask Bernadette for details. The child never anticipated questions, but when they were asked her she lent herself gracefully and readily to whatever was wanted of her.

Without pretension or pressure Bernadette then undertook

to narrate what had happened to her at Massabieille. When she spoke of the dress of the mysterious Lady, Antoinette Peyret, who was already following the details with emotion, felt her bosom swell and the tears come into her eyes.

Some months before, the guild of the "*enfants de Marie*" at Lourdes had lost its good and well-beloved president, Mademoiselle Elisa Latapie. The guild was mourning her then and for long after, for I know former members of it who, thirty years later, still shed tears over their venerated friend. Although young, Mademoiselle Latapie had obtained the confidence and respect of all. The sweetness of her character, her intellectual distinction, the generosity of her soul, drew to her spontaneously all hearts, and to the young guild members she was a friend, an adviser, a second mother. When she went along the streets every one saluted her with respect and veneration. There was universal mourning for her death. On the day of her funeral the whole town of Lourdes accompanied the coffin, and the tears of the poor more eloquently even than their words told how great had been her charity.

Now among the "*enfants de Marie*" most closely attached to Mademoiselle Latapie, Antoinette Peyret occupied the first place. She more than any other felt the agony of the separation; the image of her who was no longer presented itself to her mind continually. She was struck by the likeness between the description given by Bernadette of the dress of the Lady of the rock and that of the dress worn by the "*enfants de Marie*" on the day of their religious ceremonies. Instantly her thoughts flew to Mademoiselle Latapie, and she wondered with emotion whether the Lady who was shewing herself at Massabieille was not their former president come to ask for their prayers. From this moment Antoinette Peyret knew no repose. In the course of a conversation which she had with Madame Millet, of Lourdes, on Wednesday, 17th February, she confided to the latter her impressions and her inquietude, and together they arranged a visit to the "*cachot*."

That same day at nightfall the two women went together to the Soubirous' abode. They presented themselves just at the moment when Bernadette was begging her mother to allow her to return to the grotto for the third time. Her mother, still under the influence of the impressions of the previous Sunday, did not want a renewal of her alarms and was haranguing the child sternly.

At the sight of her two visitors she stopped, somewhat confused, but did not conceal the reason of her irritation. Madame Millet and Antoinette Peyret were almost glad to have arrived at such a moment; they did what they could to calm the mother and to show her that her fears were exaggerated. They then supported Bernadette's request and, pleading for themselves as much as for the child, they tried to make her realise that there was more danger in opposing the wish than in acceding to it. Finally they promised to accompany Bernadette to the grotto and to protect her.

"But you want to make my child a laughing-stock," cried the poor distressed mother.

"You are insulting us in even suggesting such a thing," answered Madame Millet sharply. "We will not insist, but allow us to say before we go that you are taking upon yourself responsibilities which we, for our part, would not dare to assume."

"I shall go out of my mind," answered Madame Soubirous distractedly, holding her two visitors by the hand. "I do not think that you would deceive me . . . I trust my child to you . . . you see my anguish . . . I beg you to watch over her."

This conversation has often been repeated to my sister by Mademoiselle Peyret.

The next day, before daylight, in order not to attract the attention of the curious, Madame Millet and Mademoiselle Peyret knocked quietly at the door of the Soubirous' house and Bernadette went out with them. They had scarcely taken a few steps in the street when the bells of the church announced a low Mass, and they went in. Having heard Mass they took the road towards Massabieille; few people saw them pass, for the houses were not yet open. Madame Millet held openly in her hands the traditional candle blessed at Candlemas, a candle which she burnt in her room on festivals or at the approach of heavy storms. Antoinette Peyret, on the other hand, concealed under the folds of her large black-hooded Pyrenean cloak a sheet of paper, together with pen and ink.

When they had reached the top of the *mamelon* of Massabieille Bernadette, in her hurry to arrive, left her protectors behind her and climbed rapidly down towards the grotto. Madame Millet and Antoinette Peyret, less accustomed to the path, did not reach the side of the Gave until some minutes after the seer.

They found the latter on her knees reciting her rosary opposite the recess from which the bush hung down. After having lighted the blessed candle the two women imitated Bernadette and took their rosaries. The little group knelt down and prayed in a low voice for some instants when the seer suddenly uttered a cry of joy.

"She comes, here she is!" and Bernadette, trembling with happiness, bowed her head to the earth at the same time. Madame Millet and Mademoiselle Peyret hastened to look up at the rock but for them, alas, nothing was changed.

"Let us continue to pray," said Madame Millet, "and if the invisible Lady is really she whom we believe her to be our prayers must be acceptable to her."

Bernadette had anticipated these words and her heart was already in communication with the heavenly apparition. She prayed and smiled in turn. The seer remained happy, in a gentle emotion, but that day she gave no signs of outward ecstasy. The Lady was about to speak and she wished the child to hear her voice in calm and in the full possession of her faculties.

When the rosary was finished Antoinette Peyret, still absorbed in the thought of her dead friend, the president of the guild, said to Bernadette, giving her the pen and paper she had brought,

"Please ask the Lady if she has anything to tell us and in that case if she would be so good as to write it."

The seer took three or four steps towards the rock then, realising even without turning round that the two women followed her, she signalled to them with her hand to remain behind. When she had reached the bush Bernadette stood on tiptoe and presented the pen and paper to the vision. She remained for some moments in this attitude looking towards the opening and seemed to listen to words which came from the top of the recess. She then lowered her arms, made a profound inclination, and returned to her original place. As one might expect, the paper remained blank.

Somewhat saddened Antoinette Peyret approached Bernadette and asked her what the Lady had replied.

"When I presented the pen and paper to her she began to smile; then without being angry she answered, 'There is no need for me to write down what I have to say to you.' Then she seemed to be thinking for a moment and added, 'Will you be so kind as to come here for fifteen days?'"

"What did you answer?"

"I answered, 'Yes.'"

"But why does the Lady want you to come?"

"I do not know; she did not tell me."

"But," said Madame Millet, "why did you make a sign to us to go back when we were coming up with you just now?"

"In obedience to the Lady."

"Oh!" sighed Madame Millet, distressed, "please ask her, Bernadette, if my presence here is disagreeable to her."

Bernadette raised her eyes to the top of the rock, then turned and said,

"The Lady answered, 'No, her presence is not disagreeable to me.'"

The seer began to pray, and the two women with her. In this second part of the Appearance Madame Millet and Antoinette Peyret noticed that Bernadette frequently interrupted her prayer to hold an intimate colloquy with the vision. An hour passed thus; then all disappeared.

As soon as Bernadette had come out of the grotto Madame Millet and Antoinette Peyret asked her if she had not received any fresh communication from the Lady.

"Yes," answered the child, half joyful and half sorrowful, "she said to me, 'I do not promise to make you happy in this world, but in the next.'"

"Since the Lady consents to speak to you," continued the women, "why do you not ask her her name?"

"I have done so."

"Well, who is she?"

"I do not know. She lowered her head with a smile, but she did not answer."

These dialogues have many times been repeated to me by Bernadette herself.

Bernadette was taken back to her family. Like Madame Nicolau, the miller's wife, Madame Millet and Antoinette Peyret said to the mother,

"Ah, how happy you are to have such a child."

CHAPTER IX.

FOURTH APPEARANCE (FRIDAY, 19TH FEBRUARY).

As soon as Madame Millet and Antoinette Peyret had gone, Bernadette told her parents what the Lady had said to her and of the promise she had made to come to the grotto every day for a fortnight. When they heard of this promise her father and mother were much troubled. Until then they had thought that the child's eyes had been dazzled in the grotto by some more or less brilliant vapoury form but that this form would finally vanish, even as the fantastic figures formed by the clouds in the vastness of space vanish and melt away. But what the little seer said to them now upset all their hypotheses. This vague, uncertain something of which their imagination had caught a glimpse, was a real, living being, having a will of its own and speaking like one of them. And now—(here began their difficulty)—in what spiritual category was this immaterial yet real personality which revealed itself at Massabieille to be classed?

The features transfigured in glory of the Lady described by Bernadette and the nature of the promises made by her made the child's parents think that they recognised in her the Queen of Heaven. But they soon rejected this idea as presumptuous, conscious of their own unworthiness. Then they turned over in their minds Antoinette Peyret's idea, the possibility that is of the appearance under a human form of a soul from purgatory. But the calm serenity of the mysterious being made all idea of suffering impossible in such a connection. Moreover, what purpose could a soul from purgatory have in coming to the grotto? Why should not such a soul have given utterance to its desires and its prayers when asked to do so? The presence of a soul from purgatory on the Massabieille rock did not seem probable to the Soubirous. A third possible solution of the question terrified Bernadette's parents. Certainly the Lady of the grotto showed herself externally kindly and charming, she carried in her hands the rosary so abhorred of hell, she made promises which were in their nature very like those of the gospel. But were these fine externals, these fine promises, to be trusted? Is not the spirit of evil capable of every sort of lying and deception? And moreover there were other points to be cleared up. What did the Lady's silence as to her name mean?

Distracted by their hopes and fears the Soubirous were a prey to the most terrible uncertainties. They felt themselves enveloped in the supernatural, and they did not know whether they were to welcome it or dread it. They had before them the difficult question, but they did not know how to answer it—Should they or should they not allow Bernadette to return to the grotto?

When confronted by any perplexing problem the Soubirous always asked the advice of Aunt Bernarde, their daughter's godmother, and they almost always followed it. During the course of that day, the 18th February, the little seer's mother went to her elder sister and told her of her perplexities. Bernarde listened but would express no opinion before having had time to reflect. In the evening she went to the Soubirous and told them that she had made up her mind and could not see any serious reason for preventing Bernadette from acceding to the Lady's request.

"If the vision," she said, "is of a heavenly nature we have nothing to fear; if it is some trickery of the devil it is not possible that the Virgin should allow a child who trusts her with such innocence of heart to be deceived. Moreover we have ourselves done wrong in not having already gone to Massabieille to see what is really taking place there. This we must do before anything else, and then we shall be able to form an opinion based upon the facts themselves and decide upon a future line of action."

In accordance with Aunt Bernarde's advice the mother and daughter left their dwelling in the Petits Fossés the next morning, the 19th February, at daybreak, and wrapped in their cloaks went towards the rue du Baons. They called in passing for Aunt Bernarde; then, without saying a word, they all three went with Bernadette in the middle towards the Gave. In spite of the care with which they had concealed themselves some of their neighbours who were unfastening their shutters recognised them and followed them. A little company of seven or eight persons arrived at the grotto at almost the same time as the Soubirous.

Bernadette knelt down, lifted her rosary to her forehead and impressively made the sign of the cross. A moment later the material world no longer existed for her and her soul was absorbed in the joys of ecstasy. An indescribable radiancy illumined her face and her whole being was steeped in heavenly joy.

Her mother and aunt had already been told what Bernadette was like at the grotto, but the reality far surpassed all that they had imagined. When they saw the child transfigured in ecstasy, the body bent forward as though she were about to fly away, they were seized with a nervous trembling and the mother cried,

" O God, I pray, do not take my daughter from me."

Another voice, that of some one present, said at the same time, " How beautiful she is."

Tears of emotion were in the eyes of all and all prayed in wondering silence.

Bernadette remained in ecstasy for about half an hour, and this half-hour seemed like a century to the anxious hearts of the mother and aunt; to the others present it seemed only a moment, but a moment of heaven itself.

The seer came out of her ecstasy, rubbing her eyes and overwhelmed as it were under the weight of her happiness. She turned affectionately to her mother and aunt, who took her lovingly in their arms. All three climbed up the steep ascent of Massabieille, surrounded by the women who had followed them when they left home. These women devoured Bernadette with their eyes, marvelling greatly at what they had seen. On the way back Bernadette said that the Lady had expressed herself satisfied at her having kept her promise to return to the grotto, and that she had said that later on she would have certain revelations to make to her.

She spoke moreover of a strange phenomenon which had

taken place during the vision. She said that whilst she was in prayer a tumult of sinister voices seemed to rise out of the bowels of the earth and make themselves heard above the waters of the Gave; these voices questioned, contradicted, interrupted each other, like the shouts of a quarrelsome crowd. One of the voices, dominating the others, had cried harshly and savagely, "Escape, escape." On hearing this threatening cry, the Lady raised her head and frowned, looking towards the river. At this simple movement the voices had been seized with fear, and had seemed to scatter in all directions and finally died away.

The persons who had been at the grotto had heard nothing of that which Bernadette recounted. They thought the child was mistaken and did not regard the matter as having any significance. It had a significance, however, and I shall revert to it later in the first chapter of the second part of this book.

CHAPTER X.

FIFTH APPEARANCE (SATURDAY, 20TH FEBRUARY).

By this time the news of the Appearances had become generally known throughout Lourdes and the matter was being publicly discussed. Yet up to the present, as I have already said, only some young girls and a dozen women had witnessed Bernadette's ecstasies. These women had spoken everywhere of the wonders they had seen; others caught the contagion of their enthusiasm and wished also to be present. As soon as it was known that the seer went to the grotto every morning a great number of the people of Lourdes hastened there. On the morning of Saturday, the 20th February, the excavation below the rock and the open space between the excavation and the Gave were filled with people. From this day forth the spectators could be counted first by hundreds and later on by thousands.

On the morning of the fifth Appearance Bernadette arrived at Massabieille with her mother at about half-past six. She was neither astonished nor troubled at the sight of the crowd awaiting her. She approached the rock as simply as if she had been a mere spectator, and went to kneel in her usual place. Without observing that every eye was fixed upon her she took her rosary quite naturally and began to pray. The next instant there shone in Bernadette's eyes a light which was not of the earth. The great moment had come and Bernadette was expressing her homage, her joy, her gratitude, to the hidden Lady of the rock. A superhuman grace transfigured all her movements and her own mother, who was kneeling at her side, said with tears of emotion,

"I must be out of my mind, for I simply can't recognise my daughter."

A confused murmur of wonder was already rising from the crowd, and most of those present raised themselves on tiptoe in order to get a better view of the ecstatic. Absorbed as they were in looking at the child the spectators feared to miss another sight; by a natural instinct they gazed alternately at Bernadette and at the rock. The eyes of the body saw nothing when looking in the direction of the grotto, but the eyes of the soul could see, and each one present might have said, like the ecstatic herself at one of the preceding Appearances,

"The Lady is there, the Lady is there."

After the ecstasy Bernadette, when questioned about her interview with the Lady, replied that the latter had graciously taught her word by word a prayer for her own special and particular use. When the seer was asked to repeat this prayer she answered that she did not consider herself at liberty to do so, inasmuch as the prayer had been composed in view of her own private needs. From the embarrassment with which the child spoke one could gather that the refusal was grounded upon certain spiritual scruples to which she did not like to allude.

CHAPTER XI.

SIXTH APPEARANCE (SUNDAY, 21ST FEBRUARY).

DR. DOZOUS, the doctor of Lourdes, an intelligent witness of the ecstasies of Bernadette, recounts in his book, *The Grotto of Lourdes, Its Fountain and Its Cures,* the facts which relate to the sixth Appearance. I will quote his account of it but, before reproducing it, I wish to remark that the learned physician, in going to Massabieille, thought he had to deal with nothing but one of those curious illnesses of a nervous order whose imperfectly understood manifestations often trouble uninstructed persons. He imagined that one word from him would be enough to bring light and consequently demolish the fanciful stories in circulation. He entered upon his observation with his preconceived idea, but from the very beginning he noticed that he was in the presence of a medical problem whose solution, from the scientific point of view, was by no means simple. At first he did not confess his embarrassment and returned several times to the grotto. After five or six days of minute and patient study the doctor declared publicly and courageously that the finger of God was revealed at Massabieille, and that Bernadette's malady was not one of those with which medicine can deal.

Born at a time when the Christian idea had somewhat lost its power over men's minds, Dr. Dozous had passed his life in religious indifference. Upon coming into contact with the supernatural events of the grotto he felt his soul awake and take its flight towards new regions. He renounced the sceptical opinion he had held up to that time and became one of the most ardent champions of the cause of the Immaculate Conception. The popular doctor of Lourdes died amongst his fellow-citizens, a resigned and pious Christian, 15th March, 1884, aged eighty-five. During his long career he had devoted himself disinterestedly to the relief of the poor and the poor bewailed him. No doubt the professional virtues of Dr. Dozous, as well as his great zeal in publishing the glories of the Virgin at the grotto, have been crowned in heaven by Him Who rewards even the glass of cold water offered to one of His little ones.

This is what the doctor says in his statement relative to the sixth Appearance.

"As soon as she had come before the grotto, Bernadette knelt down, took out of her pocket her rosary and began to pray, telling her beads. Her face underwent a perfect transformation noticed by all who were near her, and showed that she was *en rapport* with the Appearance. Whilst she told her beads with her left hand, she held in her right hand a lighted candle which was frequently extinguished by a very strong draught which was blowing along the Gave, but each time she gave it to the person nearest to her to have it relighted.

"I was following with great attention all the movements of Bernadette, and I wished to know what was the state of the circulation of the blood and of the respiration at this moment; I took one of her arms and placed my fingers upon the radial artery. The pulse was regular and tranquil, the respiration easy; nothing indicated any nervous excitement in the young girl.

"Bernadette, after I had left her arm free, rose and advanced a little towards the grotto. Soon I saw her face, which until then had expressed the most perfect joy, grow sad; two tears fell from her eyes and rolled down her cheeks. This change occurring in her face during her station surprised me. I asked her, when she had finished her prayers and the mysterious being had disappeared, what had passed within her during this long station. She answered:

"'The Lady, looking away from me for a moment, directed her glance afar, above my head. Then looking down upon me again, for I had asked her what had saddened her, she said, "Pray for the sinners." I was very quickly reassured by the expression of goodness and sweetness which I saw return to her face, and immediately she disappeared.'

"In leaving this place, where her emotion had been so great, Bernadette retired, as she always did, in the most simple and modest attitude."

As we see, Dr. Dozous' account shows no enthusiasm; it is the statement pure and simple of a fact examined externally only. In some of the statements the doctor betrays perplexity, but he hesitates and does not dare to make a definite pronouncement. He seeks, he gropes, he meditates. On the one hand he foresees the denials of his medical brethren; on the other he hears the demands made by his own reason. A great fight is taking place within him and he has to decide between his old ideas and the new horizons which are presenting themselves to his soul. More and more struck by the evidence of facts, Dr. Dozous finally recognises the supernatural character of the Appearances, and from that day forth, boldly facing and despising all derision, he constituted himself the devoted apostle of the grotto of Lourdes.

CHAPTER XII.

CONTINUATION OF THE 21ST FEBRUARY.

THE spectators of the ecstasy of the previous day had been numerous. Others would have been present, but fearing to be the dupes of some mystification they had decided to wait for fuller information and only went to the grotto on the next day, the 21st February. These persons were joined by some working-men from Lourdes, who thought they would employ their Sunday leisure in witnessing the events of which they had heard. These fresh visitors, added to those of the previous days who always came back faithfully, formed a considerable crowd round Bernadette on the morning of the sixth Appearance.

The seer's transfiguration threw all the witnesses of the ecstasy, as was always the case, into the deepest stupefaction. They kept silence at the grotto as being a holy place, but once back in the town they went from street to street speaking everywhere of the wonders they had seen. People came out of the houses to listen to them or stopped them at every step to question them. The listeners expressed as much enthusiastic approval at their stories as though they were recounting some happy event of a national character. If any incredulous spirit dared to contradict he was immediately forced to keep silence.

The authorities responsible for the peace of the town now began to notice the unusual stir which was taking place at Lourdes. At first they paid no attention to the affair of the grotto and thought that the commonsense of the people would make short work of the current gossip. But the commotion of the morning of the 21st February made them feel some uneasiness in regard to their official responsibilities. The mayor, the *procureur impérial,* and the police commissioner met at the mayor's office in order to see if they could not take some steps to prevent a recurrence of the manifestations which had just taken place. Certain sharp words had been exchanged between those who believed and those who disbelieved in the visions.

They exaggerated the importance of these discussions and saw in them a germ of dissension which threatened to disturb the peace of the town.

Another and more reasonable fear made the authorities anxious. The narrow space at Massabieille into which the crowd gathered presented certain serious dangers. The earliest arrivals took possession of the circular space in front of the grotto. Those who came next climbed upon the blocks of stone which stood up out of the Gave. The late comers climbed the trees and clung to the branches overhanging the hollow. The dangers of the situation may well be understood ; one false step might precipitate into the river those who were standing on their slippery little islands ; the breaking of a branch would have been enough to let the rash persons who were dangling over the abyss fall upon the spectators beneath them. No accident had happened as yet, but it would be foolish to delay taking measures until the catastrophe had occurred.

The fear of a disaster which might easily happen decided the authorities to do something. They understood however that they must proceed with caution, and that while they must act with decision they must also be careful to avoid offending popular susceptibilities. To attain this twofold end they thought that the best possible means would be to persuade the seer to go no more to the grotto. They regarded the child herself as the cause of the crowd's excitement, and so they thought that in removing this cause they would at the same time put a stop to its effects. In order to carry out their resolution the *procureur impérial*, immediately upon leaving the mayor's office, summoned Bernadette to appear before him.

CHAPTER XIII.

CONTINUATION OF THE 21ST FEBRUARY.

I.—Bernadette summoned before the procureur impérial.

THE bench of Lourdes was represented at the time of which we write by M. Dutour, who was afterwards at the court of appeal at Pau. This magistrate was respected in his jurisdiction and fulfilled with dignity the duties of his office. As is often the case with many of the best men, M. Dutour was a man of very contradictory character and had certain prejudices which spoiled his fine qualities. Thus while respectful towards religion, he warred energetically against what are called to-day clerical ideas.* In judicial matters, in which he otherwise showed considerable ability, he would hold his own opinion with the greatest obstinacy against all the other judges if they happened to differ from him. A man of such varied qualities, some good and some bad, but fundamentally honest and sincere, the *procureur* of Lourdes proceeded to deal with the affair of the grotto.

As soon as Bernadette came before him he began to question her as follows.

"My child, you are getting yourself much talked about. Do you intend to continue your visits to the grotto?"

"Yes, sir. I have made a promise to the Lady, and I shall continue going there for another twelve days."

"But, my poor child, your Lady doesn't exist; she is a purely imaginary being."

"I thought so too when I saw her for the first time and I rubbed my eyes, but now I know for certain that I am not mistaken."

"How do you know that?"

"Because I have seen her many times. I saw her only this morning. Moreover she talks with me."

"The Hospice sisters to whom you go to school would not tell a lie, yet they tell you that you are under a delusion."

"If the sisters of the Hospice saw as I do, they would believe as I do."

"Take care. Before we have done we shall perhaps discover some secret which will explain your obstinacy. It is already said that you and your parents have received presents privately."

"We receive nothing from any one."

* One Sunday at Mass he heard a curate of the parish give utterance in his sermon to certain veiled remarks about the upper classes in society; he made in particular some allusions to the State officials, whose bad examples he criticised. The *procureur* immediately took note of the young preacher's remarks and called public attention to them. By threatening to bring the curate's indiscretion before the notice of the tribunal, he compelled the Bishop of Tarbes to remove the priest in question from Lourdes.

"But yesterday you went to Madame Millet, and there you had some sweets given you."

"Quite true; Madame Millet made me take a glass of water and sugar for my asthma, but that was all."

"However that may be, your conduct at the grotto is a veritable scandal. You are disturbing the town and all this must be put a stop to. Will you promise me not to return to Massabieille?"

"Sir, I cannot promise you that."

"Is that your final word?"

"Yes, sir."

"Go away then... I shall think over what is to be done."

In the club at Lourdes to which I belong the *procureur impérial* made no mystery about his examination of Bernadette. He willingly told us of the questions and replies and even laughed over his own defeat. I ought however to add that at the time of which I speak the representatives of the Government had not yet taken up a line of hostility against the Appearances considered from the doctrinal point of view.

II.—*Bernadette summoned before the police commissioner.*

The commissioner who was in charge of the police at Lourdes at the time of the Appearances was M. Jacomet, a man of the district, aged then about forty. He had a frank, open, cheerful face and an attractive manner; he was moreover intelligent and well-educated and had a certain air of distinction about him. Every one at Lourdes, great or small, shook M. Jacomet's hand, and the unpopularity of his office did not injure his personal popularity. No commissioner was ever more successful than he in unearthing a criminal and making him confess his guilt. He exercised his skill in the chief towns in France and mounting from step to step reached the topmost rung of the Government ladder. He died at Paris comparatively young and while still occupied in the discharge of his duties.

In undertaking his campaign against the Grotto M. Jacomet had no intention of interfering in a matter in which the supernatural was concerned. He, like the *procureur impérial*, imagined that he was dealing merely with one of those many superstitions which so often attract and seduce the ignorant and uneducated.

He hoped that by his personal influence and the resources of his mother-wit he would be able to allay the excitement and prevent Bernadette from continuing her *rôle* of seer.

During the afternoon of Sunday, 21st February, without being discouraged by M. Dutour's failure in the morning, M. Jacomet went to the Place du Porche where he expected to find Bernadette coming out from vespers. Callet, the court usher, pointed out to his chief Bernadette walking in the crowd by the side of her Aunt Lucile. The commissioner, pretending to be there from curiosity, soon reached the child, and, as though taking advantage of a chance meeting, asked her to come to his office. The little girl, quite calmly and without asking any questions, followed M. Jacomet while her aunt went off to tell the family. Some one said to her jokingly in passing, "Ah, Bernadette, I expect you are going to be put in prison."

"No," said the child, smiling, "I'm not afraid, for I have nothing to fear."

Before going further I would say in passing that whilst I was living at Lourdes I occupied the same house as the police commissioner. The latter lived upon the ground floor and I upon the first floor. It is owing to the fact of our being neighbours that I have been able to give the following account.

At the moment when the seer arrived at the commissioner's my sister eagerly came to tell me the news and to beg me to come down. Bernadette's case interested me so little that I was not even curious to see her, and it is probable that I should never have left my chair if my sister had not shaken me out of it and, taking me by the arm, employed actual force. Relying on my intimacy with my neighbour I entered without knocking the room serving as pretorium, and making a sign to M. Jacomet to make him understand the object of my visit, I sat down at the side of the room. From where I was placed I could watch perfectly the features of the young seer and hear what she said.

The child before me, whom I saw for the first time, appeared to be ten or eleven years of age but she was really fourteen. Her face was fresh and round, her gaze was very sweet and very simple, the tone of her voice though somewhat loud was sympathetic. I did not notice her asthma. In a very natural attitude she kept her hands crossed upon her knees and her head slightly bent forward over her chest. She was wearing a white cloak, and her other garments though simple were clean and neat. A table with a desk upon it divided the seer from the commissioner.

When I came in M. Jacomet had just finished settling himself in his seat and was placing in front of him a sheet of blank paper and a pencil. Then he turned to the child and said to her in his most insidiously kindly manner :

" I expect you know why I have summoned you here. People have told me of all the beautiful things you have seen at Massabieille and I am so interested that I want to hear all about it. Would you mind telling M. Estrade and me how you first met the Lady of the Grotto ? "

" Not at all, sir."

" Your name is Bernadette, isn't it ? "

" Yes, sir, Bernadette."

"What is your surname ? "

The child searched for a moment, then, as one finding, she replied, " Bernadette Soubirous."

" How old are you ? "

" Fourteen."

" You're quite sure ? " said the commissioner smiling, as if to ask whether she was not exaggerating.

" Yes, sir, I am quite sure. I'm turned fourteen."

"What do you do in the house ? "

" Nothing very much, sir. Since my return from Bartrès I have been going to school to learn the catechism ; after school I look after my brothers and sisters, who are younger than I."

" So you lived at Bartrès ? What did you do there ? "

" I spent several months at my foster-mother's house ; she gave me a little flock of sheep and lambs to look after."

The commissioner in a friendly tone asked a few more questions of the child. When he thought he had secured her confidence, he said to her,

" Now let us come to what we want you to tell us, namely, the scene under the rock of Massabieille which has made so strong an impression on you. Take as long as you like in telling us about it."

Bernadette, as if in the presence of one of her own relations, told the story full of charm of the first Appearance, as recorded in the preceding pages. She entered into all the details of age, costume, face, relating to the Lady, and that with such convinced simplicity that one could not for a moment doubt her sincerity. Whilst she spoke the commissioner wrote rapidly upon his paper. Then he raised his head.

"What you tell us is very interesting, but who is this Lady who has so infatuated you? Do you know her?"

"I do not know her," answered the child with a touching simplicity.

"You say she is beautiful. How beautiful is she?"

"Oh, sir, she is more beautiful than any lady I have ever met."

"But not more beautiful than Madame N. or Madame N.?" Here the commissioner mentioned the names of those ladies at Lourdes most generously endowed with the gift of beauty.

"They can't be compared with her."

"Does this Lady move and speak, or does she remain in her place like a statue in a church?"

"Oh, she moves and smiles and speaks like you; among other things she has asked me to be so kind as to return to the grotto during the next fifteen days."

"What did you say?"

"I have promised that I will return."

"What do your parents say about these things?"

"At first, they said they were illusions—"

Catching hold of this word as it passed her lips, the commissioner interrupted her.

"Yes, my child, your parents are right, and the things which you think you hear and see exist only in your imagination."

"Others have said so to me, but I am sure that I am not mistaken."

"Listen. If the Lady of the rock was a person like other persons every one would be able to see her and hear her. How is it that this is not so?"

"I cannot explain these things to you, sir. What I can positively affirm is that the Lady is real and living."

"Since you hold to it I have no reason to prevent your believing in the existence of your pretended Lady. However, as the prefect or some other authority will probably require of me a report on this subject, let us see if I have got all your answers down correctly."

Here the commissioner took his paper of notes and began a war of traps. He tried to make the seer contradict herself.

"You said that the Lady was aged about nineteen or twenty?"

"No, I said sixteen or seventeen."

"That she was dressed in a blue robe with a white girdle?"

"Just the opposite, sir; you should have put a white robe with a blue girdle."

"That her hair fell down behind?"

"You have understood me wrongly; it is the veil which fell down behind."

And so Bernadette corrected, without boldness but also without timidity, all the mistakes which the commissioner had designedly introduced into her story. M. Jacomet understood that nothing was to be gained in this way, so he changed his tactics. Speaking to her seriously and somewhat ironically, he said:

"My dear Bernadette, I wished to let you go on to the end of your tale but I ought to let you know that I was cognisant of the story of your pretended visions before. This story is pure invention and I know who has taught it to you."

The commissioner paused and looked fixedly at the seer.

The young girl raised her astonished eyes to the man in front of her and replied,

"I don't understand you, sir."

"I will be more explicit. Is there not some one who has secretly told you to say that the Virgin appeared to you at Massabieille, and that by saying this you will not only pass for a saint but also obtain great favour from the Virgin? Be careful in your answer, for I know more about this matter than you think."

"No one, sir, has suggested to me the things of which you speak."

"I know the whole state of the case but I don't want to cause a scandal or to seek a quarrel. I don't demand any confession from you, but you must give me one simple promise. Will you assure me that you will not go again to the grotto?"

" Sir, I have promised the Lady to return there."

" Oh, indeed," said the commissioner, rising from his seat and feigning anger. " So you imagine that we are always going to listen good-naturedly to your fairy tales and give way to your obstinacy? If you do not instantly promise me not to return to Massabieille I will send for the gendarmes and have you put in prison."

Bernadette remained immovable.

I now left my place and came up to the seer.

" My child, don't be obstinate. Do what M. Jacomet asks you; if not, you know what to expect."

Bernadette understood that I had no authority to interfere and she gave no answer.

Meanwhile the door of the pretorium opened and a working-man timidly put in his head.

"What do you want?" asked the commissioner.

" I am the father of this child," replied the man, pointing to Bernadette.

" Ah! you are M. Soubirous. I am glad you have come for I was just about to send for you. You know the game your daughter has been playing for some days. Put up to it no doubt by some mischievous old woman of the district, she pretends to be inspired and gives herself up to tricks which are turning the heads of imbeciles. This comedy must finish for it constitutes a real danger to the peace of the town. I warn you that if you have not enough authority to keep your child at home I shall have enough to cause her to be shut up elsewhere."

" Oh, sir, please let me speak frankly. For myself, I have no doubt that the child is sincere in the story that she tells, but is she mistaken? That is what puzzles us. I confess to you that my wife and I are wearied out with importunities. For the last three or four days our house has never been free of visitors, and we don't know how to get rid of inquisitive persons. I am glad to have your commands as an excuse for shutting out the public. As to Bernadette, we will see that she does not go near Massabieille any more."

The commissioner congratulated the father on his good sense and dismissed him and his daughter.

Alone with M. Jacomet, I broke the silence.

"The story of this young girl is very extraordinary."

"It doesn't come from her," replied the commissioner; "it is too cleverly concocted for that."

"I don't agree with you. This young girl has been fascinated, and the picture which she has seen or thinks she has seen is still before her eyes. In reproducing it she describes what she sees."

"Not at all; she is reciting a made-up story."

"Do you think that a poor little peasant girl could recite it in such a way and with such sincere earnestness? It is impossible."

"My dear neighbour, you don't belong to the police."

"But what is the object of this story?"

"The future will tell us that."

To sum up, the commissioner suspected in the case of Bernadette a pious fraud; I only saw in it the illusive seductions of a brilliant hallucination. For both of us the supernatural was out of the question. Could there be any supernatural revelation in such an enlightened century as ours?

CHAPTER XIV.

MONDAY, 22ND FEBRUARY.

The Virgin does not Appear that Day at the Grotto.

In spite of the assurances given by Soubirous the father as to the good faith of his daughter, the police commissioner could not believe that Bernadette had no accomplice in the affair of the grotto. When he had finished the examination of Sunday he ordered all the police of the locality to keep a careful watch upon the movements of the seer, and particularly upon any dealings which she might have with any persons outside her family.

The next day, Monday the 22nd, the father and mother ordered their daughter to go straight to school, and to turn neither to the right hand nor to the left. Without a murmur Bernadette put her spelling-book in her basket and went off to the hospice. She returned home a little before midday, took her frugal meal and went off immediately afterwards to afternoon school.

When she had reached the point where the road goes from the *pont des ruisseaux* to the hospice she was suddenly stopped. " An invisible barrier," said the child afterwards, " prevented me from passing."

Several times did she try to go on but the resistance was always the same and she only felt herself left free when she turned back. Troubled and almost frightened, she thought of going home when she heard the small voice of reproach speaking to her conscience. A voice within asked her if she was faithfully fulfilling the promises she had made at the grotto. The little seer understood, her heart beat quick and fast, and without hesitating any longer she turned back.

At the time of which I am writing the gendarmerie barracks occupied the last house on the left of the street at the entrance of the town on the road to Tarbes. The house in question was only a few paces from the spot where Bernadette had stopped. The gendarmes noticed from the windows that the child hesitated to continue her road, and their curiosity was all the more aroused by the fact that they could not understand her halting before the invisible obstacle; when however they saw her turn round and go back they guessed her thoughts and hastily followed her.

Bernadette returned to the *pont des ruisseaux*, then instead of going by the street through the town she went down into the Lapaca quarter and took a path beside the fort leading to Massabieille. The gendarmes caught her up near the mill where she was born, and asked her in an authoritative tone where she was going.

" I am going to the grotto," the child replied stiffly, without slackening her pace or turning her head. The gendarmes asked no more questions, but followed her in silence.

My sister, who happened to have gone for a walk that day with some friends in the direction of Massabieille, will herself tell the story of Bernadette's visit to the grotto on the afternoon of the 22nd February. My sister wrote her account many years ago.

"When we had left the town my companions and I noticed

a number of persons collected at the spot where the path by the fort joins the forest road. All were looking down the river, and soon a cry of satisfaction was uttered by the group. 'There she is ; she's coming ! '

"We asked who was expected and they told us it was Bernadette. The child was coming along the path ; near her were two gendarmes and behind them a crowd of children. It was then that I saw for the first time the charming face of Mary's little *protégée*.* The seer was walking between the two gendarmes, calm, serene and unpretending. She passed in front of us as tranquilly as if she had been quite alone.

" My companions and I arrived at the grotto after many other persons whom we followed at a distance. Bernadette was on her knees, and the gendarmes were standing a little way off from her. They did not disturb the child during her prayer, which was long. When she rose they questioned her and she owned that she had seen nothing. The crowd dispersed and Bernadette went away also.

"While we were returning to the town we heard that the seer had gone into the Savy Mill, and wishing to see her near we went to the mill to find her. She was sitting on a seat and a woman was beside her ; I learnt that this woman was her mother. The mother was perspiring heavily ; she was pale and from time to time looked anxiously at Bernadette. I asked her if she knew the child and she replied, ' Ah ! mademoiselle, I am her unhappy mother.'

" 'Why do you call yourself unhappy ? ' I asked.

" ' If only you knew, mademoiselle, what we suffer. Some laugh at us ; others say our daughter is mad. Some even say that we are receiving money for this, and that we shall be prosecuted.'

" ' But, my good woman, if you trouble yourself about everything people say you will have your hands full. What do you think yourself about your child ? '

" ' I assure you, mademoiselle, that my child is truthful and honest and incapable of deceiving me. Of that I am certain. People say she is mad. It is true that she suffers from asthma but

* My sister had seen Bernadette go into the police commissioner's office, but she had not seen her face.

apart from that she is not ill; she eats and behaves herself in her usual way and when I ask her if she is poorly she says No. We forbade her to return to the grotto; in anything else I am sure she would have obeyed us but in this matter—well, you see how she escapes from our control. She was just telling me that an invisible barrier had prevented her going along the road to school and that an irresistible force had dragged her in spite of herself to Massabieille.' "

The wits of Lourdes, on hearing that the Lady had not appeared that day at the grotto, did not fail to make a great joke of the matter. "She is frightened of the gendarmes," they said, "and she will probably think it wise, if Jacomet has the thing in hand, to clear off from the rock and take up her abode elsewhere." At that time I belonged to the ranks of the mockers and I had no idea that I was so soon to leave them.

CHAPTER XV.

SEVENTH APPEARANCE (TUESDAY, 23RD FEBRUARY).

MY sister's friends, disappointed at not having seen Bernadette in ecstasy, had asked her mother during their conversation with her at the Savy Mill what she intended to do about the visits promised by her child to the mysterious Lady. The mother, with tears in her eyes and lowering her voice in order not to be heard by Bernadette, had replied:

"After what has happened to-day, I dare not oppose any obstacle."

That was just what the ladies wanted to know and they instantly arranged to return to the grotto the next day at the time at which Bernadette usually went there.

My sister had previously asked me on several occasions to go with her to the grotto to witness the seer's ecstasies. I had always answered that I did not share her interest in the matter and that, for my part, I had no wish to make myself ridiculous. On Monday, the 22nd, during our evening meal, without saying anything about the arrangement she had made with her friends, she returned indirectly to the charge, telling me that she was very anxious to go to Massabieille but that she did not think it suitable to walk alone along the forest road. I turned a deaf ear to her.

That same evening I paid a visit, as was often my custom, to Abbé Peyramale, curé of the parish. At that moment everyone at Lourdes was talking of the visions and naturally the conversation between the curé and myself turned upon that subject. Before leaving the presbytery, and without imagining that my words would be taken seriously, I told the curé how my sister had been urging me to go with her to the grotto.

"I don't see any harm in your doing what your sister asks," replied the curé coldly, "and if I were in your place I should have gone before now. I, like you, think that there is nothing but a child's delusion in it all, but I really don't see how you compromise your dignity by going to witness a thing which takes place in broad daylight and of which everyone is talking."

As soon as I got home I told my sister that I would do what she asked me and would accompany her next day on the Massabieille road. On starting off the next morning I found at my side not merely my sister but also her friends, those who had been with her the day before. I confess that I was somewhat abashed at having to walk through the town in the midst of this solemn cortège. On the forest road I chaffed my companions, making foolish and vulgar jokes.

"Have you brought your opera glasses? Are you well supplied with holy water? Has one of you a candle?"

At length I arrived, at about six o'clock in the morning when day was breaking, at the head of my squad of ladies and affecting an air of supreme indifference I made my first entry within the cave of Massabieille. The seer had not yet arrived but a hundred and fifty or two hundred persons were already there before us. Many women were on their knees praying and I had great difficulty to keep myself from laughing on seeing the childish belief of these simple Christians. Three or four gentlemen from Lourdes,* who like myself had come either from curiosity or to oblige their friends, had taken up their position in front

* There were, if I remember rightly, Dr. Dozous, M. Dufo, a barrister, the captain of the fort, and M. de La Fitte, formerly commissariat officer.

of the cave. My *amour propre* was relieved at finding them there.

After waiting for some minutes a confused murmur ran through the crowd and some one said that the seer was coming. The ranks opened and soon Bernadette appeared. We men made use of our elbows and cleared a way to the little girl's side. From this moment she was under our closest observation; our eyes were riveted upon her and did not leave her for an instant.

Bernadette knelt down, took her rosary out of her pocket and made a profound reverence. She did it all without the least shade of awkwardness or self-consciousness, just as simply and naturally as if she had gone into the parish church for her ordinary devotions. Whilst she was passing the beads between her fingers she looked up towards the rock as though waiting for something. Suddenly, as in a flash of lightning, an expression of wonder illuminated her face and she seemed to be born into another life. A light shone in her eyes; wonderful smiles played upon her lips; an unutterable grace transfigured her whole being. The seer's soul within the narrow prison of the flesh seemed to be trying to reveal itself to the outward sight and to proclaim its joy and happiness. Bernadette was no longer Bernadette; she was one of those privileged beings, the face all glorious with the glory of heaven, whom the Apostle of the great visions has shown us in ecstasy before the throne of the Lamb.

And we men who stood there, spontaneously, without a thought of our dignity, took off our hats and bent our knees even as the humblest peasant women. The time for argument and discussion was past for ever, and we, like all those present at this heavenly scene, looked from the ecstatic to the rock and from the rock to the ecstatic. We saw nothing, we heard nothing, but what we could and did see and understand was that a conversation was going on between the mysterious Lady and the child upon whom our gaze was fixed.

After the first transports of joy caused by the Lady's arrival the seer's attitude was that of a listener. Her movements and gestures and the play of her features quickly gave evidence of all the characteristics of a conversation. Sometimes smiling, sometimes grave, at one time the child would show her approval by an inclination of the head, at another she would appear to be asking a question. When the Lady spoke a thrill of joy seemed to convulse the girl's body; when on the contrary Bernadette made a request she would bow herself down to the ground and be moved almost to tears. We could see that at certain moments the conversation was broken off, and then the child would return to her rosary but with her eyes still fixed upon the rock. She seemed afraid to lower her eyes lest she should lose the vision of the ravishing object which she contemplated.

The seer always ended her prayers with a profound reverence to the hidden Lady. I have been in the world, only too much perhaps, and I have met models of grace and distinction. But I have never seen anyone make a bow with such grace or such distinction as Bernadette. During the ecstasy the child also made the sign of the cross at intervals, and on that same day, when returning from the grotto, I said that if the sign of the cross is made in heaven it must be made as Bernadette made it.

The ecstasy lasted for an hour; at the end of that time the seer went on her knees from the place where she was praying to just below the wild rose tree hanging from the rock. There, concentrating all her energies as for an act of worship, she kissed the earth and returned still upon her knees to the place which she had just left. A last glow of light lit up her face, then gradually, almost imperceptibly, the transfiguring glory of the ecstasy grew fainter and finally disappeared. The seer continued praying for a few moments longer but it was only the face of the little peasant child which we saw. At last Bernadette got up, went to her mother, and was lost in the crowd.

After the scene which I have just described I felt like one in a dream and I left the grotto without remembering the ladies for whom I was responsible. I could not shake off my emotion and a crowd of thoughts invaded my soul. The Lady of the rock might hide herself from my bodily eyes, but I had felt her presence and I was convinced that she had looked on me with maternal love. It was indeed a solemn hour of my life and deeply was I moved to think that I, the omniscient and superior person who had mocked and scoffed at such things, had been allowed to come so near to the Queen of Heaven.

Forty years have passed since then and with my head bowed in the dust I wonder still, oh! Immaculate Virgin, what mystery urged thy heart of love to call me so near to thee. What had I done to deserve this incomparable honour, and what have I done since to show my gratitude for thy tenderness to me? Mother, my hair is white, and I am near the grave. I do not dare to look upon my iniquities and more than ever do I feel the need of taking refuge under the cloak of thy mercy and pity. When at the last great hour I have to appear before thy Divine Son, vouchsafe to be my protectress and to remember that thou hast seen me on my knees and believing, beneath the sacred vault of thy Grotto at Lourdes, in those holy happy days when thou didst reveal thyself to Bernadette and through Bernadette to me.

Bernadette, when asked what the Lady had said to her during the seventh Appearance, replied that three secrets had been entrusted to her but that they concerned nobody but herself. The seer added that she could not reveal these secrets to anyone, not even to her confessor. Inquisitive people have often tried by insinuations, by trickery, or by promises, to get these revelations of the Virgin out of the child. But all attempts failed and Bernadette carried her secrets with her to the grave.

CHAPTER XVI.

EIGHTH APPEARANCE (WEDNESDAY, 24TH FEBRUARY).

My previous ideas were now completely upset. In the presence of the police commissioner Bernadette had astonished me; at the grotto she had conquered me. I no longer regarded her as having her mind disturbed by a phantom of the imagination; I saw the heavenly figure of the Virgin dazzling her spiritual sight. I had begun by laughing at what had happened at Massabieille, but now, after my first pilgrimage, I felt that I must consider the matter attentively and respectfully. If I had been able to follow my inclination I should have gone to the scene of the Appearances every day, but unfortunately I could not dispose of my time, and my duties often took me away from Lourdes. The 24th February was occupied in this way but on my return in the evening my sister told me what had occurred at the ecstasy that morning.

In the first place she had noticed that absolute strangers were becoming more numerous at the grotto and that the people of Lourdes continued to be present in greater crowds than ever. Bernadette had arrived at her usual time and without taking any notice of the attention she received had gone and knelt upon the stone which she had chosen on the previous days. This place was always given up by the crowd to the seer on her arrival.

Up to the present the Lady's intercourse with Bernadette had seemed to be of an entirely personal and private character, but the Queen of Heaven had wider intentions in her mind and the purport of her communications was now to be enlarged. Bernadette was doubtless the child of her choice but it was not for her alone, but for the whole world, that the heavenly Mother had come to pour forth the treasures of her mercy and pity at Lourdes. Embracing in the vast circle of her love all her earthly children, to the righteous she brought her encouragement and approval and to poor sinners those secret inspirations which speak even to the souls most indifferent to their eternal destiny. And it was of the sinners that her mother's heart was thinking on the morning of the eighth Appearance.

Continuing her account, my sister told me that while Bernadette was in her ecstasy an expression of sadness clouded her face until then so radiant with happiness. The seer was listening as to a voice which spoke from the rock ; then, like one who hears bad news, she let her arms fall while the tears rolled in abundance down her cheeks. In an attitude of humiliation she rose and ascended the slope in front of the recess placing her lips against the earth at each step. Beneath the wild rose tree she again prostrated herself and then raised her head towards the opening as if to receive a mysterious command. The ecstatic then turned to the onlookers and, with the tears still rolling down her cheeks and in a voice broken with sobs, said three times distinctly : " Penitence, Penitence, Penitence ! " This last detail I learnt subsequently, for my sister was too far away from Bernadette to hear the words she spoke. But what is quite certain is that the child herself heard them from the lips of the Lady.

Bernadette returned to her former place and fell again into an ecstasy. Whilst all were in solemn silence round her an unseemly and grotesque interruption occurred to trouble the devotions of the spectators. The quartermaster of Lourdes, followed by a subordinate, had suddenly made his way into the grotto, crying in a voice of authority: "Make room." After having forced a passage through the crowd he had taken up his position at the child's side and said to her: "What are you doing, you little actress?" Bernadette paid no attention—what was a vulgar soldier to her at such a moment?—and lost entirely in the vision she continued absorbed in prayer. Annoyed at the seer's want of respect for him, the soldier then turned towards the crowd and, putting himself in a theatrical attitude, cried: "And to think that such follies can take place in the nineteenth century!"

Struck dumb for a moment by the suddenness of this absurd remark the spectators did not at first make any protest. But when they saw that the man intended to continue his harangue several workmen drew near murmuring some words of menace. The good quartermaster immediately assumed the air of a misunderstood person, and remembering that discretion is sometimes the better part of valour, wisely stopped making an exhibition of himself.

CHAPTER XVII.

NINTH APPEARANCE (THURSDAY, 25TH FEBRUARY).

DISCOVERY OF THE MIRACULOUS SPRING.

I CANNOT help making the remark, in beginning this chapter, that man is a very versatile being and that very little is needed to disturb his judgment. He gets excited and then cools down again with very little reason and often without waiting for the guiding hand to shew him his path. This causeless haste gives birth to the inconsequences and contradictions which seem to belong to his transitory existence. Up to the present we have seen the crowd enthusiastic under the rock of Massabieille; to-day we shall find it downcast and ready to deny what it had previously welcomed with joyful belief. The moment has come when the invisible Lady is to reveal at the grotto the first manifestation of her power. The miracle took place but the spectators did not understand it; for the majority of them it was even a matter of disenchantment and offence. I myself, who was present at the mysterious scene I am about to describe, was conscious of a painful eclipse of my faith and I went away from Massabieille quite disconcerted.

On my first visit to the grotto I had carefully noted the exact spot where the seer placed herself to say her prayers. On the morning of the 25th February I succeeded in getting near that spot and this time I was again able to follow all the movements of the young ecstatic without losing a single one.

She was there then under my eyes in her angelic pose, when, after some minutes of meditation, she rose and advanced towards the grotto. In passing she pushed aside the branches of the wild rose tree and went to kiss the ground under the rock, beyond the bush. Then she came down the slope again and fell once more into an ecstasy.

At the end of some moments, the seer got up once more and seemed embarrassed; hesitating, she turned away towards the Gave and took two or three steps towards it. Suddenly she stopped abruptly, looked behind her as one who hears herself called, and listened to words which seemed to come to her from the side of the rock. She made a sign of assent, began to walk once more, but towards the grotto this time, not towards the Gave, to the left corner of the excavations. After having gone about three-quarters of the way she stopped and cast a troubled look around. She raised her head as though to question the Lady; then she resolutely bent down and began to scratch the earth. The little cavity which she hollowed out became full of water; after having waited a moment she drank of it and washed her face; she also took a blade of grass which grew on the soil and raised it to her mouth. All the spectators followed the phases of this strange scene with a painful feeling and a sort of stupor. When the child raised herself to return to her place her face was still smeared with muddy water. Seeing this a cry of disappointment and pity rose from the lips of all: "Bernadette is out of her mind! The poor child has become insane!"

Bernadette returned to her place without seeming moved and even without taking any notice of the exclamations sounding in her ears. After her face had been cleaned she resumed her contemplation of the heavenly vision, happier than ever, and with an angelic smile upon her lips.

The hour of admiration had passed; the poor little seer had lost her prestige and no more notice was taken of her except in the way of pity. The prophets of free thought had already foretold madness as the goal at which the young visionary was bound to arrive and now the fatal moment seemed to have come.

Whilst the crowd was going off from the grotto Bernadette continued, tranquil and recollected, to lose herself in the delights of prayer beneath the gaze of Her whom she loved. At length about seven o'clock, the hour when the vision disappeared, she made her impressive sign of the cross and took the road to the town.

The greater part of those present on that day departed from Massabieille with downcast eyes and hearts heavy with poignant sadness. As for me, I gave myself up to the bitterest feelings of disappointment. "Bernadette mad!" I said to myself. "Then her ecstasies were nothing but hallucinations. There was no foundation of truth in those pictures which ravished my eyes and transported my soul, nothing but my own blind folly. But if the mind and heart, the senses and all the powers of our being, conspire to seduce and deceive us, upon what testimony, my God, are we to establish our judgments and our beliefs?"

The few persons who, after the ecstasy, remained with Bernadette while she was returning from the grotto to Lourdes were not long in remarking that no alarming symptom revealed itself in the mental state of the young seer. The child talked in her ordinary fashion, spoke sensibly and with that trustful and friendly air which was one of her great charms. Convinced that the ecstatic was in full possession of her faculties, these same persons induced her to explain to them the strange scenes they had just witnessed at Massabieille.

Addressing the young child, they said to her : " Bernadette, you were very absent-minded this morning at the grotto. What was the meaning of your comings and goings ? Why did you scratch up the ground ? Why did you drink muddy water which you must have disliked ? "

Bernadette replied quite simply and naturally, and I have often heard later this same reply from her lips :

"Whilst I was in prayer, the Lady said to me in a friendly but serious voice : 'Go, drink and wash in the fountain.' As I did not know where this fountain was, and *as I did not think the matter important*, I went towards the Gave. The Lady called me back and signed to me with her finger to go under the grotto to the left ; I obeyed but I did not see any water. Not knowing where to get it from, I scratched the earth and the water came. I let it get a little clear of the mud, then I drank and washed."

" You also ate some grass. Why did you do that ? "

" I do not know. The Lady urged me to it by an interior impulse."

Some good Christians of simple and persevering faith had not allowed themselves to be prejudiced by the bizarre movements of the young ecstatic. After the departure of the spectators they had continued to say their rosary quietly under the rock without troubling about the impressions of those who had left. At the end of their prayers they noticed that a tiny thread of water, scarcely visible, had detached itself from the point where Bernadette had scratched and was trying to make a way for itself towards the Gave. It crawled along timidly and gradually, and was every now and again lost in the sand. The good women laid no stress upon this little incident.

In the afternoon of that same day, the 25th February, other persons went to the grotto and were astonished to see a ribbon of water which they had never noticed before coming down from the slope. The little current went on increasing from moment to moment and was already hollowing out a little channel in the soil. The second lot of observers witnessed the fact, but being ignorant of what had happened that morning at the grotto they did not dream of connecting it with the action of the seer. The hidden work which was being accomplished under the rock of Massabieille continued its mysterious progress and assumed greater and greater proportions. Soon the little thread of water, which only a few hours before had crept in fear and hesitation across the pebbly ground, took volume and was already flowing freely towards the bed of the river.

The next day, when the *habitués* of the ecstasies arrived, they could admire under the rock of Massabieille the abundant fountain which flows there to-day.

The news of the appearance of the source caused a great sensation at Lourdes. A large number of persons hastened immediately to the grotto to assure themselves of the reality of the fact. It was most certainly there, that fountain of blessing, that new Siloam, in which so many sick were later on to be plunged. Still somewhat muddy, the water was spreading itself out over the sloping ground. Remembering what Bernadette had said and done the day before no one doubted that this source was miraculous and a gift from heaven. The paralysed, the crippled, the blind, know its virtue to-day. The immediate result was to restore Bernadette to her former place in the public opinion and to exalt the Virgin more than ever.

CHAPTER XVIII.

THE MIRACULOUS SPRING (*continued*).

I HAVE often said and sometimes written, and that without reserve, that at the time of the first Appearances no spring existed beneath the Massabieille rock. In making this statement I was mistaken. I owe it to those to whom I made it as well as to myself to say how I came to believe this and subsequently to discover my error.

My first care on arriving at the grotto on the occasion of the Appearances of the 23rd and 25th February had been to examine its arrangement and search carefully in every corner. I found nothing which could suggest any idea of a spring. There was a little moisture on the surrace of the rocks outside on the left but this moisture must have been due to previous rain, for as soon as a spell of fine weather set in, it evaporated and no trace of it remained. There was also a muddy pool near the Gave, below the rocks looking west, but this pool which was completely stagnant and trampled by the feet of visitors to the grotto attracted no attention ; every one supposed it to have been caused by the overflow of the river which occurred there at certain periods.

When Bernadette received the order to go and drink and wash at the fountain she had not the slightest idea that any spring existed at the grotto. This is an important point and should not be overlooked. She went first of all towards the Gave ; then when the Lady recalled her she went not to the muddy pool, but under the hollow of the grotto itself looking for the fountain and only finding it after much difficulty. Putting together all these facts and all these circumstances, those who witnessed the appearance of the spring naturally concluded that the spring had come into existence and to light on the very day when the seer had scratched the earth.

There were however some persons—certain shepherds especially—who maintained that the spring had been perceived and had flowed at certain times previous to the Appearances. This they explained by saying that the fountain was visible or invisible according to the action of the Gave upon the ground below the hollow of the grotto on the days of inundation.

The first class of persons could not accept this statement of facts. They did not doubt the good faith of those who held the contrary opinion, but they thought they were mistaken. They objected that even if the spring had existed buried in the earth it could not possibly, the flow being so abundant, have reached the Gave without showing itself at the foot of the declivity where the bank was open and free from all obstructions.

This difference of opinion as to the more or less recent origin of the grotto spring continued for more than twenty years, until an authority spoke and put an end to it. Abbé Richard, the celebrated hydrogeologist, declared after a careful study of the site, that the Massabieille spring, miraculous in its discovery and in its effects, was not miraculous in its existence. His report will be found in the appendix at the end of this book.

CHAPTER XIX.

TENTH APPEARANCE (FRIDAY, 26TH FEBRUARY).

I HAVE already said how discouraged I was when I left the grotto on Thursday, 25th February. From the heights of glory whence I thought I had seen heaven on my first visit, I had fallen into the darkness of incoherence and absurdity. On the one hand I could not get rid of the impressions which my soul had originally received, and on the other I could not shake off the subsequent sight which had so completely spoilt those first impressions. I was like a man who has lost his way, and as I did not know in which direction to advance I resolved to wait until events had cleared up the situation. In accordance with this resolve I did not go to the grotto on the morning of the 26th February.

The people of Lourdes who were present at the ecstasy of that morning returned to the town with every demonstration of joy, bringing the news of the flow of the miraculous spring. The reader knows how this news was welcomed. The scene of the day before was now explained; Bernadette was shown in her true light; the holy Lady of the visions was in favour once more. For myself, I can only say that I was delivered from an awful nightmare and that I joyfully returned to my first convictions.

I give the reader the details of the tenth Appearance as they were told me.

Upon her arrival at the grotto Bernadette without any hesitation passed by the place which she usually occupied and knelt down at the top of the slope at the point where she had scratched the earth the day before. She showed no surprise at finding the new spring flowing, and having crossed herself, drank and washed there. Having dried her face with the corner of her apron, she returned to the back and knelt upon the stone which served her for a *prie-dieu.* She entered immediately into communication with Her who was the joy of her soul, reciting her rosary with devotion and self-abandonment, when the well-loved voice in a tone of sadness spoke to her these words:

"You will kiss the earth for sinners."

Bernadette was never troubled about her dignity; she immediately bent her head and with tears in her eyes put her innocent lips to the ground. She then went up to the wild rose tree and there, at the feet of Her who spoke to her, she once again bowed herself down in humility. Not satisfied with having responded personally to the Lady's request, she wished to associate every one with herself in the work of reparation. She turned towards the crowd and with a gesture of her hand ordered every one present to bow face downwards to the ground. As if the order had come directly from the mouth of the Lady herself, every knee was bent and every head touched for a moment the soil of the grotto. Those who could not bow down so low as the ground placed their kiss of penitence upon parts of the rock.

CHAPTER XX.

ELEVENTH APPEARANCE (SATURDAY, 27TH FEBRUARY).

MANY of my readers must have wondered, I am sure, about the clergy of Lourdes. What did they say and what did they think about the events taking place at the Massabieille grotto? The incidents of the 27th February will answer their questions.

The man who looks back upon his life sees the road along which he has travelled marked by graves for milestones. The tears come once more to his eyes when, among these various graves, he sees again one of a dear old friend. The former presbytery of Lourdes,* visited by death, will always be to me one of those monuments of the past which move to tears. The reader may judge of the deep emotion which overwhelms me when I say that after the lapse of thirty years I am now about to open the door and bring to light past memories.

The venerable priest who occupied this presbytery at the

* Maison Lavigne, the first on the right entering the town, after the *pont de' ı chaussée*, on the Tarbes road.

time of the Appearances was more than a friend to me—he was a father. And indeed he was that to all his parishioners. His appellation, "Monsieur le curé," was more than a mere polite formula; for the people of Lourdes it expressed beyond all else the respectful affection which they had for their good and venerated pastor. This priest, a man of deep feeling, keen intelligence and unquestioned power, has already been mentioned. The events of the grotto were to make him known far and wide. Some years later, promoted to the dignity of apostolic protonotary, the curé of Lourdes bore the title of Monseigneur Peyramale.

Among the three vicaires who shared with him the duties and labours of the parochial ministry, Abbé Pomian must be specially mentioned, for he was also chaplain of the Hospice conducted by the Nevers Sisters and continued chaplain till his death in 1893. It was there that he knew Bernadette whose catechist and director he was. As to the other two vicaires—Abbé Serre died young, and Abbé Pène followed him to the grave in 1897. These four priests made one united family in which not merely the orders but the least wishes of the head were carried out with filial readiness.

The news of the Appearances made its entry into the Lourdes presbytery very much as it made its entry everywhere, *i.e.* with the vague and nebulous character which marked the first information about it. Abbé Peyramale was not the sort of man who would pay attention to what he believed to be a child's fancy or an old woman's story. When anyone who chanced to meet him tried to discuss with him the extraordinary things which were taking place at Massabieille he would shrug his shoulders and continue his walk. At length however the moment came when the fact of the grotto assumed such great importance that he could not avoid considering it. Every morning, returning from there, a large number of persons came to look for him in the sacristy, confessional or presbytery, to tell him of their wonderment and to ask his advice as to their line of conduct in the presence of these marvellous events.

The good curé listened and sometimes asked questions but he never made any reply. He kept his own counsel and wondered what could be that strange fascination which seemed to affect all those who went near the Massabieille rock. Were his parishioners dazzled by one of those meteorological phenomena which give rise to legends and are interpreted by the vulgar as signs from heaven ? Were they not being duped by the artifices of some hidden conjurer, producing a sort of momentary play of light around the visionary ? Was not the so-called seer herself tricking the observers by putting on airs of inspired ecstasy ? Or, without having recourse to the theory of fraud, might not the young girl be the unconscious prey of one of those nervous illnesses which derange the senses and sometimes illuminate and beautify the face with an expression of spiritual joy ? All these considerations made Abbé Peyramale thoughtful and distrustful.

And yet, having made all possible allowances for the part which might be played by nature and fraud in producing illusions at the grotto, the curé of Lourdes did not forget that he was a priest. He knew that above the world of matter there exists the world of spirit, and that with that world we are in communication. He knew that from those lofty regions there descend at certain solemn hours messengers of peace, charged by God to lift a corner of that veil which hides from us the world invisible. The Queen of Heaven in particular, that glorious daughter of earth who knows the needs and ignorance of our nature, had herself more than once come down to us on such a mission. The Appearance at La Salette was of recent date, and if the Mother of God had condescended to show herself upon the Alps, was it impossible for her to show herself also in the Pyrenees ?

A secret voice urged the worthy pastor of Lourdes to incline towards the latter hypothesis. He would have been only too glad to listen to this voice, but was he right in doing so ? Allowing that a supernatural being had appeared at the grotto, the nature of this mysterious being ought to be examined. Was it good or was it evil ? Certainly, according to current talk, the Lady who showed herself to the seer wore all the insignia of the Queen of Heaven, but could one trust this specious exterior ? Was not the evil one himself capable of such witchcraft ?

In the presence of a fact capable of such different interpretations and in view of results which he could not foresee Abbé Peyramale felt that the greatest caution was needful. He continued to keep silence when in the company of his parishioners, and taking up a midway position between those who publicly proclaimed their belief in the visions and those who scoffed at them he left to Providence the task of casting light upon the mystery with which he was preoccupied.

Moreover, he made his three vicaires follow the same line of conduct. One day when they were all four together, he said to them,* " You have heard the reports which are going about respecting certain appearances which are supposed to have taken place in a grotto near the Gave. I don't know how much is truth and how much is fancy in the current legend, but it is our duty as priests to maintain the greatest reserve in matters of this nature. If the appearances are genuine and of a divine character God will let us know in His own time ; if they are illusions or caused by the spirit of lies God has no need of our intervention to reveal the falsehood. It would therefore be rash for us to show ourselves at present at the grotto. If the visions are recognised as genuine later on, we shall certainly be accused of bringing about this recognition by our own machinations. If they are subsequently rejected as without foundation, we shall be ridiculed for what will be called our disappointment. So we must not take any unconsidered step or speak any rash word ; the interests of religion and our own dignity are concerned. The present circumstances demand of us the greatest circumspection."

The good sense of the vicaires made them realise the wisdom of the curé's words, and in any case they would have naturally followed the line of conduct ordered them. The result has been that whilst the irreligious newspapers have dared to mock at the Appearances at the grotto, they have never ventured to suggest that the clergy of Lourdes ever gave the slightest grounds for being accused of plotting a miracle.

* * * * *

Whilst Abbé Peyramale and his vicaires were observing the greatest reserve, Bernadette, in accordance with the promise

* The speech which I give above has been often repeated to me by the vicaires and by the curé of Lourdes himself in our private conversations.

she had given, continued her visits to the Lady of the rock. The love of the child for her heavenly Mother was continually increasing, and it was noticed that the ecstasies, whilst losing nothing of their splendour, became more and more intimate in their character. On the morning of the 27th February the blissful contemplations of the ecstatic were somewhat longer than usual. At the end of their conversation the Lady, so the seer told us, seemed to be thinking deeply ; when she emerged from her reflections she said to her little protégée, "Go and tell the priests that a chapel must be built here."

Bernadette returned from her vision thoughtful and absorbed. It was not the mission itself with which she had been entrusted that preoccupied her most ; what most embarrassed and frightened her was having to go to her severe curé. Many a time subsequently has the simple child told me of her terror of the venerated pastor.

"Though he is so good," she has said to me smiling, "I am more afraid of him than of a policeman."

On returning however from the grotto, Bernadette, having seen her mother for a moment, summoned up all her courage and went to the presbytery. At the moment when she arrived at the house Abbé Peyramale was saying his office in the garden. At the sound of the courtyard gate he raised his head and saw a young girl coming shyly and timidly towards him. He did not yet know Bernadette, or at the most he had only caught sight of her one day at the catechism at the Hospice, at the moment when she answered to her name at the roll-call. When the child came up the priest closed his book and asked his young visitor who she was and what she wanted.

"I am Bernadette Soubirous," answered the little seer timidly.

"Oh, it's you, is it?" said the curé, frowning and scanning the frightened child from head to foot. "I have been hearing very funny stories about you. Follow me." And at the same time the stern pastor led the way into the presbytery.

In order that the reader may picture to himself with vividness the following interview I ought to say that Abbé Peyramale was a tall man with a severe face and of a striking presence. He was essentially the stern and rugged mountaineer, though his character had been softened by education, by contact with the world, and above all by grace. His words were few and his manner was cold and at a first interview he did not attract. But there were two sides to his character; the one very rough, the other very kindly and simple and estimable, and the first side was soon forgotten in the second. After the first few minutes the ice was broken and one did not know which to admire most, his original and ready wit or the natural generosity of his disposition. He had an enthusiasm for all that was noble and upright, but ugliness, falsehood and meanness disgusted him and exasperated him to the last degree. Always and everywhere he was the priest, and he never neglected an opportunity of saying the edifying word or giving the helpful counsel. You listened to him with respect, you felt the attraction of his personality, and when you left him you were his friend.

As I said, the curé of Lourdes received the little seer coldly and with his usual stiffness of manner. He left the garden and went into his house, leaving Bernadette to follow. When they had got well into the room Abbé Peyramale turned to his young visitor, and said :* "Well, what do you want?"

Bernadette, standing up and blushing, replied, "The Lady of the grotto has ordered me to tell the priests that she wishes to have a chapel at Massabieille and that is why I have come."

"But what is this Lady of whom you speak?" asked the curé, pretending to know nothing.

"She is a very beautiful Lady who appeared to me on the Massabieille rock."

"Well, but *who* is this Lady? Is she from Lourdes? Do you know her?"

"She is not from Lourdes, and I do not know her."

"And you undertake to carry such a message as the one you have just given me from a person whom you don't know?"

"Oh, monsieur le curé, but the Lady who sends me is not like other ladies."

"What do you mean?"

"I mean that she is as beautiful as they are in heaven, I should think."

* The dialogue between the curé and Bernadette is the reproduction of what has been told me several times by M. Peyramale himself.

The curé pretended to shrug his shoulders ; in reality he was controlling his emotion.

" And have you never asked this Lady her name ? "

" Yes, but when I ask her she bows her head slightly, smiles and gives me no answer."

" Is she then dumb ? "

" No, because she talks to me every day. If she were dumb she would not have been able to tell me to come to you."

" Let me know how you came to meet her."

Bernadette, in her gentle and persuasive voice, told the story of the first Appearance. When she had finished the priest said : " Go on and tell me what happened on the days following." The child gave him a detailed account of all that she had seen and heard at the grotto up to that time.

Whilst she was speaking the curé motioned Bernadette to a seat and sat down himself. He looked at her fixedly and did not lose one word of what she said. He noticed first of all that he had before him a soul transparent as crystal. He observed in the next place that the little peasant's story came from her lips clear, pure and limpid, like one of those tiny streams that trickle direct from the rock, not yet defiled by any foreign impurity. Not only did he understand that the child was telling the truth but he was moreover compelled to recognise that, simple and uneducated as she was, it would have been absolutely impossible for her to rise to such magnificent conceptions had she not been helped by some supernatural intervention.

While Bernadette, then, continued telling her story the good curé felt all his prejudices vanish one by one. When the little girl had come to the end Abbé Peyramale was more than half won over to the cause of the grotto. He concealed his impressions, however, and testing the little seer once more went on questioning her, as at the beginning of their interview, in a gruff tone of voice.

" And you say that the Lady who appeared to you ordered you to say to the priests that she wished to have a chapel at Massabieille ? "

" Yes, monsieur le curé."

" But don't you see that this Lady was laughing at you and

making you ridiculous? If a lady in the town had told you to take such a message, would you have obeyed her?"

"But there is a great difference between the ladies in the town and the Lady whom I have seen."

"I should think there *is* a difference! You imagine that a woman who has no name and comes from nowhere, who takes up her abode in a rock and has bare feet deserves to be taken seriously? My child, there is one thing I do fear, and that is that you are the victim of an illusion."

Bernadette hung her head and gave no answer. There was a moment's silence, during which the curé rose from his seat and began to pace up and down the room. He came back, put himself in front of Bernadette and said to her:

"Tell the Lady who has sent you that the curé of Lourdes is not in the habit of dealing with people whom he does not know; say that before everything else he demands to know her name, and that moreover she must prove that this name belongs to her. If this Lady has the right to a chapel she will understand the meaning of my words; if she does not understand, tell her that she need not trouble to send me any more messages."

Without giving any mark of approval or of disapproval Bernadette looked quietly up at the curé, made her little curtsey and went out. The good pastor watched her to the gate, and when she was out of sight he could not refrain from saying to himself: "This child is most certainly a child of divine providence."

CHAPTER XXI.

TWELFTH APPEARANCE (SUNDAY, 28TH FEBRUARY).

THE time during which I had been free to kneel beside Bernadette in the grotto of the Appearances was now coming to an end. The people of Lourdes and from the country round came every day to the grotto in large and larger numbers, and in order to secure a good place there it was necessary to take up one's position some time during the night. On the morning of the 28th February more than two thousand spectators were collected round the Massabieille rock, feverishly awaiting the seer's arrival. Bernadette came, clean, and neatly dressed in her Sunday clothes, accompanied by her youngest aunt, Lucile. When she passed in front of me on the top of the hill she was already holding her rosary in her hand and looking towards the low ground near the Gave with the expression of one eager to arrive. I wanted to follow her, but as she advanced the ranks of the spectators closed behind her, and like Zacchæus in the gospel, I was obliged to take up my position, not exactly in a tree, but on the edge of the rock overlooking the Gave.

From my lofty point of vantage I could see spread out before me in part of the cave one of those marvellous pictures which never fade from the memory. All around Bernadette, like an enormous crown, there extended a huge zone of human heads placed one above the other, tightly packed, leaning forward in order to see better. In the background of this living amphitheatre there stood out as a centre of light the angelic face of the seer, reflecting and passing on to the spectators the heavenly glory of the hidden Lady of the rock. By the rock itself all was solemn, silent, sublime, and on it all eyes were riveted.

When I chanced to carry my glance on beyond the compact mass of human beings to the more distant spectators who could only catch glimpses of the ecstatic, I saw many isolated details of the deepest interest. Here my attention would be struck by a hardy and stern-looking mountaineer crying like a child, there a stalwart labourer was giving vent to his emotions by twisting his stick backwards and forwards until it broke in two, near me an artisan was exhausting his vocabulary to relieve the overflow of his wonder, while in a further corner an educated gentleman who had long ceased to pray was obviously trying to bring back to his lips the forgotten formulas of early days.

One incident will show the reader the state of mind of the spectators at this moment of emotion. Bernadette had already been for some time in the delights of ecstasy, when she wished to advance to make her usual acts of reverence beneath the wild rose tree. The crowd was so dense that the persons who were in the seer's way could neither go forward nor backward. Two soldiers from the fort, who had come as sightseers, of their own accord forced a way through the crowd and got to the side of the ecstatic. Pushing back the spectators to left and right and walking backwards they cried as though giving the word of command : " Make room, make room." Then one turning to the other exclaimed, in the language of the barracks : " They dare to say that the Appearances are all humbug. By Jove, the wits of the mess will have to reckon with us."

The mysterious interview between the Lady of the rock and her little protégée on the 28th February was exclusively concerned with communications of an entirely private and personal character. Bernadette always kept silence about revelations of this sort and every one scrupulously respected her silence. In leaving the grotto after the ecstasy the seer went direct to the parish church for the Sunday Mass. She was accompanied by her aunt and many persons of the town and from the country.

I have already said that the pilgrims who came to the grotto, thinking that there was probably some occult virtue in the water of the miraculous spring, never failed to cross themselves, drink and sprinkle themselves at the stream flowing there. The crowds had trodden down the earth on both sides of this stream, and the mud made access to it difficult, tiny rivulets flowing from it in all directions. Some Lourdes workmen who had noticed these inconveniences, on the morning of Sunday the 28th February, determined to remedy them. Taking pickaxes and spades they made a proper channel for the stream and dug out a hollow basin of about one metre long by forty or fifty centimetres broad and deep at the foot of the slope leading up to the grotto. The waters of the spring flowed into this basin through a trough of oak bark. In this elementary piscina the first cures took place.

That same morning these workmen, voluntary pioneers of the Virgin, also made a zigzag path up the hill on the west behind the grotto. This path was not the same as that which now bears the name of " *chemin des lacets*." Like the latter it began at the foot of the hill, but it rose thence almost vertically in narrow, short and broken lines up to the very top of the slope.

CHAPTER XXII.

THIRTEENTH APPEARANCE (MONDAY, 1ST MARCH).

WHILE a belief in the Appearances of the blessed Virgin at the grotto became every day more living and more widespread, incredulity redoubled its efforts to misrepresent the facts and to trouble and distress minds. At the very beginning of things the irreligious newspapers had described Bernadette as an ignorant little peasant, unworthy of the slightest attention. Later, on the occasion when the miraculous spring was discovered, they published a report that the seer was mad, and in proof of their assertion they added that the sick girl herself, obeying an instinctive impulse, had felt the need of cooling her feverish head in the waters of that same spring. An incident which took place at the ecstasy of 1st March, exaggerated and misrepresented by them, was also employed in their campaign of calumny. This is what happened.

Some Lourdes person, wishing to possess an authentic and precious souvenir, had given Bernadette her rosary, asking her to use it at the grotto during the Appearances. Bernadette gladly acquiesced in this request. On the morning of the 1st March, on arriving at the grotto, the seer knelt down and took haphazard from her pocket the first rosary she found. As she was raising it to her forehead her hand was arrested and the Lady asked her reproachfully what had become of her rosary. Bernadette in astonishment lifted up her arm to show the one which she held in her hand.

"You are wrong," said the Lady, "this rosary is not yours."

Bernadette looked and saw that the rosary which she was going to use was the one which had been entrusted to her. She put it back into her pocket, took out her own and offered it to the Lady, stretching out her arm towards the grotto. The Lady made a sign of affirmation and the seer immediately began her prayer.

Ever since the day when Bernadette had invited the crowd to kneel and kiss the earth the majority of those present imitated the little ecstatic in all the acts of piety which she performed at the grotto. When she prayed they prayed with her, and when she kissed the earth they kissed it too. At the Appearance of the 1st March the crowd gave a wrong interpretation to the movements of the seer and were entirely mistaken in their imitation of her gestures. When they saw Bernadette take her rosary out twice and offer it, as they imagined, to the Lady of the rock, the people thought that an ovation in honour of the Virgin was demanded of them. All the rosaries were instantly brought out of their owners' pockets and presented and waved enthusiastically in the direction of the grotto. I who saw the scene from afar could not understand it, but I saw in it a profession of faith which touched me deeply. After her ecstasy Bernadette made known the true meaning of the signs which she had exchanged with the Lady before beginning her prayers and the onlookers consoled themselves for their mistake by knowing that the Virgin herself understood the meaning of the sentiments they had desired to express.

The incident appeared to be closed and no one at Lourdes thought any more about it, when a few days afterwards certain hostile Paris newspapers reproduced the gossip of some obscure correspondent. It was as follows :—

> "That little actress, the miller's daughter at Lourdes, collected round her again on this morning of the 1st March, beneath the Massabieille rock, nearly two thousand five hundred boobies. It is impossible to describe the idiocy and moral degeneration of these persons. The visionary treats them like a troop of monkeys, and makes them commit absurdities of every kind. This morning the pythoness was not inclined to play the seer, and to make a little variety in the exercises she thought the best thing was to play the priestess. Assuming a grand air of authority, she ordered the fools to present their rosaries and then blessed them all."

The ridicule and venomous lies of those who had undertaken to discredit the Virgin's work only had the effect of stimulating strangers to come to the grotto in yet larger numbers.

Another detail, also unimportant, puzzled the people of Lourdes even more than the incident of the rosary on the morning of the 1st March. During the ecstasy a young ecclesiastic had unexpectedly appeared at the grotto, had looked on for a moment and had then hastily disappeared. As he was the first priest who had been seen at Massabieille those present had regarded him with considerable attention, and after his departure he had been the object of much curiosity.

"It is an emissary of the Bishop, a spy of the police, a friend, an enemy," people said to each other, and the day was passed in fruitless hypotheses. The next day the young abbé again appeared at Lourdes, and, as may be supposed, was questioned. He turned out to be a seminarist from a neighbouring village, recently ordained and not yet placed. Having had to pass through the town the day before he had taken advantage of the carriage's halt to go to Massabieille. This abbé, now dead, said during his whole life that that sight of the grotto on the occasion of his first visit had been to him a vision of heaven.

CHAPTER XXIII.

FOURTEENTH APPEARANCE (TUESDAY, 2ND MARCH).

As after the Appearance of the 27th February, Bernadette rose from her ecstasy visibly preoccupied with the commission she had received from the Lady. She had in fact a new message to take to the presbytery. How would it be received by the terrible curé ?

Her aunt Basile, who accompanied Bernadette to the grotto that day, was not slow to perceive her niece's state of anxiety. On returning to the town she asked her why she was so thoughtful.

"Oh," replied the child in a constrained voice, "I really am in great difficulty. The Lady has ordered me to tell the curé again that she wishes to have a chapel at Massabieille and I am nervous at having to go to the presbytery." Nestling up to her aunt and taking her by the arm she said to her : "Dear Aunt, if only you knew how grateful I should be if you would come with me to the curé."

Aunt Basile was anxious to please Bernadette, but she was almost as fearful as her niece of the stern look and harsh words of the curé. "When I pass that holy man," said Basile Casterot in those days, " my legs tremble and I shake all over." However, measuring her niece's fears by her own, and fearing to displease the Lady, who seemed to ask her indirectly for her help, she consented to accompany Bernadette to the presbytery.

The curé gave them a cold welcome. As soon as his two visitors had come into the room Abbé Peyramale turned to Bernadette and said to her: "Well, what have you come to tell me? Has the Lady spoken to you?"

" Yes, monsieur le curé, she has ordered me to tell you again that she wishes to have a chapel at Massabieille and now she adds: '*I wish people to come here in procession.*'"

The curé's face darkened.

" My girl," he said, " this is a fitting climax to all your stories. Either you are lying or the Lady who speaks to you is only a counterfeit of her whom she pretends to be. Why does she want a procession? Doubtless to make unbelievers laugh and to turn religion into ridicule. The trap is not very cleverly laid. You can tell her from me that she knows very little about the powers and responsibilities of the clergy. If she were really the One she pretends to be she would know that I am not qualified to take the initiative in such a matter. It is to the Bishop of Tarbes, not to me, that she ought to have sent you."

" But, sir," interrupted Bernadette timidly, " the Lady did not tell me that she wanted a procession to the grotto *immediately;* she only said: 'I wish people to come here in procession,' and if I understood her rightly she was speaking of the future and not of the present."

The curé stopped short at this remark and cast a look of searching scrutiny upon the child. What was the meaning of this explanation given by Bernadette of the message? Was the curé really in the presence of a cunning actress who was throwing powder in his eyes by her airs of innocence? The gloss which she put upon the Lady's wishes was plausible and even probable, but had she not suggested it to get out of her embarrassment and to hide the part she was playing? Abbé Peyramale felt all his old prejudices revive once more, and fearing to be tricked he continued to look at the ecstatic distrustfully. The latter, on the contrary, sat quietly in her seat, showing in her face the serenity of a soul which has nothing to feign or to hide.

At last the curé broke the silence and said to the child :

" It is high time for me to get out of the *imbroglio* in which the Lady and you seek to entangle me. Tell her that with the curé of Lourdes she must speak clearly and concisely. She wants a chapel, she wants a procession. What title has she to these honours which she claims ? Who is she ? Where does she come from and what has she done to deserve our homage ? Don't let us beat about the bush. If your Lady is she whom you suggest, I will show her a means of obtaining recognition and giving authority to her messages. You tell me she stations herself in the grotto, above a rose tree. Well, ask her from me to make the tree in question burst into flower one day suddenly in presence of the assembled multitude. The morning when you come to tell me that this prodigy has taken place I will believe your word and I promise to go with you to Massabieille."

A smile from the aunt and niece was their only reply to this speech ; then, the curé having stopped speaking, they bowed and left.

A few hours later a certain inhabitant of Lourdes, one who was entirely convinced of the genuineness of the Appearances, came to see Abbé Peyramale. He found him walking in his garden lost in thought. The good priest told his visitor of the preoccupation which the seer's message was causing him. He spoke especially of the request for a procession, which seemed to him suspicious, indiscreet and untimely.

" If the child tells the truth," remarked the curé, " she who speaks at the grotto is urging me to throw off the yoke of ecclesiastical authority. If on the other hand the child is deceiving me on this point, how can I believe her word about the rest ? "

" It seems to me, monsieur le curé," objected the visitor, " that your argument rests upon a misunderstanding. Bernadette, in telling you that she was speaking of the future, was only, I think, translating faithfully the Lady's thought."

"Who can guarantee that ? "

" The logic of facts. The Lady knows that you cannot begin

to build a chapel to-morrow, and she knows in the same way that you cannot have the procession to-morrow."

"That is the logic of an optimist."

"Yes, I am more optimistic than you think; I have no doubt that there will be both chapel and procession."

"My dear man!"

"Monsieur le curé, be good enough to remember what I am going to say to you. One day, with the cross in front and with banners unfurled, your parishioners in ordered ranks and you wearing your handsomest cope will all in holy exultation go in procession to the Massabieille chapel singing *Sancta Maria* and I shall have the joy of replying to you *Ora pro nobis.*"

* * * * *

I must make a digression to say that I am anticipating events. The man who had just spoken thus was employed in an office of the Government, and in the discharge of his duty he had been obliged to leave Lourdes. After his departure great things took place in his former town. The Appearances of the Virgin were recognised officially and the chapel built. On the 5th October, 1872, an imposing national manifestation, the first of this kind, brought into Mary's city more than fifty thousand pilgrims. The next day at two o'clock in the afternoon, while the bells pealed, the curé of Lourdes, preceded and followed by an innumerable crowd of persons, came out of his church and walked in procession to the Massabieille grotto. He passed in triumph between two hedges of two hundred and fifty-seven banners, brought from every part of France, twenty deputies or senators accompamied him, and eight Bishops, crook in hand and mitre on head, came down from the chapel for which the Lady had asked to meet him on the road from the town. The visitor of the 2nd March, 1858, who had come from afar, happened to be at the side of his former curé during the procession. After exchanging meaning glances the curé lifted up his voice to sing *Sancta Maria*, and the thrice-happy pilgrim replied *Ora pro nobis.* Need I say that he who had prophesied in the garden of the curé of Lourdes was no other than the witness of the Appearances who writes these lines?

CHAPTER XXIV.

WEDNESDAY, 3RD MARCH, THE LADY DOES NOT APPEAR.*

ON the morning of the 3rd March, Bernadette said her rosary at the grotto devoutly but without any of the signs which characterised her ecstasies. She went up to the wild rose tree and said her customary prayer beneath it, kissed the ground and returned to kneel again in her usual place. Without looking any more towards the rock she bowed her head as though to collect her thoughts, remaining several moments in this attitude; then, having kissed the ground afresh, she crossed herself and rose. The persons with her began to question her as usual. The child replied simply:

"The Lady has not come to-day."

"Perhaps there will be no more Appearances?" said one of those present.

"I do not know," answered Bernadette, "but in any case the fortnight has not yet expired and I shall come back again to the grotto to-morrow."

As the reader sees, the humble child never sought to play a part or to make any pretence as to what took place at the grotto. She accepted the events just as they came. Without making a virtue of it, she was always simply submissive and simply truthful.

In view of the crowds which were sure to come into the town the next day, the last day of the fortnight, the Mayor of Lourdes on the 3rd of March addressed the following request to the captain commanding the fort:—"The presence of a large number of strangers to-morrow, market-day, of which I have been warned, compels me to ask you in the interests of public order to put the military at my disposal. Kindly arrange for the soldiers whom you can spare to come to the *mairie* to-morrow morning at six o'clock."

* Several reliable testimonies would seem, however, to establish the fact of an Appearance, not at the usual time but on a second visit made by Bernadette to the grotto later in the day.

CHAPTER XXV.

FIFTEENTH APPEARANCE (THURSDAY, 4TH MARCH). LAST DAY OF THE FORTNIGHT.

FOR some time now the public press, from the little *Lavedan* of Lourdes to the leading newspapers of Paris itself, had made known the events taking place at the Massabieille grotto. Whilst the Catholic papers prudently confined themselves to recording the facts without comment, the organs of the free-thinking party, always ready to pass judgment, described the whole thing as fanaticism, superstition and religious mummery. The more the Virgin condescended to reveal her presence at the holy rock, the more positive became the newspapers of the former class, and the more irritated those of the latter. Soon the whole press was in arms over the question and the warfare was keen. God, Who often makes our petty strifes serve His own Divine ends, made use of the clamour both of good and bad to call public attention to His Mother's work. Thoughtful people realised that as a matter or fact there must be *something* to raise all this discussion, and that if the Appearances at Lourdes were not yet fully proved they were at least deserving of study and observation. Many strangers then desirous of learning the truth, began coming to the Massabieille rock. These strangers saw heaven, as it were, opened above Bernadette, and the wonder with which they returned to their homes became contagious and spread to their neighbours. These first pilgrims were soon followed by others, and towards the end of February there were at least as many strangers present at the Appearances as people of the town.

Among these persons from a distance who had planned a visit to Lourdes a great number had reserved themselves for the last day of the fortnight, hoping that the Virgin would reveal herself on that day at the grotto by some striking prodigy. The evening before and during the night of the 3rd March, from every part of France, but especially from the surrounding towns and villages, little companies of ten, fifteen or twenty pilgrims set off in the direction of Mary's city. These caravans, converging towards the same point, united with each other as the stream unites with the river, forming at length one vast and interminable current. On the outskirts of Lourdes, along the road from Pau, Tarbes, Bagnères and Argelès, these human streams seen by the first light of day were like four great rivers ready to come into union with each other. They made their junction peacefully enough at Lourdes and then rushed like a cascade down the steep slopes behind the citadel, absorbed finally in one immense whirlpool round the Massabieille rock.

It would be difficult to say how many spectators gathered at the grotto on the morning of the 4th March. The lowest estimates made the number between fifteen and twenty thousand. To-day it is not unusual to see at Lourdes crowds of this size, but at the time of which I am speaking the railway was not yet running in the Pyrenean district and the concourse of pilgrims seemed enormous.

The authorities responsible for keeping order, though they did not believe in the Appearances, showed all the zeal and solicitude of real believers at the manifestation of the 4th March. Besides taking measures of protection for the crowd, they unintentionally gave to the close of the fortnight a splendour and solemnity which redounded to the glory of the Virgin. The garrison of the fort had been requisitioned, as I have already said. On the 4th March, at early dawn, the soldiers in full dress arrived at the mayor's office and were stationed at intervals along the Massabieille road, rifle in hand. Three or four gendarmerie brigades, summoned from outside, some on foot and others on horseback, kept the roads clear by which the seer was to come. The local brigade as a guard of honour was drawn up beneath the arcade of the grotto. The mayor, deputy-mayor and police commissioner of Lourdes, wearing their scarves, went about everywhere, giving directions with good humour. There was reason to fear accidents because of the density of the crowd and the imprudence usual on such occasions; it was noticed however that in spite of these anticipations no disaster marred this memorable occasion; for throned above soldiers, gendarmes and municipal authorities was one who was also keeping watch—the Lady of the grotto.

During these public preparations and the impatient waiting of the people what was happening in the privacy of the Soubirous' home? There nothing was happening. The master and mistress of the household were working as usual at their little domestic affairs and wondering perhaps where to look for bread to give their children that day. Bernadette, always punctual in fulfilling her engagements and conscious that the hour of the vision was approaching, rose from her bed and began her simple toilette. After having knelt for some time before the modest brass crucifix hanging by her bedside she took down her best cloak and set off for the grotto.

As soon as the seer showed herself upon the threshold of her house an electric thrill ran through the ranks of the spectators from the town up to the banks of the Gave. Everyone stood on tiptoe and the word passed from mouth to mouth: "Bernadette is coming, Bernadette is coming." The child joined the crowd without seeming to notice the attention she excited or the preparations made to keep a path open for her. As though she had been some person of great importance, two gendarmes with swords drawn took up their position in front of her to ensure her a free passage and to protect her from the troublesome attentions of the people. She walked behind them, simple, modest, tranquil and just as natural as in the days when she went with her little flock upon the hills of Bartrès.

When she arrived at the Massabieille plateau Bernadette noticed a blind girl of about her own age crying bitterly at the entrance of the path leading to the grotto. Moved with compassion she went to the blind child and kissed her affectionately. On hearing that she had been embraced by the seer the poor girl was loud in her expressions of gratitude. The people round thought a miracle had taken place and the report circulated to the effect that Bernadette had just cured a young girl of blindness. This was not however the case, and the report was soon contradicted. Finally, without any other incident, the seer arrived at the grotto at about a quarter past seven in the morning.

It would be difficult to reproduce the picture which the Massabieille hollow offered at that moment. In the lower ground near the Gave, *i.e.* in M. de la Fitte's field and on the unoccupied spaces behind the grotto, excited crowds were struggling to get as near as possible. Along the sides of the rock of the Appearances climbed daring groups of men, despising danger and keeping their places as if by miracle. Clusters of men and children hung between heaven and earth from the trees along the river, whilst the branches swayed to such an extent that it made one sick to look at them. On the other side of the Gave upon the right bank the stretch of green facing the recess was black with spectators feverishly awaiting the commencement of the ecstasy. In the far distance, on mounds and hillocks and all the points of vantage surrounding the valley, masses of onlookers were to be seen immovable as statues gazing towards the grotto ; and from the bosom of this immense, seething multitude there rose a confused and awe-inspiring murmur like the roar of the ocean.

As soon as Bernadette began her prayer the great tumultuous murmur which filled the valley ceased. As though by order of heaven every head was uncovered and every knee was bent. Held in silent awe, all hearts beat with emotion, and those present expected every moment to see some manifestation of power from on high show itself at the grotto. During this solemn time of waiting Bernadette, as though she had been alone, held loving converse with the hidden Lady of the rock. " My soul, my heart, my life are yours," her look and gesture seemed to say.

In the course of her ecstasy the seer's emotion was so great that she shed tears, and it was supposed that the heavenly Appearance was taking farewell of her. Some moments after however her face grew brighter, illumined with the rays of hope. What was the subject of this intimate converse in which joy and sorrow were revealed in turn ? Was the Lady of heaven telling her little protégée of the diverse experiences awaiting her in life ? Was she vouchsafing to her the vision of the great events which were to take place at the grotto in the future, telling her at the same time that for her the days of joy would be rare and that, buried in her retreat away from her native town, she would scarcely hear of her Massabieille rock ? Nothing has ever been told us on this subject. Bernadette remained nearly an hour in ecstasy, sometimes in the rapt attitude of St.

Theresa in communion with heaven, sometimes in the abandonment of grief of the holy women at Calvary at the foot of the Saviour's cross. The expectation of the pilgrims was not fulfilled; no miraculous sign was given at the grotto.

As soon as the seer had resumed her normal attitude the persons near her hastened to ask her how the Lady had left her.

"Just as usual," replied the child. "She smiled when she departed but she did not say goodbye to me."

"Now that the fortnight is up you will not come again to the grotto?"

"Oh yes, I shall," said Bernadette. "I shall keep on coming, but I do not know whether the Lady will appear again."

Although the ecstasy was finished and the seer had been standing up for some time the spectators continued to remain in their places. The two gendarmes who had accompanied Bernadette on her arrival resumed their office of escort and opened out a way for her through the crowd. Every one wanted to see once more the Virgin's little protégée and many touching words were spoken on all sides. Whilst the little girl was crossing the Merlasse quarter, women who had come from a distance broke the ranks of the soldiers, and regardless of the bayonets, covered with kisses the child so blessed by heaven. Then, followed by an enormous crowd giving voice to its enthusiasm, Bernadette returned to her home, indifferent to the honours paid her and without any other thought than that of having answered to the desire of that Lady whose beauty had stolen her heart.

* * * * *

In spite of the touching and splendid manifestation which had just taken place, those who believed in the Appearances departed only half satisfied with the ecstasy of the 4th March. Many had hoped that the Lady would take up the curé of Lourdes' challenge by making the rose tree of the grotto suddenly flower. Others, yet more enthusiastic, went so far as to imagine that she would show herself to the crowd that day as she had been showing herself to the seer. Thoughtful and sensible persons, who did not presume to indulge in rash expectations, put up earnest prayers nevertheless that the mysterious Lady might make her name known and give some visible sign of her presence at the grotto. To the great regret of those who believed in the visions nothing happened, and many feared that the Virgin's influence might suffer. So it is that men reason. But the Lady of the rock who had begun her work was not going to leave it unfinished. In a few more days a great revelation was to clear up the mystery and dispel all fears.

CHAPTER XXVI.

PERIOD FROM THE 4TH TO 25TH MARCH.

THE unbelievers and free-thinkers of Lourdes, in spite of the assured air which they assumed, awaited with some anxiety the last Appearance. Having no absolute confidence in the scepticism they professed, they feared one of those sensational surprises which the believers desired. During the two or three days previous to the 4th March they maintained a prudent reserve and refrained from all discussions. On the great morning itself they were to be seen scattered about here and there on the heights of the right bank of the Gave, watching with anxious eye the Massabieille rock. When their fears had passed away they raised their head and resumed their former calumnies with more bitterness than ever. The newspapers which published their letters hastened to let the world know that the comedy of the visions had finished with a great burst of laughter and that the bigots themselves, disabused of their illusions, did not dare to show themselves any more at the grotto. As to the seer herself, now that she had lost the support of the public she lived in retirement in her father's house, meditating sadly upon the fleeting glories of her rôle of prophetess. All these statements made so unblushingly by the newspapers or their correspondents were so many lies, as any one could find out for himself by going to Lourdes.

I will not say anything more with regard to the general

impressions of that 4th March. On that day the Appearances were supposed to have come to an end and pilgrims did not arrive any longer in such crowds to kneel every morning beneath the Massabieille rock. But their faith and their earnestness were no less than they had been previously. Every day and at every hour of the day they were passing backwards and forwards along the Pont Vieux road and the space beneath the grotto was never empty. On Sunday especially, when the villagers were not working in the fields, they might be seen coming in crowds along the roads to renew their homage to Bernadette's Lady. These pilgrims of the early days always received a ready and unselfish welcome from the inhabitants of Lourdes.

Coming to Bernadette we find her just as we left her upon her return from Bartrès. She had no idea that she could be the object of attention to anyone, and so she did not seek either to hide or show herself. Four times a day did she pass through the town, as she had done before the Appearances, chatting with her school-fellows. She never aimed at making an effect and therefore did not make a parade of any great outward piety, but she was free from the thoughtlessness characteristic of her age. It was innocence walking in the serenity of a peaceful conscience.

But Bernadette had not forgotten her Lady. Often she might be seen leaving her companions after afternoon-school and going quickly in the Massabieille direction. She would come up to the holy rock and kiss the ground and having cast a longing look upon the mysterious recess she would pour out her soul in an affectionate prayer. Before darkness fell she would rise with a look of happiness on her face, make a reverence of adieu and disappear as quickly as she had come. And on the days when the school was closed she would go and spend long hours with Her who had promised to make her happy, not in this life but in the next. She came no longer to the grotto, as during the fortnight of the Appearances, accompanied by the crowd and followed by ovations. She came alone, hidden in her cloak and as quietly as possible. Either from an impulse of humility or from the desire to escape notice she passed beyond the place which she occupied at the time of the Appearances and took refuge at the back of the grotto. There, absorbed in devotion, unnoticed and often unknown, she would give herself up to her meditations and say her rosary earnestly.

As soon as the Appearances of the fortnight had come to an end pious hands set up a sort of rustic altar within the interior of the grotto, placing upon it a statue of the blessed Virgin. Some medals, pictures and all sorts of pious objects were added to this statue, so that the hollow under the rock assumed the appearance of a chapel used for worship. A large number of candles burned there day and night, and the Massabieille vaults began to echo with the sound of hymns in honour of the Madonna of the Pyrenees. No pilgrim left the grotto without throwing on the ground, and later on into a box, some coin towards the erection of the chapel asked for by the Lady. No one guarded this treasure, yet no sacrilegious hand ever dared to touch it.

CHAPTER XXVII.

SIXTEENTH APPEARANCE (THURSDAY, 25TH MARCH). THE MYSTERIOUS LADY REVEALS HER NAME.

A STRONG opinion, so strong as to amount to a certainty, prevailed at Lourdes and in all the country round concerning the visions, to the effect that the Lady of the Grotto had not yet said her last word. The wonderful ecstasies, the extraordinary revelation of the spring, the account given by the seer of what was said to her and the messages she carried away all remained without explanation, if She who had appeared continued to keep silence as to her name and the object of her visits. People who had followed the course of events attentively refused to believe that a drama so evidently divine, to judge from its characteristics, could come to an end without leaving behind it anything more than a brilliant but sterile impression. The period from the 4th to the 24th March had however passed away, and no fresh event had taken place to dissipate the clouds of mystery or bring about the expected dénouement.

On this last day however, the eve of the Annunciation, a

breath from heaven stired many pious souls of the district inspiring them with the desire to go the next day to the Massabieille grotto. As a general rule on the festivals of the Virgin these good souls were wont to betake themselves for their devotions either to the ancient sanctuary of Garaison or to the no less ancient and venerated sanctuary of Betharram.* They hesitated at first as to whether they should follow this inspiration which called them from their traditional place of pilgrimage, from centres of prayer already consecrated, to a spot where the voice of liturgical worship had not yet been heard. The Lady of the rock made the persons hesitating understand, as by a secret inspiration, that She who was calling them was one with her whom they invoked at the ancient sanctuaries of the district, and that consequently their homage was directed to the same end. Instantly their scruples were appeased and the pilgrims directed their steps to Lourdes.

There were not, however, at the grotto on that day the enormous crowds of the previous days. Several men were kneeling here and there, but it was chiefly young virgins and pious matrons who formed the hidden Lady's guard of honour. In obeying the interior impulse of which they had been conscious, all these holy souls had been penetrated by the thought that some great event was about to take place at the grotto. They wondered beforehand what that event could be. Was the mysterious Lady going to raise the veil which hid her and shew herself, as they had hoped she would do on the 4th March, in all the splendour of her glory and the majesty of her heavenly perfections? Would she accomplish, by means of the new pool of Siloam, one of those wonders of healing which restore strength and joy to suffering hearts? Would she take the opportunity offered by the festival of the day itself, suggested it would seem by the very title of the Annunciation, to declare her name and reveal her heavenly origin? All these hypotheses presented themselves to the minds of the pilgrims and were the object of a thousand prayers and hopes.

That inward voice which the friends of the Virgin had

* Two places of pilgrimage very popular in the Hautes and Basses Pyrenees. One is situated in the eastern portion of the diocese of Tarbes, whilst the other on the west is in the diocese of Bayonne.

heard had also spoken, but with more intimate affection, to the heart of Bernadette. That voice was no strange voice to the child; it was the faithful messenger which always announced the coming visit of the Lady of grace and love.

During the happy days of the fortnight of the Appearances the little seer had often knelt beneath the holy rock. In obedience to the desires of her soul she often raised her eyes to the beloved recess, but alas! it ever remained empty and no heavenly light came to lighten it. One may judge of Bernadette's joy at knowing that the Mother called her to yet another meeting. Little did the child trouble herself about the anticipations of the people as to what the Lady might or might not do. Her own faith was firmly rooted, and her one and only desire was to gaze once more upon the charms of that august Sovereign who summed up in her own person all the graces and beauties of heaven.

In the family circle on the evening of the 24th March, Bernadette told her parents of the interior monition she had received and spoke as of a certainty of the happiness which awaited her next day at the grotto. Full of this thought she went to bed but sleep refused to come to her. The night seemed long and many an *Ave Maria* fell from her lips. As soon as the earliest lights of day appeared she left her bed, dressed quickly, and without troubling about the asthma from which she was then suffering, hastened along the road to Massabieille, and covered indeed she was with shame and confusion at finding the recess already aglow with glory and the Lady waiting.

"She was there," said Bernadette, "peaceful, smiling and looking down upon the crowd like a loving mother looking at her children."

"When I was on my knees before the Lady," she continued, "I asked her pardon for arriving late. Always good and gracious, she made a sign to me with her head to tell me that I need not excuse myself. Then I spoke to her of all my affection, all my respect and the happiness I had in seeing her again. After having poured out my heart to her I took up my rosary. Whilst I was praying, the thought of asking her name came before my mind with such persistence that I could think of nothing else. I feared to be presumptuous in repeating a question she had always refused to answer and yet something compelled me to speak. At last, under an irresistible impulsion, the words fell from my mouth, and I begged the Lady to tell me who she was.* The Lady did as she had always done before ; she bowed her head and smiled, but she did not reply. I cannot say why, but I felt myself bolder and asked her again to graciously tell me her name ; however she only bowed and smiled as before, still remaining silent. Then once more, for the third time, clasping my hands and confessing myself unworthy of the favour I was asking of her, I again made my request."

When the child reached this point in her story she was overcome by emotion. She continued as follows :

" The Lady was standing above the rose-tree, in a position very similar to that shown in the miraculous medal. At my third request her face became very serious and she seemed to bow down in an attitude of humility. Then she joined her hands and raised them to her breast . . . she looked up to heaven. . . then slowly opening her hands and leaning forward towards me, she said to me in a voice vibrating with emotion :

" 'I AM THE IMMACULATE CONCEPTION.' " †

In pronouncing these last words, Bernadette lowered her head and reproduced the Lady's gesture.

The great mystery of the grotto was at length revealed ! And on what a day—on the anniversary of that thrice blessed day when the archangel Gabriel came from the Most High to announce the impending advent of the Redeemer so long expected, and to salute as " full of grace," *i.e. Immaculate*, the predestined woman who was to crush the head of the accursed serpent. What a ground of hope for us, this coincidence. Angels who surrounded the Virgin in her rustic shrine, what must have been your joy on hearing your august Sovereign describe herself by one of the most glorious of her glorious titles. The vaults of Massabieille must have resounded with your hymns of praise.

The pilgrims kneeling at the grotto heard nothing but they were conscious of intense happiness within their souls. During

* Bernadette did not say in what words she had made her request.

† In patois, *Que soy er' Immaculata Counception.*

the ecstasy they hung upon the seer's lips, hoping every instant that some word of revelation would fall from her innocent mouth. When Bernadette had finished speaking an unutterable emotion seized all there present and they fell upon their knees. After having offered this first act of homage to the Lady, in transports of enthusiasm they went, some to place their lips against the holy rock, others to take in their arms as a living being or a holy relic the branches of the rose-tree hanging down from the recess. From the midst of the crowd, from the little islets in the Gave, from the top of the hill, there rose the popular invocation, *O Mary, conceived without sin, pray for us who have come to you for help.*

Very shortly after the Appearance, the town of Lourdes was full of the young seer's great news. The inhabitants shook hands on meeting in the street, congratulating one another as on a happy event which had befallen them. As to the strangers, they could not tear themselves away from the grotto ; after having said one decade they said another and when they had finished singing they began again. At length, when night fell, they dispersed in various directions, proclaiming wherever they passed the Virgin's words.

On the afternoon of the 25th March (I cannot now remember the circumstances which brought her) little Bernadette paid an unexpected visit to my sister and myself. The visit of an angel could not have caused us greater joy, and indeed the young seer was an angel, and the perfume of the mystic Rose yet clung to her person. The thoughts which filled our minds may easily be imagined, and our conversation with the child turned entirely upon the events which had taken place at the grotto. Immediately after having welcomed our little visitor we hastened to ask her about the personal details of that morning's vision. A look of happiness passed over her face and without any hesitation Bernadette told us the incidents which I have already narrated. The Virgin's attitude and gestures were reproduced in so real and striking a manner that the heavenly figure stood out clearly before our eyes. Towards the end of her story, the child was overpowered by emotion. She stopped for a moment, and then with a trembling voice and tears in her eyes, her face transfigured with joy, she repeated to us the

Virgin's ever memorable reply: "I am the Immaculate Conception."

In recording here the scene which I have just described I did not mean merely to linger over a very happy memory; I wished chiefly to give a fresh proof of Bernadette's sincerity. The poor child could not say the word *conception,* which she pronounced *coun-chet-sion.* Moreover she did not know the meaning of the Virgin's words: "I am the Immaculate Conception."*

When Bernadette had finished speaking my sister corrected her faulty pronunciation of the word "Conception." The child repeated the word after her and then turned to my sister and asked her with an embarrassing simplicity: "But mademoiselle, what do these words, 'I am the Immaculate Conception,' mean?" After such a question it is impossible to entertain doubts as to Bernadette's veracity. One may lie and deceive with words which one understands, but it is impossible to lie with words which one does not understand.

CHAPTER XXVIII.

SEVENTEENTH APPEARANCE (WEDNESDAY, 7TH APRIL).

THE Virgin had now borne witness to her own identity, but this witness, while confirming Bernadette's convictions, did not increase them. To the little seer herself, the Lady of the grotto had always been the glorious Queen of Heaven, and it was to her as such that she addressed the affectionate invocations of her rosary. By a prudence however which seemed to be inspired, during the time of the ecstasies she never pronounced the blessed name of Her who filled her soul. Whenever she spoke of her, the lady of the visions was always called the "Lady," and it was only after the Virgin had spoken that Bernadette made any change in her manner of describing her. From the day of the Annunciation onward, the gracious Vision no longer received the vague and impersonal name of

* Bernadette knew that the description of "Immaculate Conception" had to do with the Blessed Virgin, but she did not know what the expression meant.

" the Lady," but the more tender and definite name of " Our Lady of the Grotto," or " Our Lady of Massabieille."

The festival of Easter followed close upon the day when the Lady of the rock had declared herself to be the Immaculate Mother of the Divine Redeemer. Proud and happy to think that the Queen of Heaven should have chosen to become their fellow-citizen the people of Lourdes went with joy to the Eucharistic feast, and, apart from certain free-thinkers, the enthusiasm was general. During this happy festival the little girl was again the object of the Virgin's special thought, for on Wednesday in Easter week, the 7th April, we find Bernadette once more at the grotto, contemplating in the joys of her ecstasy her loving and powerful protectress.

I was not present at this Appearance of the 7th April, but Dr. Dozous has given the following description of it to his readers.

" One day when Bernadette seemed to be even more absorbed than usual in the Appearance upon which her gaze was riveted I witnessed, as also did every one else there present, the fact which I am about to narrate.

" She was on her knees saying with fervent devotion the prayers of her rosary which she held in her left hand whilst in her right was a large blessed candle alight. The child was just beginning to make the usual ascent on her knees when she suddenly stopped and her right hand joining her left the flame of the big candle passed between the fingers of the latter. Though fanned by a fairly strong breeze the flame produced no effect upon the skin which it was touching. Astonished at this strange fact I forbade any one to interfere, and taking my watch in my hand I studied the phenomenon attentively for a quarter of an hour. At the end of this time Bernadette, still in her ecstasy, advanced to the upper part of the grotto, separating her hands. The flame thus ceased to touch her left hand.

" Bernadette finished her prayer and the splendour of the transfiguration left her face. She rose and was about to quit the grotto when I asked her to show me her left hand. I examined it most carefully, but could not find the least trace of burning anywhere upon it. I then asked the person who was holding the candle to light it again and give it to me. I put it several times in succession under Bernadette's left hand but she drew it away quickly, saying: 'You're burning me.' I record this fact just as I have seen it without attempting to explain it. Many persons who were present at the time can confirm what I have said."

Dr. Dozous has neglected to give us the exact date when the fact which he observed took place. He begins his story with the vague expression, "One day." The date of Wednesday, 7th April, is however generally accepted. To be exact, moreover, I ought to say that the extraordinary fact of which Dr. Dozous speaks happened on more than one occasion. My sister, who like myself was not present at the Appearance of Wednesday, 7th April, confirms, and several other persons with her, that at one of the last Appearances of the ten which took place during the latter part of February she witnessed a fact similar to that narrated by Dr. Dozous. She remembers that at the moment when Bernadette's fingers were resting on the flame of the candle and every one present was stupefied, she called out: "Take the candle away from the child; don't you see that it is burning her?"

CHAPTER XXIX.

EIGHTEENTH AND LAST APPEARANCE (FRIDAY, 16TH JULY).

I PASS over an interval of three months to say that Bernadette was favoured with a last Appearance on the 16th July, the day of the festival of our Lady of Mount Carmel. I shall have to return subsequently to the period which I am for the present omitting, for during that time many things occurred. For the moment however I leave it, to complete the account of the Appearances.

In inviting the Soubirous' daughter to come to the grotto for fifteen days the heavenly Lady of the rock apparently undertook to be at the place of meeting indicated only during that period of time which she had assigned. At the end of the fortnight, however, by one of those inductions arising from an analysis of the events themselves, all the believers were convinced that they had not yet come to the last chapter of the Massabieille story; and in fact the Virgin appeared again on the 25th March and crowned her work by that immortal declaration of which we have spoken. But this was not enough for the Mother of Heaven. In order to accustom her little protégée gradually to the pain of separation she came back again to the grotto on the 7th April and the 16th July. I must give an account of this last Appearance.

At the time of which I am about to speak Bernadette had made her first communion, and on the morning of the feast of our Lady of Mount Carmel she had received the bread of angels for the third or fourth time. On the afternoon of that same day toward evening whilst praying in the parish church she heard the gentle voice of the Immaculate Virgin speaking in the recesses of her soul and telling her to go to the grotto. Bernadette immediately rose and ran to her youngest aunt Basile to ask her to go with her to Massabieille. Entry to the grotto was at that time forbidden by order of the municipal authority, and a palisade of wooden palings closed in the front of the cave.* In order not to infringe the prefect's regulations Bernadette and her aunt took the road leading to the meadows called "de la Ribère," and went to the right bank of the Gave, opposite the rock of the Appearances, and knelt there. While crossing the Lapaca quarter they were accosted by former neighbours, who asked them whither they were going and insisted upon accompanying them. Further on in the meadows lying below the Pau road they met several clusters of women on their knees, praying with their faces turned in the direction of the miraculous rock. As soon as Bernadette appeared all these women rose and grouped themselves in a semicircle round her. They were so glad to have the opportunity of praying beside the little seer.

Almost as soon as the child began to look towards the rock on the other side of the Gave the light of ecstasy transfigured her face and in the transports of her ravished soul she cried: "Yes, yes, there she is. She welcomes us, and is smiling upon us across the barriers!" Then instantly began between the

* I shall have to speak later on of the interferences of the civil administration in the affair of the grotto, and the rigorous measures enforced by it to put a stop to the whole matter.

Virgin and Bernadette that wonderfully beautiful spiritual communing of which I have so often spoken, like a current of light set up between the two communing souls. During her beatitude the little ecstatic seemed to be making efforts to detach herself from the earth and fly into the arms of her heavenly Mother. Her features were spiritualised by her ecstasy, and the women surrounding her thought themselves back once more in the happy days of the past.

The moment when the Virgin was about to leave the grotto, as far as her sensible presence was concerned, had now arrived. How was she to prepare the child for the trial of a separation which might break her heart ? Would the gentle Mother take a sad and tearful farewell of her ? Would she tell her that, in the dark days of her life, she would be at her side, unseen, to protect and defend her ? Would she remind her of the promise she had already given, that she would make her happy not in this life but in the next ? Nothing of all this was said, nothing was done, for the Immaculate Virgin, by an effort of sublime tenderness which all earthly mothers will understand, chose rather to be silent than to make her child's heart unhappy. During the whole of the vision she continued gracious and smiling, and when she quitted the little ecstatic she left her in the fulness of joy.

The sun was beginning to sink beneath the horizon and the shades of night were slowly creeping over the Massabieille hollow. The Virgin cast one long look of deepest love upon her little protégée and then disappeared. It was finished. Bernadette was never again to see the Mother of God except in the glory of heaven.

SECOND PART.

CHAPTER I.

COUNTERFEITS OF THE HEAVENLY VISION.

HELL could not remain idle in presence of the events which were taking place at Lourdes. The prince of darkness has been vanquished in his pride but not in his hate, and no longer daring to attack God in the plenitude of His Divine power he seeks to thwart His work and to destroy the providential order He wishes to establish. Perhaps at no period of history so much as at the present time has the genius of evil manifested so powerfully his pernicious action. He is everywhere, he insinuates himself into everything. Jealous of the glorious destiny promised to man, he turns him aside from his path by corrupting his morals, perverting his ideas, drawing him away from noble and holy affections. Ceaselessly active, he presides over secret societies, energises in the practices of spiritualism and speaks in table-turning. He has pressed modern literature into his service, while certain arts and sciences pay him continual homage.

The father of lies does not go to sleep over his triumphs, and anticipates with a jealous care any causes which may contribute to the weakening of his infernal dominion. His watchful eye travels from one end of the world to the other and searches out any weak points which seem to him threatened. In this ceaseless watchful work, was it possible that the great events taking place at the foot of the Pyrenees should escape his notice? Evidently not. The old serpent saw the grotto illuminated, and recognised, furious with rage, the Woman, his enemy, who had crushed his head with her powerful heel. At that moment all the humiliations of the past returned to his memory and drove him on to fresh outbreaks of fury. He knew by experience that it was dangerous to fight face to face against Her who is "terrible as an army drawn up for battle." He therefore resolved to make use of underhand means and to fight her not personally but in the purposes she was attempting to realise, like those secret marauders who, not venturing to attack openly an adversary they fear, set to work to ravage his domains by night. With an envious eye he observed the treasures of grace and blessing which the Queen of Heaven held in reserve beneath the vaults of Massabieille. At all costs he determined to make these riches barren and drive away from the grotto those who came to receive them. Satan set to work immediately, and we shall see him in roundabout methods disguising himself and spreading fear all about the rock of visions.

He began his exploits with the little protégée of the Virgin.

I have already said, in speaking of the fourth Appearance, that Bernadette while in ecstasy heard behind her coming from the Gave a formidable outburst of savage voices crying to her harshly: "Escape for thy life"; that the child frenzied with terror raised her hands and implored the help of the Lady of the rock; that the latter frowned and cast a terrible look at the place from whence came the sinister cries; finally, that the beings who were shouting fled away suddenly, while from afar could be heard the death rattle of their fury.

The persons who were present at this Appearance did not hear the mad cries which had filled the little seer with terror. Sure of themselves, they thought that Bernadette was mistaken and so paid no attention to her story. But Bernadette was not mistaken, and it was realised later that on the occasion in question the devil was making his first assault upon Massabieille. One knows how he and his tools were received there; they did not dare to show themselves again at the grotto until after the 7th April, that is until the time when the Virgin seemed to have left it.

The preceding story came from the lips of Bernadette herself. It was told directly by the seer to my sister and myself. Other persons at Lourdes after the Appearances spoke of the incident of the 19th February in almost exactly the same terms, and as emanating from the same source, notably Honorine***, who later on sold objects of piety not far from the grotto. Bernadette, while on a visit to Tarbes, was introduced to the Abbé Nogaro, curé of the Cathedral, and the ecstatic told him also the same story.

As soon as the Appearances of the Divine Mother had ceased* the lying spirit began again his work of darkness.

One day a young girl from the Rue Basse at Lourdes, named Marie ***, notable for her piety, came back from the grotto and said that she had heard a mysterious harmony of heavenly voices proceeding from the interior of the rock of Massabieille, producing a sort of narcotic effect upon the senses. She said and believed in good faith that angels alone were capable of producing such symphonies.

The next day the same young girl returned to the grotto with the intention of saying her rosary there and also in the secret hope of hearing once more the marvellous harmonies of the previous day. As soon as she had begun to pray sounds of unutterable beauty, sounds pure and sweet like tones which come from the lips of angels, were heard again by her ravished ears. She listened breathless to the melodious and seductive chords, when little by little but in increasing strength strange dissonances, tones harsh and strident, troubled and confused the symphony. Soon the music was lost in a tumultuous noise, an indescribable cacophony. Suddenly there was silence. Some seconds after a threatening murmur, like that of a conflict between unclean beasts, was heard in the depths of the rocks. There were stifled groanings, savage blows, the dull thud of falling combatants. Without waiting for the end of the struggle the young girl fled and for several weeks she did not dare to return to the grotto. In speaking of the occurrence she grew pale and trembled with fear.

The people of Lourdes, who at this time had no suspicion of diabolic interventions, said that the young girl was hysterical and that she had made this fantastic addition to the true history of the divine Appearances in order to acquire for herself a certain renown.

Almost at the same time a strange adventure which happened to a man of Saint Pé or of some neighbouring hamlet was much discussed at Lourdes.

This man was going quietly to the market at Tarbes and was

* I am speaking of the Appearances which ended on the 7th April, for the Appearance of the 16th July was regarded merely as a simple visit made by the Virgin to her beloved child, Bernadette.

on the road before daylight from Pau to Lourdes. When he was opposite the grotto, according to the pious custom of the people of the Pyrenees on approaching a cross, a Madonna or a chapel, the good villager took off his cap and crossed himself. He was instantly enveloped in a globe of lights which danced and played around him, and in spite of all his efforts he could neither move backwards nor forwards. Quaking with fear, he instinctively and mechanically again made the sign of the cross. The globe or balloon immediately burst with a fearful explosion and everything once more was dark. He heard in the distance mocking laughs and ironical blasphemies. Without losing a minute the traveller turned back and returned to his family.

The intellectuals of Lourdes made great fun of the surprise and fear of the peasant of Saint Pé. They explained the incident scientifically as due to will-o'-the-wisps.

Fresh stories, bearing the imprint of the marvellous, were not slow in coming to the ears of the public. The thoughtful people of the place could find no meaning in them and regarded them as fables or as dreams born of the popular imagination, which was very excited at this time. The reality had however to be faced, and the fact had to be recognised that something mysterious, unrelated to what had been observed previously and of an evil character, was making itself felt in the neighbourhood of the grotto. The visions of Bernadette, so beautiful and so harmonious, were followed by other scenes, burlesque, incongruous, sometimes terrifying. A veritable epidemic of visionaries seemed to have suddenly broken out at Lourdes; young girls and boys were especially attacked by it. When some of these children approached the excavations of Massabieille they fell into a kind of feverish contemplation and perceived within the rocks all sorts of fantastic figures. One fascinated child would see some Madonna adorned with sceptre and crown ; another St. Joseph with the traditional lily in his hand ; this one imagined he saw St. Peter ; that, St. Paul ; a third, the four evangelists. Very soon almost every saint in Paradise had taken his or her place in the march past. The personages who were made to figure in these diverse parodies, though clothed with a sort of artificial beauty, were uneasy and restless and betrayed certain involuntary convulsions which made them repulsive.

To the jugglers and mountebanks who were at work concealed in the interior of the grotto, must be added supernumeraries of a less subtle nature and of a less inventive genius. These latter were poor individuals of flesh and bone who were intentionally seeking to play a part themselves in the diabolic comedy. A village lout, for instance, aged eighteen or twenty, used to parade at nightfall on the right bank of the Gave opposite the rock of Massabieille. He would arrive at the theatre of his exploits adorned with green branches and with his face smeared with mud. Having thrown himself upon his knees and marked his breast with a huge sign of the cross he would give himself up to a thousand contortions and bellow until the grotto re-echoed with the noise. This fellow was hooted off the scenes and nothing more was heard of him.

There was talk also of the case of a servant of the town who attempted to imitate Bernadette in her ecstasies. Starting off for Massabieille she left her master's house with her head bowed down and wrapped up in her cloak. On the road she pretended to hear nothing and never replied to the questions addressed to her. At the grotto she was extravagant in her prostrations and assumed the airs of one inspired. Her smiles were grimaces and her prayers were only those of the lips. Her pantomime was so obviously made up and so awkwardly acted that everybody laughed at her. Ridiculed and disappointed, the sham seer returned into obscurity.

Significant, dramatic and harmful were the consequences experienced by those who found themselves under the fascination of the evil one. I will record certain observations made in this respect, beginning with a scene of which I was myself an eye-witness.

It occurred at the time when visions of this description were only just commencing ; no fact of this kind, so far as I can remember, had yet come to my knowledge. Two of my colleagues, the receiver and the chief clerk of Argelès, passing through Lourdes, came to see me, and after we had discussed these great manifestations of the Virgin, in which they did not believe, they asked me to go with them to the grotto which they wished to visit. We arrived at the cave of Massabieille at the moment when a young girl of the town, named Josephine ***, from the Rue de Bagnères, seemed to have fallen into a kind of catalepsy. About a dozen women were standing round her regarding her with astonishment. We drew near the group and found the young girl on her knees in the attitude of a *Mater dolorosa*. Her face, though it lacked the supernatural charm of Bernadette's, was yet very beautiful and considerably above the average of good looks. Her hands joined, she prayed; sighs broke from her breast and heavy tears were falling down her cheeks. Feverish convulsions shook her whole body at intervals.

My colleagues were so struck by this sight that they bent the knee in prayer, and before rising they both threw upon the ground a piece of money. I must confess that I myself experienced a very strong impression when I found myself in the presence of the young girl and for one instant I thought I saw before me a new and genuine ecstatic. But some secret intuition qualified my admiration and seemed to warn me that the truth was not there. I made comparisons and remembered that before the ecstasies of Bernadette I felt myself transported, whilst before those of Josephine *** I was nothing more than surprised. In looking back upon my former emotions I was conscious of a something which was truly of heaven; in analysing the latter I discovered nothing but the agitation of an over-excited organism. I departed with my doubts and uncertainties.

Josephine *** allowed us to make no mistake as to the meaning of her ecstasies. After having returned to the grotto two or three times she declared frankly that it was true that divers mysterious personages had shown themselves to her in the interior of the vault but that these personages appeared to her to be suspicious in character and of evil nature.

I will record once again the details of a fact the authenticity of which I can personally guarantee.

On one side of the house in which I lived at Lourdes with my sister, there dwelt a very respectable family, deeply attached to us and highly esteemed by us in return. One day one of the children of this family, Alex *** by name, eleven or twelve years old, now a grown-up man, came back from the grotto with his eyes starting out of his head and unable to speak. Paralysed with fear he threw himself hurriedly into the arms of his mother, seeming to demand her protection. The anxious mother hastened to question the child, but the latter only replied by signs of alarm. Thoroughly frightened the poor mother called my sister and asked her to come to her help. My sister ran up, and after some care and attention and words of comfort had been bestowed upon the child he was restored to a state of calm. When he had entirely recovered his senses, he told the following story.

"When I left the house I went to walk with some other children by the side of Massabieille. When I reached the grotto I prayed for a moment ; then, while waiting for my companions, I went up to the rock and leaned upon it, my head upon my elbow. I was there looking at those around and thinking of nothing in particular, when turning to the hollow of the rock I saw coming towards me a lady covered with gold and decked out with furbelows. This lady concealed her hands and the lower part of her body in an ashen coloured cloud, like a storm cloud. She fixed on me her great black eyes and seemed to wish to seize me.

" I thought at once that it was the devil, and not knowing what I did, I fled."

While telling his story the child still trembled in every limb and clung to his mother's dress.

Some weeks after the young Alex *** made his first communion, and on the eve of the day on which he received his God he repeated to my sister the preceding story.

A large number of people at Lourdes witnessed the following curious scenes.

A young peasant of the valley of Batsurguère, naturally awkward in manner and gait, appeared alone on certain days at the rock of Massabieille. As soon as he came near the grotto he was taken with a sort of seizure and began to turn with a giddy rapidity. When he ceased his rotatory movement he would look up in the air and seemed to be pursuing with his hands some chimerical being. During these latter manœuvres he would climb several steps up the vertical front of the rock and, contrary to the laws of gravitation, maintain his place there. Upon his return to his ordinary condition the young villager would fall into confusion and withdraw himself shyly from the grotto. When questioned he replied that he was not master of his own will and that a secret impulsion acting upon him from within the vault compelled him to do what he did.

It was at the same time that my sister was going one afternoon to the grotto to say her rosary. She met there several women who directed her attention to a young girl of eight or nine on her knees beneath the rock and apparently having a vision. The child was in an attitude of thoughtful attention and was following with her look, at the back of the rocky pier, something mysterious which seemed to bring to her lips a forced half smile. Suddenly the young visionary fell backwards and, like a hoop on a slope, began to roll in a disordered fashion from the back of the grotto to the banks of the Gave. Loud cries were uttered and several women fled. Restored to her self-possession the child could not explain the causes of her fall or of her precipitate descent.

One evening—(it was during the time when the grotto was closed)—several women were praying in a group on the summit of the hill of Massabieille. One of these women, a mother, was holding in front of her a child of three or four years whom she was clasping in her arms. Nobody was paying any attention to this child, who, moreover, was perfectly quiet and looking uninterestedly towards the Gave. Suddenly the little girl uttered a cry of surprise, left her mother, and walking straight on in front of her waved her hands towards an invisible being. An exclamation of terror escaped from the lips of all present, and the mother, like a lioness robbed of her whelp, sprang after her child and grasped her on the very edge of the precipice. One step more and the mother with her child would have rolled to the bottom of the abyss.

The young seer was almost too much of a baby to speak; she could give no explanation of the causes which had troubled her.

Some months after the facts I have just narrated, the son of a farmer, whose house was situated some hundred paces from the grotto up the stream, was seized with a strange illness which the doctors could not explain.

The child, who was about twelve years old, was of a gentle and attractive character and up to that time had enjoyed perfect health. Quite suddenly he became taciturn and irascible and his body doubled up like a shapeless ball. He grunted rather than spoke, and employed phrases whose meaning was unknown to all around him. Now and again at certain moments of the day he was seized with terrible convulsions.

We had certain relations with this farmer's family and one day my sister, meeting the father in a street of Lourdes, asked how his son was.

"He is not at all well," replied the father, "and I fear that some spell or enchantment has been cast upon him."

My sister tried to enlighten the good man and promised to come and visit the young invalid as soon as possible.

She went there indeed the next day or the day after, in the afternoon, accompanied by two or three of her friends. The visitors found the child alone, crouching forward near the fire, in a low-pitched room which served as a kitchen. In spite of ceaseless attempts to make him speak they could not obtain any answer. As the parents were at work in the fields they made ready to go away and were sitting for a moment in the yard of the house when the father appeared and asked them to come back, The ladies willingly returned, but as soon as they had reached the threshold of the kitchen they were arrested by the angry cries and furious looks of the invalid. In an access of rage he began to insult them, and to vomit forth against them the most disgusting epithets. When his anger was at its height he was raised suddenly as by a secret spring and cast, with a bound, from one end of the kitchen to the other. The visitors were frightened, and in spite of the assurances of the farmer, who said they had nothing to fear, they fled at full speed.

Father Beluze, priest of the Missions of France, was at this time preaching a course at Lourdes. He had heard of the extraordinary illness of the farmer's son and he wished to verify it for himself. He went to the place and after having watched the child in one of his attacks he did not hesitate to declare that the invalid was a prey to diabolic possession. Exorcised a few days later by the same missionary, the boy was restored almost immediately to his original good health.

In spite of his antics, his intimidations and his evil deeds, the father of lies could not chill the zeal of the inhabitants of Lourdes and of the country round towards our Lady of Massabieille; the people crowded there to prove their faith in and their devotion to the Immaculate Virgin of the rock. Day and night the prayer of the rosary resounded beneath its hollows and rose to heaven as a permanent protest against the encroachments of the destroyer.

During all this time Bernadette also came to the grotto; the counterfeit illuminations and appearances never shewed themselves to her. The evil one remembered the terrible look which had compelled him to fly at the time of the fourth Appearance. From that day forth he had never dared to attack again the little protégée of the Virgin.

At length the moment arrived when the devil perceived that all his untiring efforts to destroy the work founded by the Virgin were of no avail. The more he exercised his ingenuity in heaping cloud upon cloud upon the grotto, the more did the beloved face of the Immaculate Conception reveal itself in all its beauty and splendour. Little by little the evil visions disappeared, even as the spectres of the night flee before the break of day.

CHAPTER II.

A brief account of the original causes of the opposition to the work of the grotto—Some remarks upon M. Lacadé, Mayor of Lourdes, and M. Massy, Prefect of Tarbes—Period from the 21st February to the 25th March—The family of the Soubirous is watched—M. Rouland, Minister for Public Worship, asks for information.

The self-sufficiency and blindness of man could not fail to co-operate with the spirit of evil to hinder the work of the Virgin at the grotto. Perhaps at no time so much as at the present has the fury of opposition to the supernatural been carried so far. Proud of our intellectual progress and our modern conquests we want to probe all things, we want to bring all things down to the level of our reason. The evidence of facts is no longer enough for us; we must have analysis and demonstration;

if chemistry and mathematics are unable to solve our problems we reject them as absurd or unworthy of our attention.

The officers of the State lost their way in investigating the affair of the grotto because they refused to look beyond the world of matter. These officials, amongst whom I spent so large a portion of my life, were not at bottom bad or irreligious. They merely paid tribute, and that unconsciously, to the ideas of their time. The miraculous seemed to them a thing quite out of date, and, if they admitted it in theory in the distant ages when God needed to strike the senses in order to make Himself known, they would allow it no longer and could not understand the necessity of it in a century when the intelligence raises itself by its own strength to the loftiest conceptions.

Guided by nothing but the light of their own empty science, these officials saw in the fact of the grotto merely one of those childish illusions which can only impose upon the simplicity or folly of the common people. Out of regard for their own dignity they all of them scorned, with the exception of the police commissioner Jacomet, who was compelled to fulfil the duties of his office, the idea of going down to Massabieille to see for themselves the ecstasies of Bernadette. In the earliest days they merely mocked; but later on, when they realised that the belief in the Appearance of the Virgin had taken root and that the movement of worshippers towards the grotto went on increasing, they thought they showed wisdom in stifling the budding superstition. When the counterfeit manifestations took place the representatives of law and order were indignant and, it must be allowed, were rightly indignant. When they heard the story of the burlesque scenes caused by the spirit of evil they were strengthened in their idea that everything which happened at Massabieille was a confused tangle of unhealthy excitement and scandalous follies. Not being able to compare the true with the false, *i.e.,* the ecstasies of Bernadette with those of the possessed fanatics, they confounded the divine supernatural with the supernatural diabolic, and putting both upon the same footing treated both with the same reprobation.

* * * * *

The four men who distinguished themselves most in this

campaign of obstruction were the police commissioner, the imperial procureur, the mayor of Lourdes and the prefect, whose office was at Tarbes. I have already described the first two and I will now give some account of the other two.

M. Lacadé, mayor of Lourdes, was an honourable man in every sense of the word. A discreet lawyer and an excellent man of business, he justly possessed the confidence of a numerous clientèle. As head of the commune he was easy of approach and had the power of attracting his fellow-citizens' sympathies. At the municipal elections he almost always came in at the head of the elected candidates, and for many years the central authority had entrusted to him the administration of the town. About the time of the Appearances he was made Chevalier of the Legion of Honour in reward for his good and loyal services. From the religious point of view M. Lacadé was neither a sceptic nor a devotee ; he showed himself unmistakably friendly to the clergy.

The man who at this time presided over the destinies of the department of the Hautes Pyrenées was Baron Massy. This official bore a well-deserved reputation for being an excellent administrator and had considerable tact in dealing with persons of various political views. Devoted to his work and duty he plunged zealously into the interests of his constituency and did not care to postpone the solutions of problems. His temperament inclined him to be despotic ; his education made him affable and polite. Irreproachable in his civil life, Prefect Massy was equally exact in his duties as a Christian ; he heard Mass every Sunday and presented himself regularly at Easter at the Holy Table. Some time before the events of Lourdes, Pope Pius IX. had made him Commander of the Order of St. Gregory the Great.

A striking contrast between the acts of the leaders of the opposition and what I have just said about their personal characters will stand out clearly in the course of this story. Thoughtful and far-seeing in the ordinary business of life, they show themselves illogical and as it were blinded in the matter of the grotto. Convinced and practising Catholics, they allow in theory all power to the Mother of Heaven, while in reality they refuse her the simple privilege of showing herself to

Bernadette. Under the domination of their prejudices they have recourse to the most clumsy expedients and reveal themselves to the world as relentless persecutors.

Were these men, whose characters I have just sketched in outline, always faithful to their consciences? In other words did they, in fighting against the visions, honestly believe that they were opposing error? I can only say that I myself, knowing the loyalty of their characters, have no doubt whatever upon the subject. If at this time I disapproved of their line of conduct it was not because I regarded them as enemies of the Virgin, but on account of the means they employed to prevent others believing in what they themselves regarded as unworthy of credence.

Having made this clear I may be permitted to criticise some of their methods of resistance, without impugning the honesty of their intentions. May we not believe moreover that this resistance had its place in the purposes of the Virgin and that she herself, in rendering this resistance futile, bore witness to the fact that she had come to the grotto and meant to maintain her position there in spite of all opposition? The blessed Mother of God made use of the very barriers themselves to put an end to the heart-breaking scenes provoked by the spirit of evil.

I am confirmed in my opinion that the men in power were acting from no unworthy motive in their opposition by the fact that the Lady of the Grotto never ceased to care for them and to shelter them with her maternal protection. Of the four officials who openly declared themselves opposed to the belief in the Appearances, three died Christian deaths, M. Jacomet, M. Lacadé and M. Massy. Each one of them at the hour of death had a priest at his side and a crucifix at his lips. Of the circumstances of M. Dutour's death I am ignorant. But this I do know, that in the last years of his life he made this significant declaration to a friend: "We were fighting for the honour of religion and we ought to have conquered you. If we did not succeed—and to-day I no longer hesitate to recognise it—it was because you had the Virgin with you against us." This loyal confession of M. Dutour will certainly not have been lost in God's sight.

Let us enter now upon the history of the troubles caused by the Government officials.

* * * * *

It will be remembered that on Sunday, 21st February, the imperial procurator and the commissioner of police of Lourdes each for himself made Bernadette appear before them in order to persuade her not to return to Massabieille. It will also be remembered that neither the persuasions of the magistrates nor their menaces could move the child from her resolution and that, when compelled to speak, she replied with firmness that having promised the Lady that she would go to the grotto for fifteen days, she could not break her word. Her father on this occasion had yielded more readily to the injunctions of the law's representative. Overborne by M. Jacomet and remembering certain legal troubles which he had previously undergone, the frightened miller hastened to promise that in future he would do all he could to prevent his daughter's visits to the grotto of Massabieille. We have seen that the day after Bernadette disobeyed the commands of her father and, stopped upon her way to school as by a mysterious force, had been obliged to go back and kneel, as though in spite of herself, beneath the rock of the Appearances.

In learning that the seer had again visited Massabieille the commissioner of police thought he was being mocked by the Soubirous family. Putting aside the first thought which he had entertained of a pious plot, the idea struck him that the former tenants of the mill of Boly wished to repair their shattered fortunes by setting up their daughter as a kind of wonder-worker, in using her to exploit the popular credulity. A complete system of secret surveillance was established round the old dungeon of the Petits Fossés road. Every step of the father and mother was spied upon ; the children of the house were adroitly questioned in order that some chance revelation might be obtained from them.

At night mysterious persons came and took up their position at the doors and windows in order to see through the cracks what passed within the suspected house. Finally, under pretext of benevolence, false friends presented themselves at the same dwelling to make treacherous offers of money. All the espionage, all the tricks, all the traps of the police succeeded in proving one thing only—that the Soubirous family was not only honest but also incorruptible.

A wound yet unhealed was to cause fresh trouble however to the unfortunate family. During the year which preceded the visions Soubirous, the father, victim of an odious calumny, had been accused of stealing wood and flour, and on this charge confined for a week in the prison of the town. In order to renew the discredit which had for a short time befallen this family, the inferior police officers, perhaps going beyond the intention of their chief and wishing to excuse their tactics, reminded every one of the unfortunate affair of the theft and allowed it to be understood that the matter now being enquired into was of the same nature. They forgot to state the fact—(which fortunately was well known)—that the charge had been proved groundless and that the prosecuting lawyer himself had demanded that the prisoner should be set at liberty.

Whilst the police were pursuing these secret investigations, the attraction towards the grotto went on continually increasing. The peace officer, M. Jacomet, who was very far-sighted in matters of business, began to perceive that it would be very difficult to put a stop to it. Always alive to the duties of his charge he thought he ought to let the Prefect of Tarbes know of the singular events with were happening at Lourdes. In a letter of the 24th or 25th February he sent to his official chie the story he had heard from the lips of Bernadette and added to it his own observations. " Although the stories of the little girl," said he, " are worthy of no more attention than that which one usually gives to children's tales, it yet remains true that the country round takes them seriously and that many people go every morning to Massabieille, convinced that they are thereby performing an act of devotion."

Almost simultaneously a report of the same nature was drawn up in almost exactly similar terms by the Mayor of Lourdes and sent to the chief of the department.

The teacher of the Government school of the locality, M. Clarens, did not want to be behind the other officials of the town. He also sent to the prefecture a full account of the impression made upon him by one of his visits to the grotto.

Baron Massy read the correspondence from Lourdes with a shrug of the shoulders and, after laughing over the matter in his office, thought no more about it.

On the surface everything seemed calm during the fortnight of the Appearances. The local authorities were not however so quiet as their outward attitude seemed to imply. The ever increasing swarms of pilgrims continually arriving at the grotto bewildered them; the mayor and police commissioner in these utterly unprecedented circumstances did not know what line of conduct to follow. On the one hand it was repugnant to their feelings to protect what they considered a parade of idolatry and superstition; on the other hand they feared to abandon the crowd to its excesses. Then again, whatever line they followed, were they sure of being upheld, or rather not thrown over, by the superior authority? The two officials wanted to get out of the uncertainty and embarrassment of their situation.

On the 2nd March, in preparation for the crowds which were certain to gather at the grotto on the day fixed for the last Appearance, *i.e.* the 4th of March, M. Lacadé wrote to the prefect, but this time officially, to ask his advice or rather his directions as to the line he should take in the matter of the grotto. The next day the prefect replied calmly that there was no reason for the mayor to trouble himself about the doings of the Soubirous girl, and that the only duty of the municipal administration was to keep the roads clear and to watch over the people's safety.

It would have been impossible to have taken wiser measures and yet during this day of the 3rd March a first instinct of distrust entered into the mind of Baron Massy with regard to the events of Lourdes. An intimate friend had told him that great things were expected at Lourdes on the last day of the Appearances and the prefect had become anxious and thoughtful. He wondered whether the famous rock, before which the visionary had her ecstasies, was not being skilfully prepared for a general display of marvellous illusions at an hour arranged. Acting upon this idea he sent a second telegram to Lourdes asking the mayor to have the excavations of the grotto so thoroughly explored as to preclude any possibility of fraud being carried out there.

The next day, the 4th March, before entering into the details of the great scene which had accompanied on that day the ecstasy of Bernadette, the mayor gave an account to the prefect in the following terms of the execution of his orders.

"LOURDES, *4th March.*

"MONSIEUR LE PRÉFET,

"I received at 7 o'clock last night the telegram which you sent me, and in accordance with the instructions therein contained ordered the grotto to be visited at 11 o'clock that night by the police commissioner, an officer of the gendarmerie and my secretary; three officials of the mayor's staff were ordered to watch there until the arrival of the young girl.

"M. Capdevielle, my assistant, and the commissioner of police went to the grotto this morning at 5'clock to await the arrival of this girl in order to witness personally all that took place."*

All this watchful zeal was so much labour lost; not the slightest trace of fraud or connivance could be discovered. And I may own that I myself have always suspected the heavenly Lady of Massabieille of having inspired the prefect with this idea of a campaign of opposition which was finally to redound to her greater glory. It is clear to me that she herself more than any one else had reason to desire that the grotto should be examined carefully and watched closely, in order that it might be clearly shown and authoritatively declared in its history that no cheat or fraud was introduced into it, while she filled it with the glory of her sweet and gentle presence. If in this respect I have pronounced a rash opinion, or one in any way unworthy or unfounded, may she condescend to pardon me.

As I have already said, when the Appearances had come to an end, visitors who had no longer any reason for visiting

* Register of correspondence of the Mayor of Lourdes, in the year 1858, letter No. 61.

Massabieille at a fixed hour only came there individually or in small groups. This constant stream of pilgrims replacing each other uninterruptedly beneath the holy rock gave however at the end of the day a total of visitors at least equal to the number of those who had visited the grotto at the time of the Appearances. As nevertheless there was nothing more to fear from the danger of great crowds, and as Bernadette no longer figured at the head of these manifestations, the local authorities appeared to concern themselves no further with the affairs of the grotto.

Whilst calm reigned at Lourdes a letter bearing the stamp of the Minister of Public Worship arrived at the prefecture of Tarbes and roused Baron Massy from the repose to which he had abandoned himself.

And in passing I would just draw the reader's attention to the fact that the Virgin had no intention of taking possession of the grotto in a clandestine manner ; on the contrary, she wished to install herself there in the full light of publicity and almost (one might say) in accordance with the directions laid down by the law. With this end in view we have always seen her, and shall see her again, present herself before the legal authorities and tell them her wishes. She began by making herself heard by the police commissioner, the mayor and the imperial procurator of Lourdes. Later on we traced her to the prefecture of Tarbes ; soon we shall find her before the Emperor of the French himself. The springs and bolts of the Government are hard and stiff ; no matter, she will be able to loosen them and bend them to her purposes.

The Minister of Public Worship in 1858 was M. Rouland. This highly placed functionary had seen in the newspapers accounts of the miraculous events at Lourdes ; but, absorbed by the affairs of his department and thinking it was nothing but a matter of popular superstition, he had only given very scanty attention to the facts. The discussions and articles of the papers however made the event soon after a national matter. In the highest spheres of the Government the minister was asked for information, and M. Rouland, having heard nothing officially, could not reply. About the 10th March he wrote an urgent letter to the Prefect of Tarbes, asking him to inform him without delay as to what was passing at the grotto of Lourdes.

Baron Massy, feeling himself to be at fault, sought to excuse his silence by saying that he had feared to make demands upon the minister's valuable time by distracting his attention from serious affairs to the events at Massabieille. He then told the story of Bernadette and described the superstitious infatuation which was being shown in the country round. He ended his report by saying that since the 4th March even the keennest believers in the marvellous went no longer to the grotto and that consequently there was no longer any reason to take notice of the so-called visions.

CHAPTER III.

Bernadette is suspected of madness—Formation of a medical jury—Report of this jury—Letter from the Minister of Public Worship—Prefect Massy goes to see the Bishop of Tarbes.

At the office of the prefecture then, as well as at the office of the Minister of Public Worship, it was supposed that the Odyssey of the grotto had come to its end and this conviction lasted until the 25th March.

Great was the emotion throughout the Pyrenees and throughout the country as well, upon hearing the words received by Bernadette upon that day from the lips of the Immaculate Virgin. Up to that time those who had witnessed and marvelled at the ecstasies had quite understood, by the intuitions of their own hearts, that she who had revealed herself to the child could be none other than the Queen of Heaven. At the same time a sort of doubt, a sort of disquiet, remained in the background of their consciousness and their faith was supported only by the assurance of sentiment. Happy, a thousand times happy, were the people of the country in learning that the Virgin had spoken and that they could all in certainty give full play to their faith and enthusiasm. As soon as the great news had become known the inhabitants of Lourdes were the first to go and prostrate themselves in joyful gratitude before the rocky throne of the Immaculate Conception.

Although they only considered the matter from the material point of view, the mayor and the public commissioner of Lourdes immediately grasped the importance of the event of the 25th March. They both of them wrote simultaneously, independently of each other, to the Prefect of Tarbes to inform him of the new revelation made known by the seer and the fresh outbreak of popular enthusiasm which it had provoked.

Baron Massy was exceedingly annoyed at receiving this news from Lourdes. He understood only too well that everything was about to begin again and that it would be difficult to disabuse the simple people of the fancies to which the story of the miller's daughter had given birth. He had now moreover to reckon with the minister, and he saw himself compelled to withdraw the assurances he had too hastily given. Even his reputation as a magistrate might be liable to suffer from this troublesome affair.

The Prefect often summed up his view of the matter by saying that Bernadette was mad; but he only used the word loosely in its popular signification. In face of this new declaration made by the child he asked himself whether the epithet "mad," which he had hitherto given without meaning it seriously, did not apply exactly to the state of mind of the heroine of the grotto. This idea took concrete form in his excited brain, and he thought he had now found the key to the whole mystery.

That same evening, 25th March, M. Massy wrote to the Mayor of Lourdes to ask him to arrange for the mental condition of the little visionary to be examined by a medical jury as soon as possible and to see whether it would not be possible to send the young girl into an hospital or asylum, should medical opinion deem it advisable.

In accordance with these instructions the Mayor of Lourdes chose three doctors, two belonging to Lourdes itself and one coming from a neighbouring village, to carry out the examination requested by the Prefect. Doctor Dozous, who had followed the ecstasies and had questioned Bernadette at length, ought to have been one of the three. He was deliberately set aside as being compromised by his loyal adhesion to the supernatural character of the visions. At the same time the three doctors chosen by the mayor were all of them thoroughly honourable men and, although they did not recognise any divine intervention in the affair of the grotto, they were men who would not tamper with what they believed to be the truth.

In accordance with the instructions given them the three doctors betook themselves to the school of the Sisters and there, in the presence of the Superior, had a long interview with Berr.adette. Bernadette herself, having no idea that she was undergoing a medical examination, spoke fully and freely with all the simplicity and frankness of her soul. All that she said was open, clear and exact; any sort of subterfuge was foreign to her character. Her three inquisitors found it useless to attempt to catch her by captious arguments or embarrassing reflections; she passed over all obstacles with charming directness and irrefutable logic. The three doctors in question drew up a report which embodied the result of their observations; this is the gist of the report:

" There is nothing to show that Bernadette wished to impose on the public; this child is of an impressionable character and may have been the victim of an hallucination. A gleam of light coming from the side of the grotto doubtless arrested her attention; her imagination, naturally predisposed in that direction, gave to that gleam of light a form which had already struck her, that of the statues of the Virgin, as seen over the churches' altars.

* * * * *

" Consequently we, the signatories, think that the girl Bernadette Soubirous may have experienced an ecstatic state which has been renewed several times; that the phenomena of the visions are due to the effects of an *affection morale*.

" Is there any necessity for medical treatment?

" The affection which may we think be attributed to Bernadette cannot in any way endanger the child's health, not at least if contained within its present limits. It is probable, on the contrary, that when Bernadette has resumed the ordinary routine of her daily life she will cease thinking of the grotto and of the marvels which she recounts."

The Prefect could not fail to grasp the true meaning of the

doctors' report. There could be no further question of madness, for all doubts on that point were set at rest.

The hypothesis of hallucination was scarcely more possible. If the ray of light which was supposed to have struck the fancy of the young girl had only shown itself once it must be allowed that the power of its fascination was very extraordinary; for it had held Bernadette under its charm from the 11th February to the 25th March and had produced ecstasy sixteen times. If, on the other hand, it were admitted that the imagined ray of light by an inexplicable coincidence showed itself at the grotto every time that Bernadette went there, one was faced by a still more embarrassing alternative. How could it be possible that the people who surrounded the seer, in spite of their good faith, had never seen the famous seductive ray? The Prefect was too intelligent not to notice these various contradictions and what stood out most clearly in the doctors' report was that if Bernadette were mad and suffering from hallucination she would have to be left to cure herself.

The Mayor of Lourdes, in forwarding the opinion of the medical commission, unintentionally made the Prefect's bad temper worse by the following letter:

"The crowd at the grotto continues as large as ever and Eastertide, in which we now are, adds to it considerably. The great majority of visitors go for reasons of piety and pray to God with much fervour. I presume that this crowd will decrease after the festivals.

"So long as public tranquillity reigns and order is not disturbed I suppose there is nothing to be done. If you think otherwise please give me fresh instructions and I will follow them exactly."*

The conjectures of the Mayor of Lourdes as to the decrease of the number of pilgrims to the grotto no longer reassured Baron Massy. Precisely because of the difficulty which he foresaw in disabusing the masses of what he supposed to be a fiction, he had already written to the Minister of Public Worship on the 26th March, first to inform him of the fresh events which had taken place at Lourdes on the day before; next to ask him to approach the Bishop of Tarbes in order that the

* Register of correspondence referred to previously, letter No. 81.

latter, in virtue of his spiritual authority, might express public disapproval of the pretended Appearances of the Virgin to Bernadette. At the end of his letter the Prefect asked for instructions as to his own line of conduct.

Whilst he was waiting for the minister's reply Baron Massy had the opportunity of observing that he was not mistaken with regard to the obstinacy displayed by the crowds in the manifestation of their firm belief. Each morning, ever since the Festival of the Annunciation, Commissioner Jacomet had to report to him that continually increasing numbers of people gathered at the rock of Massabieille. The mayor, M. Lacadé, was himself obliged to withdraw the hopes he had given and on the 7th of the same month he sent the Prefect the following letter :—

"Monsieur le Préfet,

"The girl Bernadette went again this morning at about 5 o'clock to the grotto where a crowd of curious visitors had collected; she remained there for a long time in ecstasy. She prayed for three-quarters of an hour and then withdrew.

"The persons who came also prayed with much devotion.

"The most perfect order was maintained throughout. There was a considerable crowd of onlookers on the 4th and 5th of this month. We counted 4,238 strangers and 4,822 townspeople, making a total of 9,060."

(Mayor's Office, Lourdes. Letter No. 86.)

* * * * *

On the 11th April for the first time we find the Bishop of Tarbes interesting himself in the matter of the visions. Unfavourably impressed by the report of the medical inquiry which had been sent him officially, he feared that Bernadette was really suffering from the supposed hallucination, and he immediately ordered the curé of Lourdes to use all the means in his power to prevent the seer from going again to the grotto for the time being.

"Whilst admitting the possibility of the supernatural Appearances at Massabieille, I wish to be assured before all things else," said the prelate, "whether the medical opinions have not some foundation."

The next day, the 12th April, whilst the letter of the Bishop was on its way to the Presbytère of Lourdes, the Minister of Public Worship wrote on his own behalf to the Prefect of Tarbes :—

"Monsieur le Préfet,

"I have examined the two reports which you have been good enough to send me, the 12th and 26th March, with regard to the so-called Appearance of the Virgin which is supposed to have taken place in a grotto near the town of Lourdes.

"I consider it desirable to bring to an end proceedings which must finally do harm to the true interests of Catholicism, and weaken the religious sentiment of the population.

"Legally no one can set up an oratory or any place of public worship without the twofold authorisation of the civil and ecclesiastical powers. Strictly speaking, the grotto, which has been transformed into a sort of chapel, ought to be immediately closed.

"Serious inconveniences might however result from a brusque use of this power. It will be sufficient to prevent the young visionary from returning to the grotto and to take such measures as may gradually distract from it public attention and cause a diminution each day in the number of visits paid to it.

"Beyond this I cannot give you more detailed instructions ; it is before all a question of tact, of prudence and of firmness ; in this respect my advice would be useless.

"It is indispensable that you should join with the clergy in this matter. I cannot too strongly urge upon you the importance of discussing this delicate business with the Bishop of Tarbes and I authorise you to tell that prelate in my name that I consider a state of things, which cannot fail to serve as a pretext for fresh attacks upon the clergy and the cause of religion itself, should not be allowed to continue."

Armed with this letter Baron Massy went to see the Bishop of Tarbes.

CHAPTER IV.

Monseigneur Laurence—Apparent contradictions in the correspondence of the Curé of Lourdes—Visit of the Prefect to the Bishop—Divergence of views—A grave incident—Break off of relationship between the Bishop and the Prefect—The Council of Revision—Spoliation of the grotto—Illumination.

MONSEIGNEUR LAURENCE, who governed the diocese at the time of the Appearances, was one of the most remarkable of the bishops who have occupied the See of Tarbes. Sprung from a family of working people in an obscure village on the confines of Béarn, the eminent Bishop of the future had passed his youth with scarcely any school education ; at the age of twenty he could barely read and write and that was the limit of his acquirements. His natural intelligence was discovered by a variety of providential circumstances, even as the light of the rough diamond pierces through the rubbish which conceals it. Having once caught a glimpse of the intellectual horizons he found himself in his element and with giant strides he cleared the distances which separated the elementary classes from the higher school.

He distinguished himself as a pupil at the school at Bordères and the college of Bétharram, and attracted particular notice at the college of Aire (Landes), where he had been sent to complete his studies. He remained at this establishment and passed almost at once from his desk as a pupil to the chair of philosophy.

In 1821, at the age of thirty-one, he was ordained priest, and the next year he was made Superior of a little seminary just opened at Saint Pé on the ruins of the former Benedictine monastery.

Here everything had to be done, but Abbé Laurence faced bravely all difficulties. Then it was that his power of initiative and his administrative talents were revealed.

After having founded the little seminary of Saint Pé and seen it well on the road to success, Abbé Laurence left it in 1834. Monseigneur Double, Bishop of the diocese, recognising his great qualities of intelligence and sound judgment, attached him to his own person by making him Vicar-General and soon afterwards entrusted to him the direction of the seminary of Tarbes.

At the death of Monseigneur Double all the priests of the diocese, the greater number being the comrades or pupils of Abbé Laurence, asked spontaneously that he might be their Bishop, and at the age of fifty-five Monseigneur Laurence carried his episcopal cross where as a boy he had borne his shepherd's crook.

Monseigneur Laurence was of a cold, thoughtful, practical turn of mind ; he left nothing to chance, and his deeds as well as his resolutions were stamped with the seal of the highest wisdom. He had a filial devotion to the Mother of God, to whom he attributed his elevation, and in her honour he restored several sanctuaries of his diocese which the Revolution had destroyed, Garaison, Héas, Poneylaiir, re-establishing the worship of former days. He was always on the watch to further the material and moral interests of his flock, and interested himself in hospitals, founded schools for the instruction of young girls, and encouraged parochial missions. The traces of his beneficial initiative may be found everywhere to-day.

In a word, insignificant by his birth, great by his virtues, as learned as he was pious, such was the Bishop chosen by the Immaculate Virgin to make her known and proclaimed at the Grotto of Massabieille.

Monseigneur Laurence died at Rome on 30th January, 1870, during the Vatican Council. Before he left Tarbes the illness to which he was to succumb had already begun and he was begged by his friends not to undertake the journey.

"But what about my duty as a Bishop ?" replied the brave old man. "If I die, are there no cemeteries in Rome ?"

* * * * *

Whilst the Prefect was informed every day of the events which took place on the banks of the Gave, the Bishop of the diocese also received from Abbé Peyramale, curé of Lourdes, daily communications on the same subject. The curé, as we know, considered it his duty to abstain from showing himself at the grotto, and the information which he furnished came generally from the various reports which were in circulation amongst the crowd. These reports were sometimes over-enthusiastic and sometimes erred in the opposite direction. As the good curé could verify nothing himself and confined himself to passing on the stories just as they came to him his correspondence seemed to be somewhat contradictory. Sometime, for instance, he was obliged to say that what had been accepted as true the day before was found to be untrue the day after, and *vice versa*. To quote only one fact in illustration of this, it will be remembered that, until the day when she discovered the miraculous fountain, Bernadette was considered at the grotto as a veritable angelic incarnation ; the day when the fountain first began to gush forth under her fingers the seer was treated as mad ; the next day all her privileges were restored to her, and she was exalted to the position of miracle-worker or saint. These different impressions were reflected in the reports of Abbé Peyramale and were of necessity recorded.

Monseigneur Laurence was not the man to allow himself to be troubled by these divergences. While keeping upon his guard, he noticed that these reports although differing from each other often ended in agreement and so gave a new support to belief in the visions. And so he allowed the fortnight of the Appearances to pass by without coming to any hasty decision, simply praying God to enlighten him in regard to the mystery of the grotto. The day on which it was announced to him that the Lady of Massabieille had declared herself the Immaculate Conception, a great joy, followed by the light of a divine inspiration, filled the soul of the Bishop. He understood at once ; and his intelligence in holy things gave him the assurance that so bold a declaration would never have been uttered by human lips had not that declaration come from the very mouth of her to whom it referred. However he concealed his personal convictions, limiting himself to a close attention to the events taking place at Lourdes, waiting to see whether the Virgin would not confirm the revelation of Bernadette by some external manifestation of power. One day during this period of waiting the Prefect of the department sought an audience of him.

After the opening salutations, and having read the letter from the Minister of Public Worship, Baron Massy put to the Bishop the following dilemma :—

" Either the Appearances at Lourdes are genuine revelations," he said, " and deserve your sanction, or they are not and ought to be rebuked. If you regard them as supernatural, in the theological sense of the word, say so openly ; and I for my part shall be the first to bow before your decision. If on the contrary you consider them doubtful—well, I will not insult you by telling you your duty. But you must allow me to say that, whatever your opinion may be upon the events taking place at Lourdes, a clear declaration on your part is absolutely indispensable. There is a great moral unrest throughout the country, and if this unrest is not speedily dissipated by the authority of your word, there is every reason to fear that it will degenerate into discussions and regrettable conflicts."

" I do not share your anxieties," replied the Bishop, " and I must tell you at once that I cannot follow you in your desire for hasty action. If the Appearances at the grotto were unmistakably true or unmistakably false my duty would be easy, and I should let everyone know my opinion in the matter. But in the difficult conditions of the present problem, the Bishop's duty is to suspend judgment and to wait until providence has plainly revealed the truth. This will be my line of conduct in the matter of Massabieille, and if you think well you have my authority to inform the Minister of Public Worship of my decision."

" Your silence, my lord, may become a danger to the public peace."

" That is not my opinion. People pray at the grotto and prayer is never a danger."

" But if some people pray at the grotto, others mock."

" You are misinformed. I can assure you that the behaviour of those at the grotto is most reverent."

" In conclusion," added the Bishop, " do not let us waste our time in argument but let us make our positions clear. You, I have no doubt, reduce the fact of Lourdes to the simple proportions of an administrative difficulty and you are in haste to put an end to it. I, on the other hand, see in the matter a question of a much higher order, and this question I am convinced will demand from me long and continued thought. Our views are so divergent that we are far from an agreement."

"Allow me to remark, my lord, that a veritable centre of public worship has been established at the grotto of Massabieille, and that in contempt of the law. The administration cannot allow at Lourdes what it forbids elsewhere."

"Your scruples in this matter are no concern of mine. However, before you set to work, I should advise you to think your plans over carefully."

"I, like you, my lord, have rules to follow and duties to fulfil. I do not intend to neglect my responsibilities."

The Bishop and prefect parted stiffly.*

* * * * *

An incident which had no connection with the Appearances occurred sometime afterwards and definitely destroyed the good relations which had previously existed between the Bishop and the Prefect.

The Cathedral of Tarbes owned, just outside its walls, an unoccupied piece of ground formerly used as the burying-place of the canons. This piece of ground was only separated from the courtyard of the prefecture by a wall of the height of a man. Acting upon a pretended tacit authorisation from the Bishop himself, Baron Massy had the wall in question demolished and commenced building stables on the site of the former cemetery. Protests were made on all sides, and Monseigneur Laurence reminded the Prefect of the respect due to the rights of others and also to simple decency. In a letter which he wrote to him, Monseigneur Laurence, after having enumerated the moral considerations which had at all times protected the territory in question, called upon Baron Massy to restore the property he had usurped to its original condition, threatening him with a lawsuit in case he should refuse to do so. The

* The colloquy between the Prefect and the Bishop was reported to me subsequently by M. Peyramale, Curé of Lourdes, who was in the episcopal confidence. I can vouch for the strict accuracy of the conversation so far as the sense is concerned.

Prefect took no notice of the remonstrances of the Bishop but quietly continued to carry on his building operations.

Monseigneur Laurence, who combined calmness with firmness, wished to avoid the scandal of a lawsuit, and therefore wrote to the Minister of Public Worship to ask him to act as judge in the dispute. The minister recognised the justice of the Bishop's claims. The buildings were left standing, but it was decided to utilise them for another object and they became the offices of the prefecture. From this time however the Prefect refused to have anything more to do with the Bishop of the diocese.

* * * * *

Meanwhile the time of the *conseils de revision* arrived. Following his usual itinerary the Prefect came to Lourdes on the 4th May. Contrary to his ordinary custom he received none of the local authorities except those whose presence was absolutely necessary to the work to be carried out. During the inspection he was fanciful, nervous and brusque. His mind was clearly occupied with some matter quite foreign to the business in hand. It was noticed that he was impatient to end the sitting, which was as a matter of fact being carried out expeditiously. Whilst the conscripts were leaving the room, he ordered the police commissioner to call the mayors of the canton, as he had to make an important statement to them. As soon as they were all assembled the Prefect rose solemnly from his chair and made them a speech which was reported that same evening throughout the whole town of Lourdes. The speech was to this effect :—

" You cannot be ignorant, gentlemen, of the agitation which exists in the country with respect to certain so-called supernatural Appearances which have taken place near this town in a grotto on the banks of the Gave. Every day, to the great regret of all sensible persons, crowds of fanatics are to be seen making their way towards Lourdes and indulging in silly and superstitious practices at the grotto in question. These disorderly tumults and sacrilegious parodies are a danger to the public peace and do real harm to the interests of religion.

" Gentlemen, it is time that all these scandalous proceedings came to an end. Long before now I might, if I had so willed, have put in action the severe measures permitted by the law. Devoted as I am to the people for whom I am officially responsible I have preferred in the first place to appeal to their good sense and by persuasive measures bring them back to sane ideas.

" Gentlemen, you are the representatives of the Government in your respective communes, and in this capacity I call upon you to act as my mouthpiece. Say on my behalf to your good villagers that the vagaries of the visionary of Lourdes are founded upon vain illusions and only the mentally weak can possibly accept them. Use all your influence to keep them at home, and make them understand that by flocking to the grotto they are fostering superstition. Gentlemen, it is your duty to cure the peasants of the malady which infects them and to raise them morally and spiritually. Your intelligence and your devotion are equal I am sure to this task which the Government asks of you."

The good mayors listened attentively to the Prefect's harangue and to his request to them, but they kept an impassive silence. This silence was their manner of protesting ; and Baron Massy understood this so clearly that he cut short the interview and dismissed his audience.

* * * * *

The Prefect of Tarbes, finding no answering voice from the mayors of the communes in his district, in open disagreement with the Bishop, and but slightly supported by the Minister of Public Worship, did not know where to turn. In his isolated position he felt that he had lost weight and that some decisive step was necessary to restore his authority. Pious hands, as I have already said, had erected in the grotto a kind of altar which they had decorated with a number of pictures and statues. Not realising that the thoughts of the faithful soared far above these innocent ornaments, the Prefect was so blind as to imagine that in removing them he would also obliterate the souvenirs which they recalled. On his departure from Lourdes he sent for the police commissioner and ordered him to remove from the grotto all the religious objects which had been placed there in forgetfulness of the law.

As soon as the Prefect's order was known there was general consternation in the town. The inhabitants came out to their doors and discussed the news as if it were a public calamity. The police commissioner, in his search for a conveyance with which to carry out his miserable work, found it useless to ask for what he wanted or even to offer large sums of money; he was everywhere repulsed with disdain and much abuse. The postmaster of the locality, M. Barioge, at the risk of losing the privilege belonging to his office, proudly answered the representative of the law that he would not lend his horses for such base purposes. However, by dint of much searching, the commissioner found in the poorer quarters of the town a woman living alone who, terrorised by threats of prosecution and imprisonment, consented to lend her cart and humble beast of burden.* The commissioner and his assistants made their way to Massabieille, followed by the cries and remonstrances of those whom they met. No material opposition was made, however, to their operations; the persons who were at the grotto at the moment of the police officers' arrival confined themselves to a tearful protest and to prayer for the miserable despoilers.

As soon as the cart, with its contents of statues and pictures, had arrived at the mairie the public crier went through every part of the town announcing that the religious objects taken from the grotto were at the disposal of those who would come to recognise and claim them. As if the word of command had been given beforehand, all the women of the working classes crowded to the mairie, seized upon those *ex-votos* which belonged to them and also upon those which did not belong to them; then swiftly and without turning to right or left went in triumph to replace them at the grotto. That same evening when night had come, these women, in reparation of the outrage offered to the Virgin, lit up the rock of Massabieille. They spared no pains and the illumination was superb.

* By a curious coincidence which made a great impression upon the people of Lourdes, this woman the very next day broke two ribs in falling from a hayloft.

CHAPTER V.

Announcement of cures—Embarrassment of the Free-thinkers—Discussions at the Club of Lourdes—Analysis of the water of the grotto by M. Latour, Chemist of Trie—Temporary triumph of the enemies of the supernatural.

CERTAIN wise people at Lourdes, for whom the future had no secrets, informed the world with much assurance that the source of the grotto would dry up immediately the snows of the neighbouring mountains had ceased to contribute their waters. The snows disappeared, the sun of spring had dried up the ground, yet the fountain of water continued to flow with a most disappointing persistency. Every day it became more beautiful, more limpid and more abundant. Since the 25th March and even previously a large number of persons had been suddenly cured on coming into contact with the water. After a simple bathing some persons had recovered their sight; others, perfect hearing; others, the use of a paralysed limb; others, the very source of life gradually eaten away by the ravages of some insidious disease. At the beginning no regular account was taken of these cures, for those who had been healed concealed the fact carefully for fear that the cure might not be lasting, and that they might be exposed in case of a relapse to the mockery of the evil-disposed. The moment arrived, however, when secrecy could no longer be maintained and on all sides the miracles were discussed. There were certainly exaggerations and even falsehoods in the first stories which came into circulation, but it was proved that among the number of declarations made, certain true and authentic cures, attested by the neighbours of those formerly ill, had been obtained at the spring of Massabieille. The enemies of the supernatural began to be troubled; they did not know to what cause they could attribute the phenomena which took place at the grotto.

At the club of Lourdes, divided as I have said into two camps, discussions were keen and endless. We had arrived at a point where material and tangible facts were in question, not mere metaphysical theories. The converts of early days, now considerably increased in number, pointed out to their adversaries that the miraculous spring continued to flow in spite of all hostile prophecies, and they challenged them to explain its healing powers. Our opponents, being unable to deny the reality of the Massabieille spring, denied the cures *en bloc*, and for lack of arguments employed satire and mockery to support their cause.

One day, a day which the believers did not allow to pass away unnoticed, we heard that our learned opponents, several of whom belonged to the municipal council, had set on foot a proposal to the effect that the Mayor of Lourdes should be authorised to have the waters of the new stream analysed. They were thus surprised in the very act of self-contradiction. If as they said they did not believe in the reality of the cures announced, how was it that they had made up their minds to seek for the cause ? In an evening meeting we taxed them with this self-contradiction but our brave opponents refused to be logical and merely replied that they would wait till later.

* * * * *

The Mayor of Lourdes, who in everything which concerned the grotto ordered his line of conduct in accordance with the Prefect's instructions, was unwilling to carry out the resolution of his council without having first consulted his chief. Baron Massy did not merely approve of the project of analysis, he even blamed himself for not having suggested it in the first place. If the Massabieille spring should have as a matter of fact any chemical affinity with the mineral springs of Cauterets, Saint Sauveur and Barèges, whose curative properties are so great, cannot the so-called cures of the grotto be explained naturally ? Without further delay the Prefect sought to discover the scientist most fitted to carry out the wish of the municipal council of Lourdes. His choice immediately fell upon one of his friends, M. Latour, chemist at Trie, member of the general council, reputed to be one of the most distinguished chemists of the department. The Prefect congratulated the members of the Lourdes council on their excellent idea and asked M. Lacadé to send without delay some of the grotto water to the analyst whom he, the Prefect, had chosen. The water was sent to Trie at the end of April and on the 6th May following, M. Latour, who had hastened the matter, made the following report to the Mayor of Lourdes.

" *Chemical Examination.*"

" The water of the grotto of Lourdes is very limpid, inodorous and without any strong taste ; its specific weight is very much the same as that of distilled water. It contains the following constituents :

1. Chlorides of soda, lime and magnesia—abundant.
2. Carbonates of lime and magnesia.
3. Silicates of lime and aluminium.
4. Oxide of iron.
5. Sulphate of soda.
6. Phosphate—some traces.
7. Organic matter.

"We have observed in the analysis of this water a complete absence of sulphate of lime or selenite.

" This somewhat remarkable peculiarity is all to its advantage, and for this reason we regard it as very light and easy to digest and generally wholesome for the whole system.

"Without prejudging the matter, we may say that, in view of the water taken as a whole as well as of its constituent properties, medical science will before long perhaps recognise in it certain special curative qualities entitling it to be classed among the number of those waters which form the mineral wealth of our department.

" A. Latour,
" Chemist at Trie."

* * * * *

A cry of victory arose from the camp of the enemies of the supernatural. M. Latour's report furnished the key to all the mysteries and enthroned once more the rights of reason.

" Yes," cried the proud victors turning to us, " we grant you all your wonderful cures, but still you must bow before science, for science it is which can tell you by its inflexible laws the real causes which have produced the cures. However attached you may be to your seductive illusions, you must abandon them; children of the past, they have nothing to do with to-day."

"Your delight and your advice," we answered them, "seem to us somewhat premature. In the first place you must notice that M. Latour's conclusions are partly supposed by a fragile 'perhaps,' and this gives them a character of doubt. Moreover, even admitting that the chemist's analysis is correct, there still remains a problem which you will find it difficult to resolve—that of the instantaneousness of the cures. We certainly have never heard that the waters which are so rich minerally in our department have ever followed the succinct and rapid methods of the Massabieille waters in the cure of the different maladies. However that may be—in order to keep the discussion to the point in question, and to prevent you from wandering from the subject—we recognise to-day that you have acknowledged, though explaining them in your own way, the extraordinary cures which have taken place at the grotto. Remember your admission and we will see if you continue to say the same thing later."

But they paid no attention to what we said.

In the enjoyment of their transitory success these partisans of a natural solution had an eye upon the future and were already converting Lourdes into a thermal station. They fondly saw in their mind's eye at the foot of the Massabieille rock an immense establishment for restoring health to the sick; all around were wonderful casinos for the idle pleasure-seeker in search of fashionable amusement; elsewhere sumptuous hotels, comfortable apartments, shops filled with thousands of articles to take the fancy; everywhere in the streets, in the squares, all along the promenades, movement and life.

With regard to the decorative side of the picture, our opponents were true prophets. Those future splendours which they saw through the prism of their imagination have become realities. The rock of Massabieille, the hills which surround it, have seen spring up, as by enchantment, noble buildings, majestic and superb. But our philosophers were very far from imagining that these buildings were to be surmounted by a cross and that instead of favouring idleness, gaming or vice, they were to be the houses of prayer and penitence and all the works of sanctification. It is true indeed that vast crowds are to come to Lourdes, but who could see that so many sick, given up for dead by their doctors, should come to the grotto and there find renewed life ?

CHAPTER VI.

The gifts of money left at the grotto are handed to the Municipal Receiver of Lourdes—A false interpretation given by the police to the words of the Curé Peyramale—The Prefect of Tarbes issues a decree forbidding all access to the grotto—Protest of the workingmen of Lourdes—Destruction of the barriers—Intervention of the Curé—Pacification of troubled minds.

ALTHOUGH wounded in his *amour propre*, the Prefect of Tarbes did not manifest publicly any resentment at the mortification he had suffered from the hands of the women of Lourdes on the occasion when the grotto had been stripped of its ornaments. He had the good sense to understand that he could not fight with women of that class ; moreover, even had he wished to do so, he foresaw the difficulty there would be in legally defining the offence of which they had been guilty.

Alleging as a pretext the fact that his previous orders had been forgotten—(a forgetfulness which in his opinion was much to be regretted)—the Prefect wrote, but without bitterness, to the Mayor of Lourdes two or three days after his return to Tarbes, to ask him to take away from the grotto the gifts of money which the generosity of the pilgrims had placed there and to see in future that these gifts were collected every evening and placed without any deductions in the treasury of the municipal receiver. In these wise instructions Baron Massy, the keen-sighted administrator, could be recognised and everyone throughout the district applauded the prudent measures taken by him. Up to that time it is true nothing had been taken from the Virgin's treasure, but who could answer for the future ? In any case was there not urgent need to anticipate the danger and temptation of covetousness ?

To the credit of the municipality of Lourdes it is to be recorded that these sums, which did not amount to anything of great value, were afterwards handed to the diocesan authorities and employed subsequently in the erection of the chapel for which the Lady of the Grotto had made request.

As soon as the month of May, the month of Mary, had arrived, a veritable and ceaseless procession of pilgrims was established upon the Massabieille road. The beauties of nature, so attractive at this season, united with the religious sentiment to increase the charm of the walk to the grotto. The road which led there was bordered with two hedges scented with the perfumes of box, hawthorn and wild roses. The trees, then covered with their new foliage, sheltered the passers-by with their delicious shade. The rocks themselves clothed in their adornment of fresh moss seemed anxious to charm the visitors' eyes. Not one of those who at Lourdes believed in the heavenly Appearances—(and the believers were in the majority)—failed any day to go and pray in their hours of leisure at the holy grotto.

The evil one, however, furious at the homage offered to our Lady of Massabieille, did all he could in his mad rage to put a stop to the devotion. The reader will remember what I have already said about the terrifying visions. It was just at the time of which we speak that hell opened all its batteries to deceive, seduce and frighten the fervent servants of the Virgin. The moment came when timid souls could only approach in trembling fear the rocks now haunted by the spirit of lies ; their hesitation became greater still when the curé, one Sunday speaking from the pulpit, advised the mothers to watch over their children and to prevent them from going to play near Massabieille. He even turned out of the sacristy and the catechism a boy, a server, who had disobeyed his orders.

Man often finds it difficult to comprehend the means of which God makes use to carry out His purposes. This is excellently illustrated in the following circumstance.

There were present at the sermon of Abbé Peyramale two police officers who interpreted the preacher's words in the opposite sense to that intended by him. They imagined that the good curé was making a pronouncement against the reality of the Appearances, and that he was urging his parishioners not to return any more to the grotto. Now the curé had been most explicit in his sermon; without any circumlocution he had spoken of the evil one and of his malefic influence at Massabieille with all the liberty of apostolic times. He had warned his people to mistrust Satan's devices; then, noticing the trouble of his congregation and not wishing to leave them in doubt concerning his real opinion, he had added:—

"Take courage, my brethren; the machinations of hell will never prevail against that which God has determined to establish. It is useless for the spirit of darkness to try to obscure the events of the grotto; in spite of anything he may do they will be made manifest in all their truth and beauty to the glory of the Queen of Heaven."

One would have thought that these last words would have prevented any possible misconception, and yet the two officers continued in their mistake. They went off to tell their superior, M. Jacomet, what they imagined they had heard, and M. Jacomet himself, confirmed in this opinion by the incident of the boy who had been turned out of the catechism, hastened to inform the Prefect of the words so wrongly interpreted which he had heard that day. M. Jacomet told the Prefect in substance that the clergy of Lourdes, disabused at last of the silly fancies which until then they had accepted as facts, publicly dissociated themselves from the fantastic tales of the grotto and urged the faithful to have nothing more to do with the extravagances which took place there.

The Prefect at the time of his last visit to Lourdes, that is to say at the time of the council of revision, had been informed of the appearance at Massabieille of new visionaries and of the absurd mimicries in which they indulged. He had laughed and replied that he regarded the doings of the new seers as the natural continuation of the comedy played by Bernadette; the only difference so far as he could see was that the original actress, the little daughter of the miller, had played her part skilfully, whilst these later actors were but coarse and awkward imitators. He was however delighted at this complication, for from his point of view it heaped confusion upon confusion and gave reason for hoping that the legend of the visits of the Virgin to Massabieille would perish by its own exaggerations and absurdities. When he learned from the mistaken reports of the police that the clergy of Lourdes were publicly denouncing the Appearances and urging their people to keep away from the spot where they had taken place, he thought that his anticipations were about to be fulfilled. For some days he turned his attention in the direction of the episcopal palace waiting to hear the Bishop pass some censure upon the false miracles on the banks of the Gave. Finding that he waited in vain and that the spiritual authority remained immovable, he determined that he himself, a simple layman, would put a stop to the scandals which in his opinion were perverting the moral and religious sense of the country.

It was in accordance with the clear over-ruling of Providence that Baron Massy displayed such zeal against the infant sanctuary. The time had come when God would no longer permit the evil one to continue profaning the humble grotto which the Virgin had sanctified by her presence.

The man who summed up in his own person the various forms of opposition directed against the grotto was, as I have already said, loyal but prejudiced and misinformed; he was uncompromising in his hostility. And it was precisely this formidable adversary, the highest representative of public authority in the country, that God chose to carry out, and that at the cost of his own suffering, the projects he had planned.

The reader does not need to be reminded that Baron Massy saw in the supernatural events, divine or diabolic, taking place at Massabieille nothing but a confused mass of swindle and pantomime. He was therefore naturally inclined to wage war against that which he believed to be nothing but a silly superstition, but in setting to work he failed to realise that he was acting in obedience, not so much to his own inclination, as to the impulses of a divine will.

Remembering the failure of his early enterprises Baron Massy had become cautious. He thought it wise, before beginning again his attacks upon the grotto, to furnish himself with a weapon more definitely legal than those of which he had made use previously. He sought for this weapon, but in vain. Then that secret hand which was directing events caused him to find that for which he sought in the report of the analysis of M. Latour, of Trie.

This report said that the water of Massabieille appeared to be possessed of curative properties and that *perhaps* medical science would not be long in making use of it.

On the other hand it was notorious that the people of Lourdes and its environs, without troubling themselves about the opinion of the learned, went openly to the miraculous spring to drink there and bathe the sick.

Combining this last fact with the report of the chemical analysis the Prefect saw his opportunity to resume once more his attacks upon the grotto and that without fear of exposing himself to defeat. He remembered that the regulation of mineral springs belongs to the State and that consequently, until the superior authority had pronounced an opinion, he had the right to forbid the public using the waters of Massabieille. As soon as the report of M. Latour was in his hands he prepared a notice according to the terms of which, not merely the miraculous spring, but all the grounds of the commune surrounding the rock of Massabieille were forbidden to the public. In order to lose no time he affixed the signature of the Mayor of Lourdes to this notice and sent it to the printer.

Owing to his hasty action and the liberty he had taken Baron Massy encountered his first obstacle. The Mayor of Lourdes, who until then had passively obeyed the orders which came to him from the prefecture, felt his dignity wounded on receiving the placards, where he found his name displayed without his permission having been previously obtained. He wrote a strong letter to the Prefect in which he said that he allowed no one to make use of his signature, and rather than sanction the rigorous measures of the notice he would cease to be mayor.

The Prefect did not expect this resistance and was therefore obliged to come to an arrangement with his subordinate. After a correspondence of some days, in which the one magistrate renewed his demands and the other his refusals, some mutual friends intervened and brought about an understanding. It was agreed that the Prefect by the wording of the notice should set the mayor free from all responsibility, and that the latter merely *pro forma* should allow his signature to appear. In consequence of this arrangement the old notices were destroyed, and on the 8th June, on the walls of the town and on a notice-board erected on the summit of the Massabieille rock, appeared the prohibition to this effect :—

"The mayor of the town of Lourdes,

"In accordance with the instructions addressed to him by the superior authority;

"In accordance with the laws of the 14th to 22nd December, 1789, of the 16th to 24th August, 1790, of the 19th to 22nd July, 1791 and of the 18th July, 1837, with regard to municipal administration:

"Considering that it is necessary in the interests of religion to put an end to the lamentable scenes which take place at the Grotto of Massabieille, situated at Lourdes, on the left bank of the Gave;

"Considering moreover, that it is the mayor's duty to watch over the public safety;

"Considering that a great number of townspeople and strangers come to draw water from a spring in the said Grotto;

"Considering that there are good grounds for supposing that this water contains mineral elements, and that it is prudent, before allowing it to be used, to wait until a scientific analysis has made known the medical purposes for which it may be employed;

"Inasmuch, moreover, as the law places under the control of the Government the working and developing of mineral springs;

"Decrees—

1. The taking of water from the aforesaid spring is forbidden.
2. It is also forbidden to walk upon the communal ground of Massabieille.
3. At the entrance to the Grotto a barrier of palings will be erected to prevent access to it. Notice-boards will be also put up, bearing these words, 'Entrance into this enclosure is forbidden.'
4. The Police Commissioner, the gendarmes and other officers of the commune are charged with the execution of the present decree.

"Given at Lourdes, at the Mayor's Office, the 8th June, 1858.

"A. LACADÉ, *Mayor.*

"Seen and approved,

"O. MASSY, *Prefect.*"

* * * * *

Acts of oppression always cause intense irritation, and the people of Lourdes became furious upon reading the decree which forbade access to the grotto. A general outcry arose from all quarters of the town and even those who were least inclined to recognise the action of the Virgin at Massabieille censured the Prefect's action as harsh, vexatious and imprudent. The women cried out in the streets that they would never submit to commands which were an insult to the gracious Mother of God.

There was, however, one important part of the population, the most redoubtable for its physical strength, which had not yet made its voice heard. I refer to the quarrymen, very numerous at Lourdes, and believing strongly in the miraculous Appearances at the grotto. When the proclamation of the Prefect was published they were at work in the various yards surrounding the town, and they knew nothing of the embargo put upon the grotto until their return home in the evening. Isolated from each other, they could not exchange opinions on the subject, and that night the town remained calm.

Next day the slate and stone cutters, though somewhat excited, returned peacefully to their quarries. Gathered together in groups, the proclamation became the subject of every conversation ; it was universally condemned and words became hot.

"What business is it of the Prefect whether we believe or don't believe in what has happened at the grotto ? What right has he to prevent our drinking at one stream or at another ? Are we free men, or are we slaves ? "

The order for revolt had been given and the quarrymen, without exception, resolved that the barriers erected in front of the grotto should disappear.

That evening before returning to the town the quarrymen waited for each other, and having all met together they sanctioned as a body the plan of rebellion they had planned individually. The most level-headed of the assembly remarked, however, that they ought not to do anything hastily, and that before having recourse to extreme measures they would do better to content themselves with a peaceful manifestation. This suggestion was accepted and it was agreed that upon leaving work on the 10th June all those who intended to take part in the manifestation should meet near the old bridge and go from there to the grotto.

And so on that day at sunset these rough champions of the Virgin's cause might be seen, hammer on shoulder, descending from the heights which look down upon the town and making their way towards the appointed place of meeting.

Arrived at the spot agreed upon, they formed into two ranks and began to march toward the grotto. Those who were at the head of the column flung to the winds, with vigorous voice and to the traditional tune of the Pyrenees, the opening invocations of the litany of Our Lady. Immediately a formidable *Ora pro nobis*, like the distant roar of the ocean, awoke the echoes of the town and of the surrounding mountains. The men advanced in this way repeating their invocations up to the summit of the Massabieille hill, crossed the boundary set by the Prefect's notice-board, and by the slope where to-day there is a path in zigzags, came down near the Gave.

There they laid down their tools and standing up they sent above the barriers their final prayers to the Lady of the Rock. At nightfall the order for departure was given and each one returned peacefully to his own home.

As the mayor of Lourdes did not wish to make himself unpopular with his fellow-citizens and the police commissioner did not feel himself strong enough to resist the working-men's party, they both pretended to know nothing of what had happened at Massabieille. The stone and slate cutters, in order to rouse the local authorities from their torpor and force them to realise the purpose for which they were working, repeated their peaceful demonstration, a second and a third time, between the 10th and 16th June. At the end of this time, finding that their course of action remained fruitless and that no attention was paid to their demands, they determined to give a more energetic expression to their protest.

On the evening of the 17th June, as had been agreed, the hardy quarry workmen came down once more towards the grotto, walking with a resolute air and letting all the world know that this time something more than a mere commonplace manifestation was to be expected. Gathered together around the rock of the Appearances they looked at each other as if to count their numbers and to give mutual encouragement; then, without a single word, they took their tools, approached the barrier of boards and broke it up into splinters. Having finished their work they returned peacefully to the town.

The next day, 18th June, the mayor of Lourdes gave the Prefect the following account of the devastation committed at Massabieille on the previous evening.

"The police officer who went to the place at 5 o'clock this morning found the barrier destroyed, and the boards and stakes lying on the banks of the Gave. Only the notice-board was left untouched. I have given orders that so much of the wood as has not been destroyed should be collected and I will see that the barrier is put up again. I will have enquiries made concerning the authors of this outrage. The grotto is isolated and somewhat away from Lourdes; it will therefore be necessary, to prevent such occurrences in the future, to have this grotto guarded during the night."

The palisade was in fact reconstructed at the mayor's commands, and in accordance with the instructions given by the Prefect, a permanent watch upon Massabieille was set up.

But anyone who imagined that the workmen of Lourdes would be discouraged by the failure of their first attempts could know very little of the hardy mountain character of these people. How was it that they managed to elude the vigilance of the guardians of the grotto? However it may have been, the fact remains that on the 27th June and the 5th July following the barriers again disappeared without the authors of the destruction ever being discovered.

Two successive telegrams were despatched to inform the Prefect of the fresh devastations committed at the grotto. In the first he was told that not merely the barrier but also the notice-board erected on the summit of Massabieille had been thrown down; in the second, which betrayed the mayor's evident discouragement, the Prefect was further informed that notice-board, planks and stakes had all been thrown into the Gave and carried away by the current.

* * * * *

Open war was thus waged between the Prefect and the workmen of Lourdes. The *amour propre* of the Prefect would not allow him to be mocked by men who were under his authority ; the workmen on the other hand would not allow him to attack their religious independence without good reason.

The barriers were set up again and fresh instructions came to the mayor of Lourdes, ordering him to see that a stricter watch was kept and that a summons was taken out against any person entering the Massabieille enclosure. This obstinate persistence of the Prefect raised the anger of the workmen to its height. They loudly proclaimed their irritation against the chief of the department and did not hesitate to say to the local authorities themselves : " It is no longer the police, it is we ourselves who will be responsible in the future for watching over the grotto and woe be to him who attempts to dislodge us ! "

At the very moment when tempers were at their hottest and conciliation seemed no longer possible a man arose in Lourdes to avert the danger of the situation. This man, the nobility of whose character the reader already knows, was no other than the curé Peyramale. One day a friend told him that he had overheard in the street this sinister remark : " The police had better take a census of their members, for before long they will have to fish them out of the Gave as they have already had to fish out the planks of the barriers ! "

This was enough at once to stir into action the worthy pastor of the parish. He instantly went into the different quarters of the town directly inhabited by the working class, and there, passing from house to house, he preached peace everywhere and reminded his hearers of the respect due to the decision of the superior authority. He felt however that his task was unfulfilled, for at the time when he paid his visits the men were at their places of work outside the town and he had only the women to speak to. The good curé went home and took his mid-day meal in haste ; then he sallied out again in the direction of the hills surrounding the town.

In all the workshops he was received with respect and sympathy, for the good workmen knew by experience that, in days of trial, the curé was their best and most faithful friend When, however, he spoke to them of peace and of the danger of insurrection against the Prefect's orders he noticed that their faces grew dark and that his advice was not listened to as respectfully as usual. He returned to the town somewhat saddened and depressed, not knowing how far he could consider his mission successful. All through the following night his mind was very anxious about the future and this uneasiness weighed upon his sleep like a heavy nightmare.

The next day which was Sunday, he rose early, determined to preach at the first Mass, a Mass chiefly attended by the working people. He went up into the pulpit and made the events then disturbing the town the subject of his discourse. Speaking directly to the quarrymen, who were in a body at the back of the church, he blamed them for their violence and told them that they were doing more than any barriers to hinder the work of the Virgin at the grotto. He told them that their devotion was a mere outward devotion of display, and that it seemed to him that there was much more pride than true religious zeal in the course of action they were pursuing. "Take care," he said, "the authorities of the Government are aware of your criminal intentions and they have their eye upon you. Make no mistake; they have armed forces at their disposal; at the very slightest outbreak on your part they will in all probability put them into motion to crush you."

These words called forth certain signs of disagreement. As though on springs, Abbé Peyramale raised himself in the pulpit to his utmost height and speaking with increased energy said: "I observe that there are certain obstinate men here in church who wish to make this town a town of blood. Be it so then, but I warn them that the first blood they will have to shed will be that of their pastor. Henceforth they will have to reckon, not with the police, but with him who is speaking to them at this moment. From this day forward—(for I have no fear of their hammers and crowbars)—I will station myself on the road to the grotto and woe be to those who try to force a passage. If they come *en masse*, they will be able I know to trample me under their feet, but I shall at least have the right to brand them as cowards; if they come singly, and one of them begins the fight with me, I give him fair warning that it is not he who will gain the victory." Without adding another word the curé came down from the pulpit.

The working-men of Lourdes were proud of their curé because he was able, when occasion called for it, to speak the energetic language of the people amongst whom he lived "He has the courage," they said, "to tell us the truth to our face, and we know that he is not the man to go back when once he has made up his mind." At the end of the reprimand which I have just quoted the turbulent quarrymen looked at one another, smiled, and owned themselves vanquished. These strong children of the mountains, who would not have feared to fight with armed battalions, did not dare to resist the admonitions of their beloved pastor. When the Mass was finished they waited outside the church, and then and there, sealing the compact amicably with their horny hands, promised the curé not to return any more to the grotto, not at least as law-breakers. From this moment peace was restored to the town, and every, one at Lourdes, whether believer or unbeliever, blessed Abbé Peyramale for his successful intervention.

CHAPTER VII.

Ruses of the women of Lourdes—The guardian Callet—Summonses—Justice of the Peace—Two illustrious lawbreakers—Prosecutions abandoned—A meeting with Louis Veuillot—Trickery of the Imperial Procurator of Lourdes—Court of Appeal of Pau—A fresh defection in the camp of the free-thinkers—An odious legend.

THE women of Lourdes had been the first persons to utter the cry of revolt against the Prefect's proclamation. When they found that their husbands were proceeding to violent measures and were giving voice to sinister threats, they were afraid and tried to calm them. After the peaceful solution of the crisis one would have expected them to keep calm. But nothing of the sort; they thought that their husbands had gone too far and acted too hastily, in surrendering unconditionally to the curé's demands. In their opinion the men might have provisionally given up their right to make use of the water of the spring, inasmuch as the nature of this water—(so at least it was said, rightly or wrongly)—was yet under discussion, but they ought to have held out for freedom to pray under the rocks of Massabieille; prayer, said they, can do harm to no one. The women of Lourdes having once taken up this position, their view was bound to manifest itself in action. The good souls agreed universally themselves to take up the work laid down by their husbands, but as they were too weak to offer any material resistance they planned a campaign of craft.

After the barriers had been re-erected for the fourth time the watch over the grotto was specially entrusted to an officer of the Mairie named Callet. He was a good-natured, obliging man, not by any means one who took pleasure in being disagreeable; he had however once been a soldier and as such, trained under military discipline, he intended to see that orders were obeyed. The cunning women of Lourdes saw at once the guardian's weak side and the advantage to be taken of it.

Every day, according to arrangement among themselves, they left the town and made their way towards the basin of the Gave, divided into two distinct squads. When those who formed the advanced guard had reached the top of Massabieille they pretended to pray for an instant; then under some pretext or other they called Callet on to the top of the knoll. Callet, suspecting nothing, and only too glad to interrupt for a moment the monotony of his watch, fell in with the wishes of the treacherous pilgrims. As soon as the guardian was well engaged in conversation on the summit, the women who had remained behind, upon a prearranged signal, passed quickly through M. de la Fitte's field, crossed the bed of the canal which had stopped Bernadette, and entered the grotto. When they had satisfied their devotion they returned, went up to the group which was holding Callet in conversation, changed places with their companions and gave them the opportunity by means of the same trick of saying their prayers also in the grotto.

This stratagem was repeated several times and the matter was a joke throughout the town, but the good Callet himself noticed nothing. At length the local chief of police, better informed, told him about it and reprimanded him severely.

From this moment Callet turned a deaf ear to all solicitations and became inexorable. Crafty and artful in his turn, he contrived to take out ninety-four summonses during the month of July and early days of August. About forty of these law-breakers consisted of strangers who, in going to or from the thermal stations at the end of the valley, had not wished to pass through Lourdes without visiting the grotto in spite of the strict prohibition then in force. Callet gave the police commissioner every evening a list of the offenders of that day, and as writing was not his forte, he left to his superior the task of drawing up in a legal form the statement of offences committed.

The local justice of the peace was overwhelmed by the number of summonses with which he had to deal. In order not to let business accumulate and without troubling about degrees of culpability he adopted a method which was both speedy and simple. On a day fixed he ordered all the accused of the week to appear before him; then, including them all in the same sentence, he condemned them all and each to a penalty of five francs, the expenses of the prosecution being shared between them.

The women of Lourdes never took these law proceedings seriously. They went to the court as they might have gone to a circus, some knitting stockings, others with their distaff. The idlers of the town also took a great delight in these meetings for they were often of a most amusing character.

Things began with the arrival of the justice of the peace, a man of unimpeachable honour, but nervous and entirely under the thumb of the authorities. He took his seat, fussy and angry, rang the bell, and sharply ordered the warrant to be read.

"Call the first defendant," he would say.

"What is your name?"

"Why, surely your honour knows my name; I am your neighbour; don't you recognise me?"

"Remember that you are here before the judge. Answer my question."

Very often the merry defendants purposely concealed their

real names and gave their family nicknames. This aroused general amusement.

"If these demonstrations are repeated," the judge would say, "I will have the court cleared."

Then turning once more to the defendant:

"Do you acknowledge the truth of the charges made against you in the summons?"

"Yes certainly, but I deny Callet's right to summon us."

"What do you mean?"

"I mean that Callet shuts himself up in the grotto and prays there to his heart's content; everyone knows it; and he has no right to refuse to others that which he grants to himself." *

"Not so much talk. Is it true, yes or no, that you obtained entrance to the grotto by forcibly breaking in?" (*A l'aide d'effraction.*)

"By the help of fractions! (*A l'aide des fractions.*) Oh! your honour, I have no learning, and I didn't use fractions, so far as I know."

"You are an idiot. I ask you if you got into the grotto by breaking down the boards of the barriers?"

"I? Certainly not, Lord love me. We poor weak women don't do like the quarrymen. And by the way, your honour, why aren't the quarrymen summoned as much as we? You must know that they didn't go there for nothing."

"Silence; that's not your business. Tell me what you went to the grotto for. To play the fool?"

"Your honour, we do at Massabieille exactly what you do at church on Sunday. Nothing more. I tell you straight."

"Do you imagine you are honouring the Virgin? You are pouring contempt upon her."

"But, your worship, when you put on your best coat and

* It was a matter of common knowledge that Callet, every day before mounting guard, took his rosary from his pocket and recited it before the grotto. Laying to heart the injunction of the Gospel, "Render to Cæsar the things that are Cæsar's, and to God the things that are God's," Callet had made it his rule to give no offence either to the Police Commissioner or to our Lady of Massabieille. Was he to blame?

Callet died in 1899, burdened with years and infirmities. To the very last he remained guardian of the grotto, and was always delighted to give pilgrims all the information for which they asked with regard to the origin and successive transformations and developments of the pilgrimages.

go to pay a visit to some grand lady in the town, do you think you are pouring contempt on her?"

Such was the habitual tone of the proceedings in court, and they generally ended in an outburst of laughter.

* * * * *

Two incidents occurring on the same day, and unforeseen by the authorities, put a stop to this ceaseless flow of summonses and fines.

On the afternoon of the 28th July Callet saw coming down from the heights of Massabieille a lady in mourning, evidently a person of some distinction; she was accompanied by two younger ladies whose dignity and charm of manner also attracted attention. It seemed to be a mother and her two daughters. All three went and knelt quietly near the Gave, outside the barriers. Callet instinctively took off his cap and approached the little group with visible embarrassment.

"Madam," said he, "you are doubtless not aware that it is forbidden to come here."

The lady raised her head and summed up Callet at once.

"You do not seem malicious," she said. "I am a stranger, and I shall not often come to Lourdes. Allow me I beg of you to go into the grotto with my two daughters and I shall be very grateful to you."

"But, madam, I shall have to summon you."

"Oh, I don't mind about that. Take out the summons and I will pay for it. Only let me enter."

Callet's opposition was clearly weakening. He scratched his ear, looked all round to see whether the outline of the police commissioner might not be visible on some neighbouring hill. Then hesitating and fearful he unfastened a board and let the three ladies enter.

They knelt down and said their rosaries together aloud. Having prayed for some time they drew near the miraculous spring and drank from it out of the hollow of their hand; they approached the wild rose tree which hung down from the recess and broke off a little branch; then, making a last sign of the cross and a profound reverence, they prepared to depart. As soon as they were outside the barriers Callet, still most respectful, came up with his note-book in his hand and asked the lady to be so good as to give him her name.

"I am the wife of Admiral Bruat and the governess of the Prince Imperial," answered the stranger simply.

A thunderbolt falling upon the rock of Massabieille would not have astonished Callet so much as did this declaration. His hands trembled so violently that it was impossible for him to write the lady's name. Madame Bruat could not help smiling; she took the note-book with a laugh and wrote her name in it. The three visitors nodded to Callet pleasantly and took their departure.

* * * * *

Some minutes later a new arrival, a man of between forty-five and fifty, appeared on the path leading down to the grotto. Stoutly built, he walked slowly and firmly. His face was pitted with the marks of smallpox but its expression was striking and intelligent. Without taking any notice of the guardian, the unknown man went straight to the barrier which he found still open, and without more ado entered the grotto.

"Hi, you there," cried Callet, thoroughly angry this time, "did you not see the notice-board on the summit of the slope?"

"Yes my good fellow and I even read your mayor's proclamation."

"Well, I like your impudence. I shall summon you and you must give me your name and description."

"I am Louis Veuillot, editor of the newspaper the *Univers* at Paris!"

Callet, who knew more about admirals than he did about men of letters, succeeded better this time in writing down the name of the celebrated journalist.

Louis Veuillot took off his hat on going into the grotto, examined the conformation of the rock which had now become so famous, and gazed for a long time at the recess; then collecting his thoughts he gave himself up to meditation. When a quarter of an hour had elapsed he raised his head, cast one last look all round the grotto, and went off forgetting to salute the guardian.

Irritated by this want of politeness Callet began to growl between his teeth, calling Veuillot "cad" and "bounder." The journalist meanwhile climbed up the Massabieille hill.

* * * * *

The police commissioner frowned when glancing down the list of law-breakers summoned that day. Although he was nothing but the instrument of the superior authority, he wondered whether he were wise to summon two such important persons as Madame Bruat and the powerful editor of the *Univers*. Might he not be accused of intemperate zeal and lack of respect for social position? In his perplexity he went to ask th advice of the mayor. The mayor did not dare to pronounce an opinion on such a thorny matter; moreover, not wishing to become responsible for a position of affairs which he had not created, he told the commissioner to put his difficulties before the Prefect. The Prefect for his part was no less embarrassed. If on the one hand he prosecuted Madame Bruat and Louis Veuillot he had to fear the Government repudiation of his whole action in the matter and the criticism of the press; If on the other hand he did not prosecute them, he would be charged with partiality and respect of persons and would lose all influence over the people for whom he was responsible. His natural pride inclined him to the first course of action, but he had to consider his official position and from this point of view he realised that the approbation of the minister was absolutely necessary. He therefore decided to obtain this approbation and informed the Minister of Public Worship that he was faced by a difficult alternative; he must either prosecute Madame Bruat and Louis Veuillot or he must prosecute no one. The Minister without entering into details replied at once that he was to prosecute no one.

From this moment the summonses ceased and no more fines were inflicted.

* * * * *

The reader will allow me I think to tell the story of my meeting Louis Veuillot on this occasion of his first visit to Lourdes. It is one of my pleasantest memories.

The day had been very hot. In the evening I was walking near the stream of Lapaca with one of my brothers, a curé in the Tarbes diocese, and my neighbour Abbé Pène. As we were passing in front of a bathing establishment Louis Veuillot came out of it, approached us, saluted us, and asked if the clergy with me belonged to the staff of the parish. Abbé Pène at once said he was one of the vicaires,* and the editor of the *Univers* seemed delighted.

"I have been to the presbytery," he said, "but I did not see the curé, who is away and does not come back until to-morrow. I wished to ask him about the strange events of which everyone is speaking, and which took place I am told in a grotto near here. I should be very sorry to leave Lourdes without having obtained authentic information from a reliable source. I hope that as the curé is away his vicaire will be so kind as to give me the information I want."

Abbé Pène told Louis Veuillot that the clergy of Lourdes had made a point of keeping away from the grotto during the time of the Appearances.

"But here is M. Estrade," he added pointing to me. "He has seen with his own eyes the greater number of Bernadette's ecstasies and you will find no witness better informed or more reliable. You may trust him on all points."

"That's lucky," said Louis Veuillot; and taking me by the arm he added, "You are the very man I want, sir."

Then turning to the two priests he said: "I am going to deprive you of him. There is nothing more for you to learn from this gentleman and I am anxious to know everything. I want to listen to him quite free from distraction. Moreover," he added, with a smile, "we are laymen, and should prefer to be left free in our discussion. It is most probable that I might say something which would shock you."

I was still under the influence of my first impressions and I began my story with so much warmth and enthusiasm, betraying so intense a faith, that Louis Veuillot interrupted me immediately.

"I do not doubt your sincerity, sir," he said to me, "but

* It must be remembered that the French "curé" corresponds to the English "vicar," and the French "vicaire" to the English "curate."

let me give you a word of advice to begin with; don't be so positive in your opinion but wait until the bishop has spoken. It is only he who, in virtue of his office, has grace to distinguish the true from the false in things of this nature. And his task is not easy. The bishop needs much prudence, tact, knowledge, and above all illumination from on high. My profession of Christian journalist has compelled me to give a certain amount of time to the study of mystical theology and I have found it both interesting and instructive. In the books which treat of this science a great number of marvels are described which at first sight seem to be divine facts but are in reality only diabolic tricks or merely human artifices. I must confess that I have myself been taken in and that is why I am so suspicious now. One day I heard that a marvellous trance medium had been discovered in Germany and it was represented to me that I might perhaps do a service to the cause of religion by going to witness *de visu* the reality of this phenomenon. I immediately packed my bag and went off to the other side of the Rhine. I arrived at the clairvoyante's house and watched her ecstasies in amazement; I treated her with great respect and had no idea that I was being completely humbugged. Some days after, when I was back again in Paris, I learned that my ecstatic maiden w as a clever actress and that her morality left much to be desired."

Having said this, M. Veuillot asked me to excuse his interruption and begged me to continue my story which he followed with the deepest interest to the end. I could tell from his emotion that I had gained my cause and of this I was quite certain when he asked me to write down for him all that I had heard and seen at the grotto at the time of my first visit there.

This account, sent to Bagnères de Bigorre where Louis Veuillot was spending the summer with Monseigneur de Salinis, Archbishop of Auch, was reproduced in full two or three days after in the columns of the *Univers* which had not till then, I think, spoken of the Appearances of Lourdes. Some years later I found in the *Mélanges* of Louis Veuillot (vol. 4, p. 348) some traces of my communications under the anonymous signature of " A witness."

The editor of the *Univers*, so terrible in his journalistic polemics, was charming in his private conversation. I have kept a delightful recollection of him. It was time, after our long talk about Bernadette's visions, to return home. We once more joined Abbé Pène and my brother and the conversation turned upon the subject of confession. As the matter was not one upon which I could express an opinion with authority I held my peace and listened, then suddenly Louis Veuillot turned to me and asked me: "And you, do *you* often go to confession?"

Amazed at this unexpected question I stammered something, not knowing what to say.

Abbé Pène took pity on me and told my inquisitive questioner that I went to confession before the great festivals.

"That is something," said Veuillot, "but it is not enough. I go to confession every fortnight, and though my back is broad, when the end of the fortnight arrives I feel the need of hurrying to free myself from the load I carry. You act otherwise, and that proves one thing, viz. that your burden is less heavy than mine."

Having said this he shook my hand and said good-bye to us.

* * * * *

I have said that after the minister's reply there was no more talk of summonses. I am wrong and must rectify my statement.

The imperial procurator of Lourdes, who had become one of the bitterest partisans of the opposition, regretted continually that he had not been able to exercise any legal authority over the affairs of the grotto. He sought for an occasion and found it in a contemptible incident. M. Dutour, who until then had been regarded as a clear-sighted and sensible magistrate, lost much of the public esteem.

One day some wit, who was never discovered, started a report to the effect that the emperor and empress intended to make a pilgrimage to Lourdes and that before beginning their journey they had asked for prayers to be made at the grotto. This report, passing from mouth to mouth among the people of the working class, was arrested on the lips of three good women, as harmless as they were credulous. The procurator, through some mental obliquity which it is difficult to understand, thought he saw in the idle story an indirect advertisement of the grotto and an insult offered to the royal family. Without realising that he was acting ridiculously he summoned the poor simple women and ordered them to be taken before the police-court for circulating false information.

When the case came up the judges smiled and only listened for form's sake. They acquitted two of the defendants and only condemned the third to a small fine for some insulting word spoken to the police-officer. The verdict completed the irritation of the procurator. Already annoyed at the attitude taken by the tribunal on the opening of the case, he immediately brought the case before the court of appeal at Pau hoping thereby to restore his prestige.

On the day fixed for the trial a great number of the women of the capital of Béarn, many of whom had been present at the ecstasies of Bernadette, ran to meet the defendants from Lourdes, received them in triumph and accompanied them with enthusiastic and noisy sympathy to the court-house. The attorney-general, finding himself in the presence of a manifestation which if opposed might degenerate into a public outbreak, and recognising moreover that his subordinate's lawsuit had nothing serious about it and that petty self-assertion was the motive which had urged it, declared, as soon as the judges of the court had taken their seats, that he did not intend to go on with the matter. Thunderous applause broke out in the court and several persons on leaving cried out, "Long live our Lady of the Grotto."

The acquitted women, after having been entertained at Pau for several days, returned to Lourdes crowned with laurels. The people in the streets went up to them and welcomed them, congratulating them on the result of the lawsuit. M. Dutour was obliged to swallow his humiliating defeat in silence.

* * * * *

M. Dutour's prosecution of the women of Lourdes reminds me of a defection from the camp of the free-thinkers which took place at that time and which caused a great impression in the locality. The deputy of the imperial procurator, M.

de L., fell ill of consumption, a consumption which was bound to terminate fatally. The young lawyer of whom I speak was a delightful man, and the speeches he made at our club debates were always courteous and conciliatory. Although he had not expressed any very decided opinion with regard to the events of the grotto, our opponents claimed him as one of their adherents. As soon as the sick man realised the gravity of his illness he sent for Abbé Peyramale and made his confession. Upon the return of the curé, who had gone to bring him the Viaticum, M. de L. raised himself, and said in a clear voice, "Monsieur le curé, before receiving my God I have a confession to make, and I am glad to make it in the presence of all in this room as it gives me the opportunity of humiliating myself. Although I was thoroughly convinced of the truth of the Appearances of the Virgin at Massabieille—(and I had reasons of my own for my belief)—I had not the courage to confess my faith."

At this moment Abbé Peyramale stopped him and calmed his scruples; then, deeply touched, he gave him the Holy Communion. M. de L. recovered from this first attack, but some time afterwards, in the Landes, he died piously in the bosom of his family.

* * * * *

Here I may as well once and for all dispose of a miserable and odious lie, invented by certain evil minds in the cafés for their own amusement and to excuse their unbelief. This foolish story born of a foul imagination and reproduced by certain unscrupulous and vulgar journals attacked at the same time the reputation of one of the most honourable families in Lourdes and the belief in the supernatural Appearances of Massabieille. The story was to the effect that, at Bernadette's first visit to the grotto on the 11th February, 1858, the seer had suddenly come upon a certain lady of Lourdes, whose name was given, in the company of a certain cavalry officer. This unfaithful wife, in order to put the little girl off the scent and so escape recognition, immediately took up the attitude of a statue of the Virgin and uttered strange words in a prophetic manner. In 1892, on the occasion of the notorious novelist Zola's visit to the grotto, the gutter press dished up once more the legend of the guilty wife. I was myself at Lourdes in September, 1892, and I was much concerned at the harmful influence the persistent repetition of this foul legend might produce on ignorant persons. I had a vague idea that the lady whose memory was thus libelled—(for she had already departed this life)—at the time of the Appearances was confined to her bed by the birth of a child. In order to be quite exact I went to the mayor's office and asked to see the birth registers of the town. And I made a happy discovery. The lady accused of unfaithfulness to her husband had given birth to a daughter on the 8th February, 1858, three days before the first Appearance of the Virgin at the Grotto. The birth in question is numbered 13 in the register of births of Lourdes. The finding of this proof put a stop to the calumny. It was communicated to the press, with a threat of legal proceedings, and nothing more was heard of the matter.

CHAPTER VIII.

Clamours of the press—A fresh analysis demanded by the inhabitants of Lourdes—Result of the analysis made by M. Filhol, chemist at Toulouse—Intervention of the Emperor Napoleon III.—The barriers removed—The Prefect of Tarbes and the Police Commissioner are transferred elsewhere.

SIMULTANEOUSLY with the events which I have just related, a question was being raised which concerned the deepest interests of the grotto. I refer to the doubts which still existed concerning the nature of the Massabieille waters.

The reader will remember the joy manifested by the opponents of the supernatural at the arrival of the analytical report of M. Latour, of Trie. This joy was reflected in an infinity of journals, from the little *Lavedan* of Lourdes and the *Ere impériale* of Tarbes, the organ of the prefecture, up to the Paris newspapers most in vogue at the cafés. On all sides it was said that the fairy-tale of the grotto would soon be resolved into the simple and commonplace affair of a buvette.

The inhabitants of Lourdes (excepting the unbelievers), daily witnesses of the miracles which took place at the fountain, did not let the witticisms of the free-thinkers or the opinions of science trouble them. Simply taking a commonsense view of the matter they maintained that the Massabieille water could not contain any curative mineral elements, certainly no elements which could produce a sudden cure. They scoffed at the experiments of the Trie chemist, and loudly demanded a fresh analysis and one carried out by abler hands.

The promoters of the first analysis moreover, regarding their triumph as assured, desired nothing better than to confound a second time the blind believers in the marvellous. Would not a fresh analysis they asked themselves, free from all restrictions, crown their initiative with complete success? Were their ideas of building mad, and their projects of fortune for the town to remain unrealised? Might they not, circumstances being propitious, expect to have a column erected to their honour beside the fountain of Massabieille, a fountain still beneficent though no longer clerical?

The Mayor of Lourdes had then no choice but to carry out the wishes of the inhabitants and he was all the more ready to do this as he saw, without committing himself definitely to either of the two parties, that a new era was in any case about to open for the town. If on the one hand it was shown that the water of the grotto cured in virtue of the mineral elements constituting it, Lourdes would become *ipso facto* a thermal resort. If on the other hand the water cured by virtue of something outside the common laws of nature, then Massabieille with the added charm of its legend would become a place of pilgrimage. In fine, whatever might be the result of the new analysis the town could not fail to profit by it

The mayor had already written in anticipation to the Prefect to ask his advice as to the man best qualified to undertake the final official analysis of the grotto water. The Prefect replied that the best known chemist in the south was M. Filhol, one of the most eminent members of the Toulouse Faculty of Sciences. He advised the mayor to approach him, not merely because M. Filhol was a highly esteemed savant, but also because he had made most of the mineral springs of the Pyrenees the subject of a thorough and conscientious study.

Immediately upon receiving the Prefect's reply the mayor

summoned a meeting of the town council in order to obtain from it an authorisation to make the necessary researches as to the true character of the Massabieille water. Without touching on the religious side of the question, he laid before the meeting the interest which the town had in knowing clearly and finally the chemical constitution of this water and he suggested M. Filhol as the specialist best fitted to give entire satisfaction in this respect. The council raised no objection to the mayor's suggestions, and resolved unanimously as follows :—*

"In the year one thousand eight hundred and fifty-eight, and on the third of June, the town council met in the place where it generally held its meetings, under the presidency of M. Lacadé, mayor.

"Present, Messrs. Normande, Capdevielle, deputies, Claverie, Latapie, Cousté, Duprat, Dupont, Rouy, Rives, Labayle, Cesta, Lapeyre, Pagès.

"The mayor, after having opened the meeting, laid the following facts before the Council.

"There has been discovered at Lourdes on the left bank of the Gave a spring of water said to be possessed of curative properties.

"This water has been analysed by M. Latour, a distinguished chemist of this department, who has found it to be possessed of such properties that medical science may *perhaps* class it among the number of those waters in which this district i so rich.

"The town has a great interest in knowing the elements of which it is constituted, as well as its properties.

"Under these circumstances I ask for your authorisation in order that I may submit it to a fresh analysis.

"The council, considering that the mayor's proposal should be agreed to ;

"Considering that M. Latour's report states that the Massabieille water appears to contain mineral elements ;

"Considering that having already M. Latour's opinion it is clearly to the town's interest to have the water analysed afresh by an equally distinguished chemist in order to have the opinion of two specialists ;

* An exact copy from the minute-book of the town council of Lourdes in the year 1858.

"Has resolved that the mayor be authorised to have this water analysed by M. Filhol, chemist at Toulouse, and to pay the fee out of funds at his disposal for that purpose.

"Having nothing more to lay before the council the mayor closed the proceedings and those present signed."

(Here follow the signatures.)

The mayor then wrote to M. Filhol to ask him to undertake the analysis in question. The letter is numbered 129, and dated 16th June, 1858. M. Filhol at once replied that he would carry out the analysis, and he began work almost immediately.

The people of the labouring classes in the town, absorbed at this time in the war undertaken against the barriers, gave but scant attention to the verdict asked for from science with regard to the Massabieille water. They had seen Bernadette in her ecstasies; they had seen the sick rise up healed from the miraculous fountain; that was quite enough for them.

But it was very different with the intellectuals, as represented at Lourdes by the members of the club of the Café Français. All minds there were in a state of restlessness and awaited with feverish impatience M. Filhol's reply.

Believers were in fear that the Appearances themselves might be disputed and faith shaken if the analysis gave unfavourable results. And the opponents themselves were not entirely comfortable as to the consequences of the step which they had urged. They feared for their dignity and for their schemes. Both parties therefore held their peace and during some time there was a cessation of their irritating disputes. It was the anxious silent moment which precedes the thunderbolt.

M. Filhol's report seemed very long in coming. At last one day the news spread in every quarter of the town, like a spark put to a train of gunpowder, to the effect that the conclusions of the official chemist were known and that the supernatural was victorious. A great number of people hastened to the mairie to make sure of the truth of the report; then they withdrew, radiant or crestfallen, according to the opinion they had supported. The statement of the analyst was clear and precise. The water of the grotto contained nothing but the elements of ordinary water; it was good drinking water but nothing more.

This is what the eminent chemist said in his report.

"I, the undersigned. . . certify that I have analysed a certain water coming from a spring which flows from a grotto in the environs of Lourdes."

After having detailed the reagents employed to decompose the water M. Filhol added :—

"From the foregoing facts, I conclude that the water of the Grotto of Lourdes contains in solution,

1. Oxygen.
2. Nitrogen.
3. Carbonic acid.
4. Carbonates of lime, magnesia and a trace of carbonate of iron.
5. A carbonate of silica of alkali, chlorides of potash and sodium.
6. Traces of sulphate of potash and of soda.
7. Traces of ammonia.
8. Traces of iodine.

The quantitative analysis of this water has been carried out by the ordinary processes, and gives the following results :—

A kilogramme of water.

Carbonic acid...	8 c.c.
Oxygen	5 c.c.
Nitrogen	17c.c.
Ammonia	traces
Carbonate of lime	O gr. .096 mil.
Carbonate of magnesia	O gr. .012 mil.
Carbonate of iron	traces
Carbonate of soda	traces
Chloride of sodium	O gr. .008 mil.
Chloride of potash	traces
Silicate of soda, and traces of silicate of potash	O gr. .018 mil.
Sulphate of potash, of soda	traces
Iodine	traces
Total	O gr. .134 mil.

"From the foregoing analysis I conclude that the water of the Grotto of Lourdes may be considered in its composition as a water for drinking, similar to the majority of the springs found in the mountains, the soil of which is rich in limestone.

"This water contains no active substance capable of giving it marked therapeutic properties; it can be drunk without danger.

"Toulouse, 7th August, 1858. Signed, Filhol."

In the letter accompanying this report M. Filhol wrote to the mayor of Lourdes :

" The extraordinary results which I am informed have been obtained by the use of this water cannot, at least in the present condition of scientific knowledge, be explained by the nature of the salts whose existence is revealed by analysis."

* * * * *

Great was the disappointment in the camp of the adversaries of the supernatural when they learnt the final opinion of science. Our local philosophers, taken in their own nets, were stricken in the inmost recesses of the soul. They could no longer deny the cures at the grotto for they had openly recognised them, and on the other hand they did not see what line they could take in order to avoid the humiliation of their defeat. As strategists uncertain of their ground, who yet would not abandon their flag, they took a turn in another direction and employed quibble instead of argument. They said that it was not uncommon to come across sudden cures of which the cause could not be explained ; that, under the stress of a violent emotion, paralytics had walked, the dumb had recovered speech ; that in fact all the secrets of nature had not yet been revealed to us and that what appeared a mystery to us to-day might to-morrow become a commonplace truth. What would they not have said if they could have known the marvels accomplished in our days in the schools of suggestive healing ?

Talk and subterfuge are but blunt weapons and truth disdains the use of them. Those who believed in the supernatural virtue of the waters of Massabieille replied, not by mere theories, but by actual concrete facts. They brought before the notice of their antagonists a crowd of cases of illness such as cancers, open wounds, stiff or deformed limbs, diseases in which the imagination could play no part, which had yet been cured instantaneously and radically at the grotto by the action of its health-giving waters, and they challenged their adversaries to explain these phenomena and to say once for all what they thought of them. Our obstinate opponents still rambled on vaguely and would not keep to the point at issue.

The few survivors of the time of which I speak, formerly antagonists, are now enrolled as happy believers under the banner of the Immaculate Virgin. Many a time during the last few years have I found one or other of them come from afar to worship at the grotto and to kneel humbly on that holy ground. I have come close to my old friend and former antagonist and pointing up to the white Madonna above us our eyes have met in a look full of intelligence and meaning; memories of the past have risen up before us; now, thank God, our understanding of each other is perfect and unhindered.

* * * * *

The minister having put an end to his campaign of summonses and a master of science having now pronounced the water of Massabieille to contain no curative properties, the Prefect of Tarbes ought logically to have ceased his hostile attacks upon the grotto. He did not cease however; and if until then the harassing methods he had adopted could be excused on the grounds of the sincerity and earnestness of his opinions, it was now clear that he was acting purely from caprice and obstinacy.

The Prefect had given two reasons for forbidding access to the grotto; the fear of seeing religion compromised and anxiety for the public health. In face of the clear declarations of science Baron Massy had to abandon his second reason, that of anxiety for the public health; he tried therefore to give more weight to the pretext of the danger threatening religious beliefs. In order to justify his continued prohibition he again said that the grotto had been made into a place of worship and the law thereby infringed, and that it was all the more important to put a stop to this worship because it sought to honour a system of lies and superstitions.

When M. Filhol's report arrived the Prefect, fearing that his previous orders would now be disregarded, instructed the mayor to make no change with regard to the arrangements at the grotto, charging him especially to maintain the barriers and still have them guarded but not to take out any summonses. The grotto of Massabieille consequently continued closed during two long months, from the first days of August till the beginning of October.

A detailed account of the annoyances to which the pilgrims were subjected would be wearisome to the reader. I will spare him this and come at once to the conclusion of these miserable quarrels.

I have said in the course of this story that the day was to arrive when our Lady of Massabieille would bring about the intervention of the chief of the state himself. That day was approaching.

Napoleon III., as was his custom every year, took up his residence at Biarritz to spend the sea-bathing season there. The inhabitants of Lourdes and its environs, weary of the high-handed action of Baron Massy and the bondage in which he held them, took advantage of the Emperor's presence in their neighbourhood to bring their complaints before him. They found certain men of influence in the district who were glad to act on their behalf. Napoleon III. spoke little but acted speedily. He listened impassively to the story of the events which had taken place at the grotto of Lourdes, but when he was told of the absurd annoyances and petty persecutions carried on by the authorities of the department he frowned and rang at once for his secretary. He briefly ordered him to telegraph to the Prefect of Tarbes to the effect that the barriers preventing access to the grotto of Lourdes were to be taken down immediately and that he was to cease interfering in the matter of the Appearances.

On the 5th October the barriers were removed by those who had put them up and the following notice was affixed to the walls of the town of Lourdes.

"The mayor of the town of Lourdes,

"In view of the instructions addressed to him by superior authority, gives notice,

"That the order of the 8th June, 1858, is repealed.

"Given at Lourdes, at the mayor's office, 5th October, 1858.

"A. LACADÉ, Mayor."

* * * * *

Some weeks after, the *Moniteur Officiel* gazetted the removal of M. Massy, Prefect of Tarbes, to Grenoble, and soon afterwards, by order of the minister, M. Jacomet, police commissioner at Lourdes, was appointed to Arles (Bouches du Rhône).

CHAPTER IX.

An unexpected visit from the Bishop of Montpellier—His impressions at Lourdes—A commission appointed by the Bishop of Tarbes to inquire into the facts of the Grotto—Outcry of the free-thinking press—Work of the commission—Doctrinal judgment relative to the Appearances of the Virgin at Massabieille.

A HOST of events had taken place during the summer of 1858. I must go back in order to record them in their chronological order.

About the middle of July there came to Lourdes a certain eminent person whose theological knowledge entitled him to express an opinion on things supernatural. This man was Monseigneur Thibaud, Bishop of Montpellier.

Having gone to Cauterets for the waters he had heard very much about the grotto of Lourdes and the marvels which took place there, but he had been given very conflicting accounts. Before returning to his diocese he wanted to form his own opinion on the spot itself and discover what was true out of the thousands of reports in circulation on the subject of the Appearances.

One day, then, without having previously announced his visit, he knocked at the door of the Lourdes presbytery. Abbé Peyramale was delighted to satisfy his legitimate curiosity. After having heard what he had to say the Bishop at once allowed that there were good reasons for believing that the Virgin had appeared at Massabieille. He asked to see Bernadette and she was sent for.

The innocent appearance of the child, her modest look and smile, made a favourable impression upon Monseigneur Thibaud. He welcomed her kindly, made her sit down near him and, after having spoken a few words of encouragement, asked her to tell him the story of the favour bestowed upon her.

Whilst Bernadette spoke the prelate, bending forward, listened eagerly and made no movement except to wipe away the tears which came unbidden to his eyes.

When the little girl had finished her story, the Bishop was entirely convinced of the reality of the Appearances of the

Blessed Virgin at Lourdes. However, he still kept Bernadette for some time longer, and when the moment for her departure had arrived he gave her his blessing with a voice which betrayed emotion and respect.

After the child had gone Monseigneur Thibaud turned to the curé and his vicaires who were present at the interview and said to them : " If the story of this child is not true, then we can be sure of nothing that our understanding brings before us for belief. What ! Is it possible that a poor peasant girl without any intellectual culture, a creature as simple as a flower of the fields, should come and recite to us a poem which would do credit to the most richly gifted imaginations ? No, it is not possible, and wha that young girl recounts she has seen and heard."

The pious curiosity of Monseigneur Thibaud was not yet satisfied. Before leaving Lourdes he wanted to know the opinion of some of those who had been present at the ecstasies of Bernadette. I was sent for and had the honour of giving my testimony ; he kept me nearly two hours. I was still in the fire of my first enthusiasm and after having spoken for some long time I ended my story with the following words :

" Monseigneur, I have seen celebrated actresses act in great theatres ; they were but grimacing statues by the side of Bernadette. They represented with exaggeration the passions of earth ; but the ecstatic at the grotto, like an angel, mirrored the joy and beatitude of heaven."

" That's it, that's it ! " cried the Bishop. " Others, sir, have spoken to me as you have spoken. But what is there surprising in it ? Had not the little seer before her eyes that Immaculate Virgin who is the wonder and delight of the hosts of heaven ? "

Monseigneur Thibaud was of a keen and ardent nature. In the room of the hotel where he had received me and where several priests were waiting he walked up and down, saying continually, " But what is Monseigneur Laurence doing on his episcopal throne at Tarbes ? What is the meaning of his continued inaction ? I understand that at first extreme reserve was necessary, but to-day, now that the facts are so widely known, why is he so slow in recognising them or at least in looking into them ? Is he afraid of a Prefect ? Does he fear the mockery of an idiotic and degenerate press? Does he suppose that all the inhabitants of Lourdes are suffering from an hallucination? I had not intended to stop at Tarbes, but now my conscience tells me that, as a brother Bishop, it is my duty to see him. If the Bishop of Tarbes still hesitates to believe in the Appearances at the grotto I will tell him to come here, and do what I have done. I defy him to leave Lourdes unbelieving."

Did Monseigneur Thibaud carry out his intention and visit the Bishop of Tarbes? That I know not; but what I do know is that, a few days after the departure of the Bishop of Montpellier (to be exact, it was Sunday the 1st August), Monseigneur Laurence, in all the churches of his diocese, caused an order to be published to the effect that an ecclesiastical commission was appointed to examine into the authenticity and nature of the events which had taken place at the grotto of Lourdes.

The document in question was as follows:

"*Order of Monseigneur the Bishop of Tarbes, appointing a commission charged with the examination of the authenticity and nature of the events which have taken place during the last six months or thereabouts, on the occasion of an Appearance, real or alleged, of the most blessed Virgin in a grotto situated to the west of the town of Lourdes.*

"BERTRAND SÉVÈRE LAURENCE, by the mercy of God and the grace of the Holy See, Bishop of Tarbes, to the clergy and faithful of our diocese, health and benediction in our Lord Jesus Christ.

"Certain events of the greatest importance concerning religion which have stirred the diocese and been discussed far and wide have taken place at Lourdes since the 11th February last.

"Bernadette Soubirous, a young girl of Lourdes of the age of fourteen, is said to have had certain visions in the grotto of Massabieille situated to the west of that town; the Immaculate Virgin is said to have appeared to her; a spring of water is said to have flowed there; the water of this fountain, drunk or applied as a lotion, is said to have caused a great number of cures. These cures are described as miraculous; people have come in crowds and continue to come every day, both from our own and from neighbouring dioceses, to seek from this water the cure of their various illnesses, while invoking the Immaculate Virgin. The civil authority has taken cognisance of the matter; from all parts since last March the ecclesiastical authority has been asked to pronounce an opinion concerning this spontaneous pilgrimage.

"We thought at first that the time had not yet arrived when we could profitably consider this matter; that in order to give that settled judgment which is expected of us we ought to proceed slowly and deliberately, distrust the enthusiasm of early days, allow time for minds to grow calm, give place for reflection, await that illumination which can only come from a thoughtful and enlightened observation.

"Three classes of persons appeal to our decision but with different views and intentions.

"There are those, first of all, who refuse to look into the matter and see in the facts of the grotto and in the cures attributed to the water of the spring nothing but superstition and jugglery and a means of making dupes. It is evident that we cannot be of their opinion on *a priori* grounds and without serious examination; their newspapers at once cried out, and very loudly, that the affair was one of superstition, fraud and bad faith, affirming that the facts of the grotto had their *raison d'être* in base self-interest and greed and thus wounding the moral sense of all Christian people. The party of negation, with its accusations of bad faith, finds no difficulty in solving problems; that we allow, but its line of argument is both dishonest and unreasonable and more apt to irritate minds than to convince them. To deny the possibility of supernatural facts is to follow a school of thought now out-of-date; it is to reject the Christian religion and to stick in the rut of the materialistic philosophy of the last century. We Catholics cannot in such circumstances take counsel with persons who deny God the power of making exceptions to those general laws which He has established for the government of the world, the work of His hands, nor can we enter into discussion with them as to whether such and such a fact be supernatural or not, since they begin by laying down as an axiom the statement that the supernatural is impossible. Does this mean then that we reject a sincere, conscientious, open-minded discussion in the light of science on the fact now in question? Certainly not; on the contrary we most heartily desire it; we wish these facts to be first of all submitted to those strict laws of certitude which a sound philosophy admits; we wish in the next place to decide if these facts are supernatural and divine and to summon to the discussion of these grave and difficult questions specialists who are versed in the sciences of mystical theology, medicine, physics, chemistry, geology, etc.; lastly we wish science to speak and let us hear what it has to say. We desire above all things that nothing be omitted whereby we may arrive at the truth.

"There is a second class of those persons who neither believe nor disbelieve the events of which they hear but who suspend their judgment. Before they pronounce their opinion they wish to know the decision of the competent authority and they honestly and earnestly ask for that decision.

"Finally, there is a third very large class of those who have already formed their convictions with regard to the present facts, convictions premature but decided; they are awaiting with eager impatience the authoritative decision of the Bishop of the diocese upon this serious matter and though they expect from us a decision favourable to their pious sentiments, we are sufficiently assured of their submission to the Church to be certain that they will welcome our judgment, whatever it may be, so soon as it is made known to them.

"To guide and enlighten the religion and piety of so many thousands of the faithful, to satisfy a public need, to clear away doubts and to calm minds, we accede to-day to the requests which have been made for so long from all parts, we invoke light upon the facts which have so deep an interest for Christians, upon the cult of Mary, upon religion itself. For this purpose we have resolved to establish in the diocese a permanent commission to collect and register the events which have occurred or may occur in the future at the Grotto of Lourdes, to bring those events before us and inform us as to their character and thus to furnish us with the necessary facts whereby we may arrive at a solution.

"For this cause, the Holy Name of God being invoked, we have ordained and do ordain that which follows:

"Article I. A commission is established in the diocese of Tarbes in order to inquire :

1. Whether any cures have been effected by the use of the water of the grotto of Lourdes, either drunk or used externally, and if these cures can be explained naturally or must be attributed to a supernatural cause ?
2. Whether the visions which the child Bernadette Soubirous professes to have had in the grotto are genuine, and if so whether they can be explained naturally or whether they have a supernatural and divine character ?
3. Whether the object seen in the visions has made any requests, or revealed any desire to this child ? Whether the child has been told to communicate them ? If so, to whom ? and what are the requests or desires revealed ?
4. Whether the spring now flowing in the grotto existed before the vision which Bernadette Soubirous claims to have seen ?

"Article II. The commission will lay before us only facts which have been established by solid proofs ; it will furnish us with circumstantial reports upon these facts, containing its opinion thereon.

"Article III. The rural deans of the diocese will be the chief correspondents of the commission. They are asked to bring to its notice (1) facts which may occur in their respective deaneries ; (2) persons who may be able to testify to the existence of these facts ; (3) those who by their learning may assist the commission ; (4) the doctors who attended the sick persons before their cure.

"Article IV. After having taken depositions the commission will be able to investigate cases. Witnesses will be examined on oath. When the investigation is made on the spot two members at least of the commission will proceed to the place in question.

"Article V. We urgently recommend the commission to call to its assistance men skilled in the sciences of medicine, physics, chemistry, geology, etc., in order to hear them discuss the difficulties which may exist from certain points of view and to know their opinion. The commission should neglect no means whatever of obtaining light and information and of arriving at the truth, whatever that may be.

"Article VI. The commission will be composed of the nine members of the Chapter of our Cathedral, the Superiors of our large and small seminaries, the Superior of the Diocesan

Missioners, the Curé of Lourdes, and the professors of dogma, ethics and physics of our seminary. The Professor of Chemistry of our little seminary will be often appealed to.

"Article VII. M. Nogaro, canon, archpriest, is appointed president of the commission. Canon Tabariés and Canon Soulé are appointed vice-presidents. The commission will appoint a secretary and two vice-secretaries from among its members.

"Article VIII. The commission will begin its work immediately and will meet as often as it may think necessary.

"Given at Tarbes at our episcopal palace under our seal and signature and countersigned by our secretary the 28th July, 1858.

"Signed BERTRAND SÉVÈRE,
Bishop of Tarbes.

"By order, FOURCADE,
Canon, Secretary.

In reading this document one cannot but admire the spirit of frankness and wisdom which characterises it. There is nothing roundabout, mysterious or equivocal in it; everything is to be done in the light of day according to the rules of sanity and reason, and it is clear that the Bishop's one desire was to get at the truth, whatever the truth might be. He entrusted the study of the great problem which was exercising him to men whose theological knowledge and ripe age would guarantee the wisdom of their judgment. After having put on one side those pretended philosophers who denied not merely the miracle in question but all possibility of a miracle, the Bishop ordered the committee which he had just formed to seek to associate with itself true *savants*, to pay attention to what they said, and when the opportunity offered to oppose their opinion against the credulities of the vulgar and the self-assertions of the ignorant. Finally, to make sure of the sincerity of the testimony given, he appealed to the religious sense and advised that no declarations concerning the grotto should be accepted unless made under the binding responsibility of an oath. When these various precautions had been taken (and surely the care of man could go no further), the Bishop shut himself up in his oratory and prayed to God,

Who is the source of all light, to enlighten the commission and lead it along the path of truth.

* * * * *

On the publication of the episcopal order the free-thinking journals, both in Paris and the country, embarked upon a new campaign, crying out that the intrusions of the clerical authority were a scandal. According to them the line taken by the Bishop of Tarbes was an insult to reason and could not fail to arouse the bloody conflicts of the ages of ignorance. At the very least the prelate in question ought to be prosecuted in the Court of Appeal and declared unworthy of the functions he exercised. Only two Paris newspapers, the *Univers* and the *Union*, defended the Bishop of Tarbes and without expressing any opinion upon the particular case of Lourdes supported energetically the principles and teaching of the Church in the matter of miracles. Louis Veuillot especially pounded with his resistless logic the fetichism of universal and immutable laws. In this combat he let fall the most happy and piquant phrases. One day in an attack upon the *Siècle* he began a leading article as follows: "The *Siècle*, which has taken this morning into its service a hired theologian," (*théologien de louage*) — this phrase "hired theologian," could only have been thought of by him. On another occasion the editor of *La Presse*, M. Guéroult, concluded a diatribe against the miraculous with these words: "If any one assured me that a supernatural event, even one most striking, was taking place at this very moment next door to my office on the Place de la Concorde I would not turn aside to go and see it." Louis Veuillot replied, "If some one told M. Guéroult that in the name of Christ a great miracle was taking place on the Place de la Concorde he would not go. He would do well because he has made up his mind to remain an unbeliever; in the presence of such a sight he might find it difficult to discover a materialistic explanation which would excuse him from going to make his confession."

Finally this noisy tempest, like those which preceded it, calmed down, without having done much harm either to the grotto or to the tranquillity of the Bishop of Tarbes.

* * * * *

The commission of inquiry although constituted at the end of July only began its work in the third week of November. The grotto having continued to be closed until the end of October, the Bishop's delegates were unwilling to infringe the Prefect's orders and made a point of not coming to Massabieille until after the barriers had been taken away. At the date of which I speak, when the causes of conflict had been removed and peace had been once more restored, the principal members of the Chapter of Tarbes came to Lourdes and there began their first investigations.

After having said a Mass of the Holy Ghost in the parish church they summoned Bernadette and, in presence of the general public, made her undergo a long and detailed examination. The child was just what she always was in her replies, simple, clear, exact and convinced. With much emotion she drew the portrait of the heavenly Lady, recounted in their smallest details the different words spoken to her during the Appearances and narrated with inexpressible grace the scene in which the Virgin had revealed herself under the name of the Immaculate Conception. When the president of the commission asked her whether, in her soul and conscience, she could assert with an oath the truth of her declarations, Bernadette seemed to collect herself for a moment; then with a gravity which struck all present she raised her hand and replied, "I swear."

This first interview gave the committee of enquiry the impression not merely that Bernadette was not lying, but that she was not mistaken or deluded. Continuing however their investigations, the members of the committee went to the miraculous grotto to examine its structure and its different optical effects. They wondered for a moment whether some fantastic form or some reflected light might not have fascinated the child's eyes. After having explored the locality and made all sorts of experiments they had to abandon this hypothesis and recognise that there was nothing in the grotto which could produce any such illusions.

Bernadette was there. She was asked to point out the exact spot in the recess where the mysterious Lady had appeared, the place where she had seen her for the first time and finally her different movements when discovering the "spring."

The child showed in all this such exactitude and simplicity that, seeing the perfect agreement between what she recounted and what she pointed out, it was impossible not to accept her evidence.

On this occasion moreover a great number of persons were heard by the commission on the subject of the more or less plausible existence of the miraculous spring. In regard to this matter the depositions of the witnesses, as I have already said, were divided. Many of the river fishermen and of the men who worked on the banks of the Gave declared that in rainy weather they were accustomed to take shelter in the grotto but had never perceived any sort of spring. Certain shepherds and farmers of the neighbourhood stated on the contrary that they had seen water flowing on other occasions some long time previously. All, however, were unanimous in agreeing that when the Appearances first began to take place no spring was visible and that its sudden gushing forth under the fingers of a child was evidently something outside the ordinary laws of nature.*

During this same day several persons of Lourdes miraculously cured at the grotto were summoned to the presbytery to bear witness by their presence to their new condition and to recount the circumstances under which they had recovered health. M. Dozous, the doctor of the town who had attended the greater number of those persons during the time of their illness, attested before the ecclesiastical jury the marvels which had taken place and allowed that medical science found it impossible to give an explanation of these marvels. On leaving Lourdes the members of the commission carried away with them the conviction that the finger of God had been manifested at the grotto.

But it was not only at Lourdes that the episcopal delegation carried on its investigations. It betook itself to all parts of the district where cures had been obtained by the use of the Massabieille water. Every possible precaution that human wisdom could suggest was taken in this second chapter of the enquiry to arrive at the complete and exact knowledge of the truth. In order to be on their guard against the pitfalls of bad faith or

* See in the appendix at the end of the book a study on the grotto by Abbé Richard.

the extravagances of a false religious zeal, the members of the committee of enquiry before studying the cures themselves sought the most reliable information possible with regard to the morality, the habits and the temper of mind of the persons cured. They asked if the illnesses from which they had previously suffered were a matter of general knowledge and whether the restoration to health had taken place in the presence of witnesses and by virtue of the immediate action of the water of the Lourdes grotto. When these first questions were answered satisfactorily they went to the homes where the Virgin had so graciously bestowed her favours. The examinations always took place in the presence of the various doctors who had attended the respective invalids, and if the men of science without prejudice expressed any doubt about the supernatural character of the cures they were at once put aside and not recorded.

The work of the commission lasted four years. The harvest of miraculous facts thus reaped was rich and varied; but as it was impossible that the enquiry should go on for ever it was necessary to give up the examination of a great number of cures in which the power of the Virgin had been manifested. The delegates of the episcopal authority went in a body and with the solemnity suited to the circumstances to inform Monseigneur Laurence of the result of their patient and laborious observations. The marvellous cures recorded in their report were not merely most striking and recognised as such by medical science, but the greater number had received that seal which time imprints upon all that is durable. In laying down their charge the members of the commission could say to their Bishop, only changing the scene, that which Jesus Christ had said to the disciples of John: "At the waters of Lourdes the lame walk, the deaf hear and the dumb recover their speech."

Finally, on the 18th January, 1862, there was published *The Charge of Mgr. the Bishop of Tarbes, giving judgment on the Appearance which has taken place at the Grotto of Lourdes.*

In a brief summary the prelate spoke of the divine Appearances recorded in the two Testaments, recounted the Appearances of the Blessed Virgin in the Church's history, and told the story in substance of the Appearance at the Grotto of Lourdes. Then reminding his people that judgment on supernatural facts could only be pronounced after long and careful study, he stated at length the reasons for the decision at which he had arrived, developing his arguments amply, luminously and irrefutably. And he added: "The event of which we are speaking to you has been for four years the object of our anxious study. We have followed it in its different phases and been advised by a commission composed of holy, learned and experienced priests who have questioned the child, studied the facts, examined and weighed everything. We have also sought the opinion of scientists and we are finally convinced that the Appearance is supernatural and divine, and that consequently she whom Bernadette has seen is the Most Holy Virgin herself. Our conviction is based, not merely upon the testimony of Bernadette, but more especially upon the events which have taken place and which can only be explained by divine intervention.

"The testimony of the young girl is in every way as satisfactory as possible. To begin with, her sincerity cannot be doubted. Who that has questioned her can fail to admire the simplicity, the candour, the modesty of this child? Whilst everyone is talking about the wonders which have been revealed to her she alone keeps silence; she only speaks when she is questioned and then she recounts everything without affectation and with a touching simplicity, and she replies to the numerous questions addressed to her without hesitation, giving answers clear and precise, very much to the point and bearing the stamp of intense conviction. She has been tested most severely but no menaces have ever shaken her; she has responded to the most generous offers by a noble disinterestedness. She never contradicts herself; in all the different examinations which she has undergone her story never varies; she never adds to it or takes from it. Bernadette's sincerity cannot then be disputed. We may add that it never has been disputed; even her opponents, when she has had opponents, have paid her that homage.

"But if Bernadette has not deliberately deceived us has she not been deceived herself? May she not have thought that she heard and saw something which she did not hear or see? Has she not been the victim of a hallucination? How is it possible to believe such a thing? Her wise responses show that the child possesses a clear mind, a calm imagination, a commonsense above her age.* The religious sentiment has never shown itself in her under the form of excitement; no one has ever discovered in this young girl intellectual disorder, mental vagaries, eccentricity of character or any hysterical affection which might predispose her to creations of the imagination. She has seen the Appearance, not merely once, but eighteen times; she saw it first of all suddenly, when nothing could have led her to expect the vision, and afterwards during the fortnight when she expected to see it every day, for two days she saw nothing, although she was in the same place and in exactly the same circumstances. And then again, observe what happened during the Appearances. A thorough transformation took place in Bernadette; her face wore a new expression, her eyes lighted up, she saw things which she had never seen, she heard a language which she had never heard, a language whose meaning she did not always understand but which never left her memory. All these circumstances taken together make it impossible to believe in the theory of hallucination; the young girl has then really seen and heard a being who called herself the Immaculate Conception and as this phenomenon cannot be explained by natural laws we are bound to believe that the Appearance was supernatural.

"The testimony of Bernadette, important in itself, gathers yet fresh force from the marvellous facts which have taken place ever since the beginning of the Appearances. These marvellous facts are indeed the complement of the Appearances. If the tree is to be judged by its fruits we may certainly say that the Appearance of which the young girl tells us is supernatural and divine, for the results it has produced are supernatural and divine. What has happened, my brethren? Scarcely had the fact of the Appearance become known than the news spread with the rapidity of lightning. It was known that Bernadette was to go to the grotto for a fortnight and the whole country was in commotion; crowds of people flocked to the scene of the Appearances, the solemn moment was awaited with pious

* Bernadette's intelligence was only remarkable when she spoke on the subject of the Appearances.

impatience, and whilst the young girl, beside herself in ecstasy, is wholly absorbed by the object of her contemplation the witnesses of this prodigy moved to the very depths of their soul are united in one common sentiment of admiration and of prayer.

"The Appearances have ceased, but the crowds still come. Pilgrims arrive, not merely from places near, but from distant countries, and hasten to the grotto ; men and women of all ages, of all ranks, of all conditions of life, are to be seen there. And what is it that has brought all these visitors ? They have come to the grotto to pray and to ask certain favours of Immaculate Mary. They show by their devotion that they are conscious of that divine breath which stirs round this rock, henceforth so celebrated. Christian souls have been established in their faith ; the cold and indifferent have been restored to the practice of religion ; obstinate sinners have been reconciled to God, our Lady of Lourdes having been invoked on their behalf. These wonders of grace, so many and so various and so permanent in their results, can come from no one but God Himself. Are we not right then in believing that they confirm the truth of the Appearances ?

"If we pass from the healing of souls to the healing of bodies we find fresh wonders to record. Bernadette had been seen to drink and wash herself at the spot pointed out to her and this circumstance aroused general attention. People naturally supposed that this might indicate that supernatural virtue had descended upon the Massabieille spring. With this thought in their minds the sick made use of the grotto water, and not without success ; several persons whose maladies had stubbornly resisted the most persistent treatment suddenly recovered health. These extraordinary cures caused a great sensation and they were spoken of far and wide. Sick people from all countries asked for the Massabieille water when they could not go themselves to the grotto. How many sick have been cured, how many families made happy. If we were to call upon them to give their witness, voices innumerable would testify with heartfelt gratitude to the healing power of the water of the grotto. It is impossible to enumerate here all the blessings received, but we are bound to make known to you all the fact that sick persons, given up by their doctors and declared incurable, have been restored to health by the Massabieille water. These cures have been effected by the use of a water which, according to the reports of skilful chemists who have analysed it carefully, contains no natural curative powers. These cures have taken place, some instantaneously, others after the water has been used several times, either as a drink or applied outwardly. Moreover these cures are permanent. What is the power which has worked them? Is it to be found in the organism itself? Science consulted on this matter has replied in the negative. These cures are then the work of God and they are in direct relationship to the Appearances; the Appearances are the point of departure, for they attracted the attention of the sick and inspired them with confidence. There is thus a link between the cures and the Appearances; the Appearances are divine, because the cures bear the mark of God's hand. That Appearance consequently which called herself the Immaculate Conception, which Bernadette both saw and heard, is none other than the Most Holy Virgin. Well may we say then the finger of God is here.

"How can we fail to be struck by the dispensations of providence? At the end of the year 1854 Pope Pius IX. proclaimed the dogma of the Immaculate Conception. The winds carried to the ends of the earth the pontiff's words; the hearts of Catholics rejoiced and the glorious privilege of Mary was celebrated everywhere by festivals whose memory will remain with us for ever. And now about three years later the blessed Virgin appearing to a child says to her: "I am the Immaculate Conception. I wish a chapel to be erected here in my honour." Does it not seem that she herself wished to consecrate with her approval in the face of all the world the infallible decree of Saint Peter's successor?

"And where does she wish the permanent record of her approval to be set up? At the foot of the Pyrenees, where so many foreigners from all parts of the world meet together to seek health from our thermal waters. She invites believers of all nations to come and honour the new temple which is to be built to her.

"Inhabitants of the town of Lourdes, rejoice. Mary our

Queen looks down on you in gracious love. She desires a sanctuary to be built at the gates of your city where she may shower down her blessings. Thank her for this proof of affection which she gives you, and since she bestows on you a mother's love, show yourselves her devoted children by imitating her virtues and by following more faithfully than ever your religion.

"Moreover we are glad to recognise the fact that the Appearance has already borne abundant fruits of salvation in your midst. You have seen with your own eyes the events at the grotto and all the blessings bestowed there and no power can ever shake your faith. We have admired your wise self-restraint, the docility with which you have followed our counsels and submitted to the civil authority when, during several weeks, you had to forgo your visits to the grotto and do violence to your feelings, in spite of that marvellous sight which you had seen during the fortnight of the Appearances.

"And you all, our brethren of this diocese, open your hearts to the message of hope. A new era of grace begins for you and you are all summoned to receive your share of the blessings promised you. In your prayers and in your hymns you will henceforth join the name of our Lady of Lourdes to the blessed names of our Lady of Garaison, of Poneylaiin, of Héas and of Piétat.

"From the heights of these holy sanctuaries the Immaculate Virgin will watch over you and shield you with her protection. Yes, dear brothers and fellow-workers, if with our hearts full of confidence we keep our eyes fixed upon this Star of the sea, we shall pass through the storms of this life without fear of shipwreck and safely reach the harbour of eternal joy.

"For these reasons, after having conferred with our venerable brethren the dignitaries, canons and chapter of our Cathedral Church ;

"The holy name of God being invoked ;

"Taking as our guide the rules wisely laid down by Benedict XIV. in his treatise on the Beatification and Canonisation of Saints in order to distinguish true appearances from false (Book III., ch. 51) ;

"In view of the favourable report which has been presented to us by the Commission established to enquire into the

Appearance at the grotto of Lourdes and the facts relating to it ;

"In view of the written testimony of the doctors whom we have consulted concerning the numerous cures obtained by the use of the water of the grotto ;

"Considering in the first place that the fact of the Appearance, whether in relation to the young girl who has told us about it or in relation to the extraordinary results it has produced, can only be explained by the intervention of a supernatural cause ;

"Considering in the second place that this cause can only be divine, inasmuch as the effects produced are on the one hand visible signs of grace, such as the conversion of sinners, on the other hand results outside the ordinary laws of nature, such as miraculous cures, and can therefore only proceed from the Author of grace and the Lord of nature ;

"Considering lastly that our conviction is strengthened by the enormous crowds of the faithful who come spontaneously to the grotto, who have not ceased to come ever since the first Appearances and whose purpose is to ask for blessings or to give thanks for those already received ;

"In order to give an answer to the legitimate impatience of our venerable Chapter, of the clergy and laity of our diocese, and of the many pious souls who have for so long a time demanded of the ecclesiastical authority a judgment which for reasons of prudence we have delayed to give ;

"Wishing also to satisfy the desires of several of our episcopal brethren and of a great number of distinguished persons outside the limits of our diocese ;

"After having sought the light of the Holy Spirit and the assistance of the blessed Virgin ;

"We have declared and do declare that which follows :

"Article 1. We judge that Mary, the Immaculate Mother of God, did really appear to Bernadette Soubirous on the 11th February, 1858, and on certain subsequent days, eighteen times in all, in the grotto of Massabieille near the town of Lourdes ; that this Appearance bears every mark of truth and that the belief of the faithful is well grounded.

"We humbly submit our judgment to that of the Sovereign

Pontiff who is charged with the government of the universal Church.

. . . . .

"Article 3. In order to carry out the wish of the blessed Virgin, expressed more than once at the time of the Appearances, we propose to build a sanctuary upon the ground adjoining the grotto which has now become the property of the Bishops of Tarbes.

"The building of this sanctuary, in view of the steep and difficult nature of the site, will be a slow process and will necessitate considerable expenditure. We need therefore in order to carry out our intention the assistance of the clergy and laity of our diocese, of the clergy and laity both of France and of foreign countries. We appeal to their generosity and especially to all devout persons of every country to whom the cult of the Immaculate Conception of the Virgin Mary is dear.

. . . . .

"Article 8. This our Charge is to be read and published in all churches and chapels.

"Given at Tarbes on the 18th January, 1862, Festival of the Chair of St. Peter at Rome.

"(Signed) BERTRAND SÉVÈRE,
Bishop of Tarbes."

* * * * *

The doctrinal judgment of the Bishop of Tarbes made a great sensation and was welcomed with joy everywhere. The spiritual energy of the nation was stirred by the assurance that the Queen of Heaven had come once more to visit her ancient kingdom of the Gauls. It was an event of happy omen, for the Virgin had appeared to Bernadette with a smile upon her lips, and the first fruits of blessings to come had already fallen from her hands. As soon as it was known by the Bishop's voice that the Lady of Massabieille asked for a chapel and desired that processions should be made on that spot one spontaneous cry of generosity and filial love rose from the breasts of all. "Do you, our Mother," they said, "the Queen of Heaven and Sovereign of the world, ask nothing more of us than a humble chapel? Have you forgotten that we are the eldest children of the Church and the descendants of the Crusaders? No, we hope to honour ourselves by offering you a temple truly worthy of your greatness. You invite us to come and visit you in that rustic dwelling which you have chosen for yourself in our mountains. You have spoken, and all France is waiting, ready to come and receive the benedictions of your maternal heart."

Christian France carried out all that was demanded of her. Spontaneously, unanimously, she gave of her best, and money arrived at Lourdes in abundance to erect the sanctuary asked for by the Immaculate Conception. As to our Lady's second demand, we know how fully that has been answered. Who can count to-day the innumerable crowds who pass in procession before the sacred rock of the Massabieille hill?

CHAPTER X.

BERNADETTE AFTER THE APPEARANCES.

I. HER LIFE AT HOME.—THE SOUBIROUS FAMILY.

After the Appearances had ceased Bernadette resumed her former ordinary life, without the slightest idea that the events which had recently brought her into notice could attract any sort of homage or attention to her personally. Whilst from one end of France to the other, and even in distant countries, thousands and thousands of voices pronounced again and again the name of this privileged child, she alone seemed to know nothing of it all. She could not understand that one should take an interest in her poor little self. In order to preserve her from the attacks of pride, providence, watching over her, thought fit to leave her her moderate mental powers, her poverty, and even her ceaseless attacks of asthma. Bernadette then took up once more the ordinary course of her daily life, remaining always the humble daughter of the Soubirous, the simple and innocent shepherdess of Bartrès.

Every morning she might be seen going to school, as she had done before the Appearances, carrying a basket containing the stockings she was knitting, her crust of black bread and a dog's-eared spelling-book. During the play-hour she laughed and sang and jumped with her young schoolfellows in the courtyard of the hospice. When the time arrived for her to be prepared for her first Communion there was no striking difference between Bernadette and the other children. She like the rest was sometimes thoughtless and at other times wrapt in devotion, sometimes giddy and at other times fervent. At the confessional she was serious and earnest without being sanctimonious. In all things, to put it shortly, she went to God simply and naturally, with the confidence of innocence and the trustful familiarity of love.

Bernadette approached the Holy Table for the first time on 3rd June, 1858, in the chapel of the hospice, where she had received her religious instruction. On the occasion of this holy festival the people of Lourdes hoped that the little seer would be allowed to enjoy one of those heavenly ecstasies which had been the marvel of the crowds at the rocks of Massabieille. But nothing of the kind took place. Bernadette, her hands joined, approached the altar, received her God into her childlike soul and returned to her place without giving any sign but that of a deep and immense happiness. At the grotto Bernadette fulfilled a public mission ; here she was accomplishing an action, most solemn certainly and comparable to no other action, but an action of private life.

Some time after, however, Abbé Peyramale told how on a certain Sunday, whilst he was giving the Holy Communion in the parish church, his attention had been attracted by a halo of brilliant light over the head of a young girl upon her knees. He looked and found that it was Bernadette.

* * * * *

During the visit which the happy child paid us at the time of her first Communion, my sister said to her : "Tell me,

Bernadette, which of the two things was the greatest joy to you; the receiving of the good God in your Communion or the conversing with the blessed Virgin in the grotto?"

Bernadette hesitated for a moment and then replied:

"I do not know; the two things go together and cannot be compared. All I know is that I was intensely happy in them both."

* * * * *

And this reminds me of a number of answers made by Bernadette during her private intercourse with us. These answers, which fell quite naturally from her mouth, were thoroughly characteristic of the child. I will give one or two of them as they occur to me, regretting that I cannot reproduce them in the picturesque patois which Bernadette spoke so well.

But in the first place I must say that, towards the end of the Appearances, my sister and I sought to attract the little seer to our house in order to obtain from her the most intimate personal information about all that had happened at the grotto. We found her at first timid and reserved, but she soon opened out before the warmth of our sympathy and became our little friend. For nearly two years she paid us an almost daily visit and let us read her pure, transparent soul.

I must repeat what I have already said, that Bernadette showed but a limited intelligence in the ordinary subjects of conversation; when however the talk turned to the grotto and the things relating to it she was a different person. She was then no longer her ordinary self and answered with a charm and an appositeness which delighted her questioners.

* * * * *

One day when she was talking with us I said to her: "Tell me, Bernadette, did the Lady of the Grotto speak to you in French or in patois?"

"Oh, patois."

"Bah! Do you mean to say that a lady of such lofty rank knows patois?"

"Yes." Then she added proudly, "And it was the Lourdes patois which she spoke."

* * * * *

Another day, referring to the promise of happiness which

the Virgin had made her, a missioner of Garaison, Father Vignes, wanted to know what the seer thought of it and said to her in our presence: " Since the Lady has promised to make you happy in the other world you need not take any trouble, but can rest confidently on her promise."

" Oh, monsieur le curé," she said, " you are going on too fast. I shall be happy, yes, but only if I am careful to do what I ought to do and to walk along the straight path."

* * * * *

On another occasion, in speaking to Bernadette of the secrets with which the Virgin had entrusted her, I said to her: " Are you quite sure that the secrets are known to no one but yourself? We were as near to the Lady as you were."

" Oh, I am quite sure that you have not heard them, because it was not like we are talking now."

"What do you mean?"

"When the blessed Virgin entrusted me with her secrets she spoke to me here, and not through the ear"—and when she said " here," Bernadette pointed to her heart.

" I don't understand you."

" And I cannot make you understand me. Look here. All those persons who were round me at the grotto were as though they were a hundred yards away; and persons at that distance would see that we were talking, but would not understand what we said."

" Bah, you are talking nonsense."

The child said no more but smiled.

* * * * *

Inquiring as to details about the Appearance of the 18th February Bernadette said: " The Lady asked me to come to the grotto daily for a fortnight."

I interrupted her and said: " Tell us the very words of the Lady."

" The Lady said to me: Will you have the goodness?"

Then the child stopped in confusion, lowered her head and added, " The Lady addressed me as *vous*."*

* * * * *

During the time when the official opposition was so bitter, returning one day to my house, I found Bernadette in conversation with my sister.

" Have you heard ? " I said to her. " All your frauds have been at last discovered and it has been decided that you are to be put in prison. Moreover, as I have backed you up they add that I am to follow you there."

Bernadette understood the joke. " Oh ! " she replied, " that would suit me splendidly. In the first place I should save my parents the cost of my board and lodging, and then you would be there on the spot to teach me to read and to repeat my catechism, like the Sisters at the Hospice."

* * * * *

" Tell me, Bernadette," my sister asked her one day, " did the Virgin look only at you when we were all at the grotto ? "

" Oh ! no. She looked at everybody and with much affection. Sometimes she seemed to look at each person individually and her gaze seemed to rest upon certain there as though they were old friends."

* * * * *

The day when the members of the commission appointed by the Bishop went to the grotto, the president put to Bernadette this question.

" You have just told us that at the moment of discovering the spring you had eaten a blade of grass. Why did you do that ? "

" I do not know. The Lady impelled me and made me understand I was to do so."

" But, my child, only the animals eat raw grass."

" Oh, monsieur l'Abbé, you are mistaken ; we eat salad raw. Certainly," she added, smiling, " we do add a little vinegar and oil."

* Children and inferiors in France are usually addressed in the singular, *tu*.

But I must stop, for if I was to recall all these interesting sayings my book would become too voluminous.

* * * * *

I said, at the beginning of this chapter, that after the Appearances had ceased Bernadette returned to her customary occupations. In saying this I mean to insist upon the unalterable modesty and simplicity of the seer, but of course the fame attaching to her necessarily modified the conditions of her obscure and peaceful existence. No stranger willingly passed through Lourdes without seeing and hearing the little protégée of Mary. At the times when the carriages going to Cauterets, Saint Sauveur or Barèges made their stop at Lourdes there was a real procession to the Soubirous' house. When Bernadette was not to be found there all the travellers would hasten to the Hospice. It would be difficult to realise or enumerate fully all the annoyances to which the poor child was subjected during the three or four years which followed the Appearances. Returning home after her lessons she had barely time to snatch a meal. Whilst she was at school the bell announcing a visitor was continually ringing. Ten or twenty times a day she had to begin again her story. At certain moments, wearied out and suffocated with her asthma, she showed no signs of emotion, and recounted the most beautiful scenes in the history of the Appearances as though she was saying a lesson learnt by heart. Without any pity for her exhausted condition her hearers, the women especially, hung on to her desperately and tenaciously. Some would ask of her a souvenir; others would give her their rosaries to touch; certain would even fall on their knees and ask for her blessing. Bernadette would remain patient and smiling in the midst of all these attacks and would often find the happiest phrases with which to protect herself. Once when a visitor kept on asking her for her blessing the child replied: "But, my dear lady, you see I have no stole; please wait until I have received the Bishop's authorisation."

* * * * *

One last trial, the greatest trial of all, awaited Bernadette at the end of the audiences which she had to give. The distressing poverty of the Soubirous family was known to everyone.

On his or her departure each visitor naturally wished to leave with Bernadette some little token of sympathetic pity. The child refused, humbly indeed, but not without making it quite clear that she was not to be shaken in her refusal. Prayers, tricks, even violent measures were employed to overcome the delicacy of the child. But nothing could shake it and although often worn out Bernadette always emerged victorious from these attacks.

One day a lady, a stranger of distinguished appearance, came to our door to ask if she might see the little heroine of the grotto who was with us at that moment. We received her into our house and introduced our little visitor. She overwhelmed us with gratitude, and was delighted to find that she could converse freely with the Virgin's little protégée. She made her talk, and remained for more than an hour hanging on her words. When the lady rose to leave she kissed the child and, with graceful delicacy, slipped a packet of money under the fold of her apron. Bernadette jumped as if a hot coal had fallen on her and let the lady's present fall. Ashamed of her brusque movement, the child picked up the packet of gold pieces and gave it back politely to the charitable stranger; and the most earnest entreaties could not make her accept anything.

Some days after (this event took place in the presbytère of the parish) the Bishop of Soissons, going either to Cauterets or Barèges for the waters, stopped at Lourdes to hear all about what had happened at the grotto. He saw Bernadette, and had a long conversation with her. He too, like Monseigneur Thibaud, was much impressed by the little seer's narrative. At the end of the interview the Bishop took from his pocket a rosary with a gold chain and gave it to the child.

"Oh! it's much too good for me," said Bernadette. "I thank you, Monseigneur, but I cannot accept it."

"But my child," said the Bishop kindly, "my present is not so disinterested as you suppose, for in giving you my rosary I had the intention of asking for yours in exchange."

"Why certainly," said Bernadette. And immediately with charming gracefulness she drew her modest rosary from her pocket and put it into the hands of her distinguished visitor. It was useless for the latter to insist. He had to leave Lourdes without persuading the child to accept his rosary though he took away hers with him.

* * * * *

Many people at Lourdes believed at the time that one of the secrets entrusted by the Virgin to Bernadette was an express command that she should refuse any present of money or any gift whatsoever in relation to the events of the grotto. I cannot say how far this popular opinion was correct, for the little seer, as we know, carried with her to heaven sealed within her own breast the confidences of our Lady. I can only say that nothing less than a superhuman strength of soul could have enabled Bernadette to withstand successfully the attacks of charity, and that if she really was forbidden to accept anything she kept the command given her to the very letter.

A yet more heroic example, and one which shows to what heights Christian delicacy can rise, was given by the father and mother of Bernadette. During the period which preceded the Appearances the Soubirous, husband and wife, went out every day to work at anything which might be given them and by their toil they managed to earn just enough to supply bread from day to day for themselves and their numerous family. Ever since the hour when the events of the grotto had brought Bernadette before the public the family's affairs had become worse and from bad they had become critical. The house of the Soubirous was continually invaded by visitors and being unable to attend to their ordinary occupations, owing to these distractions, they often suffered from hunger. The poverty of the unhappy family had always inspired pity and this pity was now intensified by the sight of the famine-stricken faces. It was natural then that charitable souls, after their pious curiosity had been satisfied by the little seer, should wish in return to succour the physical misery of the family. I have already related the efforts made to overcome the delicacy of Bernadette. When these efforts had failed the visitors usually turned to the master and mistress of the house, hoping that they at least would accept their liberality. But they were mistaken; the father and mother were equally firm in their refusal and nothing could shake their resolution. Sometimes it happened that certain generous persons could not make up their minds to accept these refusals. They would pretend to be indifferent; then at an opportune moment they would secretly lay their offerings down on a chair or table or shelf. But it was all lost labour. The Soubirous took as much trouble to protect themselves against the enterprises of charity as other people take to protect themselves against the surprises of theft. Everyone then could see that the accusation made against the former miller, to the effect that he made money out of the mystical vagaries of his daughter, was unfounded.

But what was to be done? That was the thought which weighed upon the hearts of all. Was the Soubirous family to be left to perish of hunger because of the delicacy of the parents' conscience? This difficult problem, in spite of the most ingenious efforts of charity, remained without solution during nine long years.

One would have imagined that the position of the Soubirous already so hopeless could scarcely become worse, yet a trouble more terrible than all their previous troubles was to fall upon the unfortunate family. Early in the month of December, 1866, the devoted wife of François Soubirous, she who had been so dearly loved by husband and children, was attacked by sudden and serious illness and passed away peacefully on the 8th December, 1866, on the very festival of the Immaculate Conception itself, after four or five days of suffering.* The grief of the children was very keen as may be imagined but the poor unhappy father, struck as it were by a thunderbolt, fell into a sort of numbed prostration. He remained for some time helpless and overwhelmed; then remembering as by instinct that his labour was still necessary for the little ones around him he pulled himself together and took up his work once more to give bread to his young family.

No one at Lourdes was more grieved at the misery and misfortunes of the Soubirous family than Abbé Peyramale.

* Bernadette loved to recall this happy coincidence and found great comfort in it. At the very hour when Bernadette's mother passed away, Vespers of the Immaculate Conception were being sung in the chapel of the crypt for the first time.

Sharing the opinion of his parishioners to the effect that the unfortunate household only refused offers of help in obedience to the secret orders which had come to it from the grotto, the good pastor earnestly prayed the Mother of mercy to withdraw in some measure her stern commands. At length, after having waited for some time he thought he saw in a chance circumstance Heaven's reply to his earnest prayers.

One day when the good curé was traversing the poorer quarters of the town he happened to hear that the Lacadé mill situated on the Lapaca stream was for sale, and that the owner was looking for a purchaser. This news struck him like a ray of light. He immediately thought of Bernadette's unfortunate father. He knew how anxious Soubirous was to take up again his former business of miller, not merely because the work was to his liking, but also because it would give him the opportunity of watching over his children and supplying their needs. The zealous pastor, without losing a minute, sought out Father Sempé, the superior of the grotto, and some hours later the two priests found themselves in the presence of the Bishop of Tarbes. Mgr. Laurence had long known of the want and poverty of Bernadette's family. When therefore he learnt the object of the priests' visit he was of opinion that the purchase of the mill should be arranged without delay, and he undertook to make himself responsible for the sum required. The affair was carried through and by virtue of a deed executed on the 29th August, 1867, in the presence of M. Daléas, notary at Tarbes, François Soubirous, father of the little seer, became owner of the Lacadé mill. From this moment the Soubirous family was set free from its former privations and, save for the void left by the mother's death lived comparatively happy.

Every one at Lourdes approved of Abbé Peyramale's generous initiative and all were grateful to the good curé for his kind action to the Soubirous, as being a sort of public service to the town itself.

CHAPTER XI.

BERNADETTE AFTER THE APPEARANCES (*continued*).

II. BERNADETTE AT THE HOSPICE OF LOURDES.

BERNADETTE had left Lourdes some time before her mother's death and she was not at home when her family entered into possession of the Lacadé mill.

To make her biography complete I must go back some way to the period when she was still living with her parents in the old *cachot* of the rue des Petits Fossés.

Her father and mother were very anxious about Bernadette at this time. In spite of all the care they could bestow upon her, she remained weak and ailing. Her parents had hoped for a long time that as soon as she had passed the critical age of childhood she would grow stronger. But their hopes were disappointed.

Bernadette paid no attention to her own health. Every day according to her wont she went to school, and after school when circumstances permitted would put on her cloak and go to the grotto to pray. Thus she passed her time at Lourdes and nothing occurred to disturb the current of her existence.

The Sisters of the Hospice of Lourdes were much attached to their pupil. The lovable character of the child, her innocence, the unspeakable memories which her presence recalled, called forth their sympathies. These good women had already noticed with anxiety that Bernadette looked more delicate every day. They attributed the progress of ill-health to want of nourishment and with this thought in their minds they resolved to take the child under their hospitable roof. After having obtained permission from their superiors they went to the parents of Bernadette and, putting the matter from the point of view of health, represented to them how necessary it was that the sick child should have a change of residence.

They offered to receive her into their house and to take care of her as though she were their child. The Soubirous gratefully accepted the suggestion and Bernadette followed the sisters.

The separation was not a painful one, for the child was only going a short distance from her father's house, and moreover it was arranged that she should have the opportunity of seeing her family nearly every day.

Bernadette entered the Hospice of Lourdes nominally as a sick person without means, but as a matter of fact she was not put under the ordinary régime of the sick and poor. The sisters looked upon her as a sacred trust committed to their charge, and the superior of the house, inspired by this idea, put her in a little room of her own, sunny and bright, and gave her a special place at the table of the school boarders.

In spite of all the affectionate attentions lavished upon her, Bernadette became no better, but rather grew worse. Soon after her arrival at the Hospice she had so sharp an attack that the chaplain, Abbé Pomian, thought it necessary to give her the last sacraments. The doctors of the place, summoned in haste, agreed unanimously that there was no hope for the young girl. They prescribed although without hope a very strong remedy which might produce a reaction. After their departure, the sisters who surrounded Bernadette made her take a spoonful of water from the grotto. The sick girl immediately recovered the power of speech and almost directly afterwards felt herself cured. The sisters said the cure was miraculous, but as Bernadette was subject subsequently to the same attacks followed by the same sudden restoration of strength we can hardly use the term in this connection.

In taking under their protection Mary's little protégée the sisters of the Hospice had hoped to deliver her from the troublesome visitors who plagued her and wore out her strength. But the good women had not allowed for the obstinate importunity of the public. They refused as much as possible the requests for interviews made to them, but generally the visitors brought introductions from such important personages that the sisters had finally to give way. Bernadette sacrificed herself cheerfully in this matter, and remembering the goodness of the Virgin to her, she was sweet-tempered with all. She told quite simply what she had seen and what she had heard, without additions or omissions. If any one appeared to disbelieve or made some idle objection the child would reply gently,

"I am not learned and I cannot discuss it. I have told you what took place at the grotto, and you must decide what to think of it."

* * * * *

To all outward appearance Bernadette during these interviews was not unhappy, but as a matter of fact when the conversation degenerated into small talk or futile remarks, the poor child suffered tortures. Something which she once said will help the reader to understand the moral and physical weariness these interviews caused her. One day when she was in bed with one of those attacks to which she was so subject a lady of Lourdes came to see her.

"You are always ill, my dear Bernadette," said the lady to her on coming into the room. "Poor child, how sorry I am for you."

"Don't be sorry for me," said the sick girl brightly. "I can't take a very cheerful view of life with this fever on me, but I certainly prefer it to my interviews with visitors."

"You must remember, my child, that you are fulfilling a duty laid upon you by the Virgin."

"Oh, I willingly fulfil that duty, but there are some people who come to see me and hear me, just as they might go to a menagerie to see and hear certain curious animals."

Bernadette passed through her eighteenth and nineteenth years in alternately good and bad health. During this time she grew a little, and learnt, not without difficulty, to read and write. She lived happy from day to day without thought as to her future.

* * * * *

In the year 1863, Monseigneur Forcade, Bishop of Nevers and superior-general of the Ladies of Charity of that town, came to Lourdes to visit the sisters of the Hospice, who were under his authority. After having given his blessing to the community he asked the superior about Bernadette. Some moments later, whilst inspecting the establishment, he found her busy cleaning vegetables in the kitchen. He was delighted with the gentle and modest appearance of the young kitchenmaid and spoke some kind words to her in passing.

When evening arrived he sent for her to the reception room and asked her to tell him of the wonders which she had seen. Monseigneur Forcade had been convinced of the genuineness of the Appearances by reading the doctrinal decision of the Bishop of Tarbes, but when he heard Bernadette he became enthusiastic. A moment's silence followed the story of the young seer and the Bishop was clearly considering an idea he had in his mind. He was anxiously wondering what would become of this innocent flower before him when transplanted, unprotected, into the world and its atmosphere of corruption. He gave expression to his thought, and said to Bernadette:

"Yes, my child, you have received great graces from the blessed Virgin; what are you going to do for her in return?"

"Monseigneur, I have never thought of doing anything but what I am doing here, work and pray with the kind sisters."

"But, my dear child, you are only here for the time being and the good sisters cannot keep you with them for ever."

"Not if they take me as their servant?"

"They cannot do it, for the servants of the Order are bound by vows and you are not bound."

Bernadette hung her head.

"Come my child," continued the Bishop, "open your heart to me. Have you never thought of entering the congregation of the good sisters who take care of you?"

"No, Monseigneur, or if I have ever thought of it, it has been to regard it as impossible."

"Why impossible?"

"Because I am too ignorant and because I am penniless."

"It is true," replied the Bishop, "that as a general rule a certain sum of money and a certain amount of education are necessary, but the rule is not inflexible in the case of a real vocation."

"I understand you, Monseigneur, and thank you, but before coming to any decision I must have a long time for reflection."

"God forbid, my child, that I should hurry you into a hasty resolution. All I ask you to do is to examine your conscience carefully as to what the Virgin wants of you. Pray the good Mother to give you light, follow her inspirations, and then if you are really drawn towards the cloister, *i.e.*, to a life of self-sacrifice, write to me, and I on my part will pray God to show me what we ought to do."

The interview ended thus and made no apparent difference in Bernadette's daily life. She went about her work as usual and continued to fulfil her religious duties, no less fervently but certainly no more fervently than before. The sisters had been forbidden to talk to her about her future plans or to influence her determination. But whilst every one imagined that Bernadette would never consent to go far away from the grotto, her conscience was working inwardly and preparing her for the life of self-sacrifice. After a year of meditation and prayer Bernadette asked to see the Mother Superior alone.

"Mother," said she gravely, "I have reflected for long before God and the blessed Virgin on the words which were spoken to me as you doubtless remember by the Bishop of Nevers. I have formed my decision to-day, and if it be possible and I am not unworthy, I beg you to write to Monseigneur to say that I desire to live and die a sister of your Order."

"Blessed be this day," cried the Superior embracing Bernadette with tears in her eyes. "I have for a long time been praying secretly with you and awaiting this happy hour. Yes, my dear Bernadette, we shall be only too happy to receive you in our midst, for are you not already our dearly loved child?"

A few days later Monseigneur Forcade informed the Superior of the Hospice that the doors of the noviciate of the mother house of St. Gildard, at Nevers, were open to the Virgin's protégée, and that he authorised two of the Lourdes sisters to accompany the postulant on her journey.

But the Immaculate Virgin seemed to will that Bernadette should yet continue to be her apostle at the grotto, or at least she seemed to wish to prove that the girl was entering the convent without any external constraint or compulsion. For the young aspirant was attacked by a succession of illnesses which kept her at Lourdes until the summer of 1866. During this period of waiting and when her health allowed she joined with much fervour in the devotions of the community and began to prepare for the religious life.

At length the moment arrived when Bernadette had to tear herself away from her family, the grotto and the good sisters who had brought her up, and bitter and terrible was the separation.

On the eve of her departure she went to her beloved Massabieille Grotto, accompanied by two or three sisters from the Hospice. At the sight of the holy place her whole body was convulsed with emotion. She broke out into sobs and burst into a flood of tears. She bowed her face down to the earth and at the same moment the cry of anguish fell from her lips :

" My Mother, my Mother, oh ! how can I leave you ! "

She tried to pray but the poor child was utterly prostrate and her rosary hung limply from her powerless hands. She drew near to the rock above which was the sacred recess which had received the Appearance, and time after time she pressed her lips to it, as though she wished to leave there the imprint of her soul. She returned and knelt outside the grotto and gazed with a look of burning love upon the spot where she had seen the Queen of Heaven. But alas ! that beloved face which had formerly made the child glad with her smiles was no longer there, and Bernadette broke again into fresh torrents of tears.

The sisters thought it wise to take her away and put an end to this distressing scene. They came up to her gently and told her that it was time to go.

" Oh, let me stay," she said beseechingly, " it is for the last time. I beg of you, dear sisters, allow me a moment longer."

The delay was allowed and again allowed, but at last the sisters took Bernadette affectionately by the arm and led her away. The young girl, bathed in tears, tore herself away at last from that beloved spot which she was never to see again ; then with heroic resolution she dried her eyes, cast one last look upon the grotto, and walked quickly away towards the town. When she was once more calm the sisters said to her :

" But Bernadette, why were you so distressed ? Don't you know that the Virgin is everywhere and that everywhere and always she will be your Mother ? "

"Yes, I know that," she replied, "but at Lourdes, dear sisters, the grotto was my heaven."

The next day, early, Bernadette went to say good-bye to all her family. On entering the house she fell into her mother's arms and fainted. After she had recovered consciousness she remained seated on her mother's knees and gazed lovingly upon all the members of her family, who each in turn came and kissed her, weeping. Suddenly the sound of carriage wheels was heard outside the door. As though moved by a spring, Bernadette jumped up, tore herself from her parent's arms and disappeared hastily, saying several times: "Good-bye, good-bye."

She stopped for an instant outside the Hospice where her weeping benefactresses awaited her to give her their last embraces. Two of the sisters got in with her and then the carriage drove off. Bernadette was never to see Lourdes again upon earth.

CHAPTER XII.

BERNADETTE AFTER THE APPEARANCES (*continued*).

III. BERNADETTE AT THE CONVENT AT NEVERS. HER LIFE AS A RELIGIOUS. HER DEATH.

THE Mother and sisters of the convent at Nevers awaited Bernadette with much the same emotions with which they would have awaited the arrival of an angel in their house. They rejoiced in the thought that they were soon to have for their friend and companion her who had been honoured with the vision of the Mother of God and who had held converse with the Queen of Heaven. What wonderful stories they were to hear! Surely, in telling them of the Appearances, the seer would reveal to them the splendours of eternity! The convent at Nevers then was filled with joy, and sister proposed to vie with sister in welcoming Bernadette, when a scruple or rather a fear arose in the Superior's breast. She wondered whether the attentions paid to the young postulant might not injure her spiritually and intoxicate her with pride. She communicated her anxieties to the older sisters to whom she turned for counsel, and they sharing the Mother's views agreed unanimously that it would be wiser to treat Bernadette as an ordinary postulant.

The day after they had come to this decision the two sisters from Lourdes, who had accompanied Bernadette, knocked at the Mother's door and announced to her the young postulant's arrival. Great was the Mother's emotion and to recover her calm she sent away the two sisters and fell on her knees before her crucifix. So she remained for some time; then when at length her self-control had returned she went down to the parlour where Bernadette was waiting, alone and heavy-hearted. She gave an uninterested look at the young girl and began to question her as if she had never heard of her.

"Are you the postulant from Lourdes?"

"Yes, Mother Superior."

"What is your name?"

"Bernadette Soubirous."

"What can you do?"

"Nothing very much, Mother Superior."

"But, my child, what are we to do with you then?"

Bernadette did not reply.

"Who is it who has recommended you to us?"

"The Bishop of Nevers."

"Ah, that holy man has sent us many others. Come, my child, I will take you to the refectory where you will have supper with the Lourdes sisters; then to-morrow morning, if you are not too tired, you will go to the kitchen and help the lay sister to wash up."

The Mother assigned this menial office to Bernadette for the purpose of testing her humility. But Bernadette stood in no need of such a test. At the convent she had never stopped to think what duty might best suit her; she always went to the task assigned her as cheerfully and readily as if she had been left free to choose it.

Upon her entry on the noviciate Bernadette received the name of Sister Marie Bernard, and the name so happily chosen combined in itself the names of the Virgin who had appeared to her and that of the happy seer.

Sister Marie Bernard, already familiar with convent life, had no difficulty in submitting to the requirements of the rule. Hers was a gentle, persevering piety; she showed neither the excessive ardour so common with novices nor the reaction of lassitude and discouragement which follows the excess. Always simple and unpretentious, she attracted the sympathy of every one, and the Nevers like the Lourdes sisters became attached to the young novice, not merely because of the extraordinary favours she had received, but still more because of her natural charm.

The air of Nevers seemed to have a beneficial effect upon Bernadette. During the first few months of her stay there she recovered strength and looked really well. But alas! this state of things and the hopes which it inspired did not last long.

One evening after leaving the refectory the poor child vomited blood to such an extent that every one there gave her up. The doctor of the house, hastily sent for, said at once that there was no hope. He tried various remedies, but with no result. The Mother Superior in anguish and grief sent to inform Monseigneur Forcade of Bernadette's alarming state. In spite of the late hour of the night the Bishop crossed the town on foot and hastened to the sick girl. He could not give her the Viaticum, for the excessive vomiting continued, so he administered to her the sacraments of the dying. After praying for a long time, and giving her one last blessing, thinking that all was finished, he left her bedside with tears in his eyes.

Whilst he was going down the stairs the Mother Superior who accompanied him expressed her keen regret at seeing Bernadette die before receiving the veil and being professed.

"Well, but what is there to prevent it?" replied the prelate quickly. "Yes, I will certainly grant this last privilege to the Virgin's protégée."

The Bishop returned to the bedside of the sick girl.

"Sister Marie Bernard," he whispered in her ear, "the Virgin of Lourdes is not yet satisfied; she wishes to see you arrive in heaven wearing the uniform of your profession. Gather up all the forces of your soul and prepare to make your vows. If you understand me, make me a sign to that effect."

Bernadette instantly cast up to heaven a look of gratitude. The Bishop immediately recited the customary prayers; then he solemnly invited the novice to answer, or better still to give her heartfelt adhesion to the undertakings to be pronounced in her name. The sick girl, unable to speak, nodded her head.

After the ceremony she fell into a comatose state which appeared to announce the last agony. But her hour was not yet come. Whilst the sisters of the house were grouped around her bed to receive the last sigh of their beloved companion, the latter was in a peaceful and restorative sleep and soon her breathing became freer and more regular. After some hours of rest Sister Marie Bernard awoke smiling and began to speak. Nourishment was given her immediately and at the end of two or three days Bernadette was completely convalescent.

But alas ! like all those sealed with the seal of the elect, the poor child only escaped one trouble to fall into another. The words of the Virgin to her : "I do not promise to make you happy in this life, but in the other," were to be completely fulfilled. She had scarcely recovered from the attack which threatened her life when she received news which pierced her inmost soul.

Without any preparation, she heard suddenly of her mother's death. She fell to the ground and remained in a faint for some length of time. A few months ago she had left her mother at Lourdes still young and in perfect health, and at their farewell she had promised to come and see her either at Nevers or at any other convent where she might be. Many tears did the young sister shed secretly in her cell, but tears are compatible with resignation, for Bernadette, in spite of her natural grief, was a worthy child and follower of her who suffered at Calvary. She often repeated :

"My God, You have willed it, I accept the cup You have given me. Your Holy Name be blessed."

Her illness and terrible trouble, the one coming after the other, threw Sister Marie Bernard into a state of chronic weakness. For some time she was dispensed from all rule and put under a special régime of medical care and treatment.

When she recovered her strength she had, notwithstanding her having been professed *in extremis*, to re-enter the noviciate in order to complete her religious formation. She prepared for the final giving-up of herself with a pious self-abnegation in which there was joy rather than any sense of sacrifice. At length, after much meditation and prayer, Bernadette renewed her vows in the presence of Monseigneur Forcade in the church of the Mother House of St. Gildard, at Nevers, on the 30th October, 1867.

A few days after her profession Sister Marie Bernard was transferred from the kitchen to the hospital belonging to the convent. Without having ever spoken of her wish to any one she had always secretly longed to nurse the sick. Who better than those who suffer themselves can sympathise with the pains of others? The young professed sister had now all that she wished for, but the poor child's strength was not equal to her devotion and she soon succumbed under the weight of her task. The doctor of the house remarked to the Superior that Bernadette would be more in her place in the sick bed itself than in doing the work of a nurse. The Superior understood and immediately relieved Sister Marie Bernard of her duty, entrusting to her the care of the community chapel.

Sister Marie Bernard revealed unexpected capacities in the discharge of her new office. She showed at once exquisite taste in the decoration of the altars and she soon became very clever with her needle. Some of her embroidery is still preserved in memory of her, and in delicacy of idea and skill of execution it is equal to the most perfect work of the kind.

The humble modest sister passed the greater part of her life within the shelter of the sanctuary. There, absorbed in meditation, she worked from morning till evening under the eye of God and of His Holy Mother. No shadows obscured her faith, and she felt herself taken up into the life of the Holy Family.

Whilst the devout sacristan found her joy and happiness in the decoration of the images of the saints whom she loved, the angels were preparing for her that diadem which she was to wear eternally. Bernadette had already suffered greatly. Now that she was drawing near to the end of her life she found that the various maladies which had existed for so long in germ attacked her in all directions and with great severity; asthma, tumours, rheumatism, spitting of blood, disease of the bone, everything seemed to combine to weaken and destroy her already delicate constitution. The poor child was often completely worn out and sometimes, in offering her sufferings to the God of the tabernacle, she would fall helpless upon the sanctuary steps. She was very much ashamed of these fainting fits, and said to the sisters who nursed her: "It's very silly of me, dear sisters, to give way so easily and I am sure you must be shocked at me."

The cup seemed to be full, and yet the patient sufferer was still far from the end of her troubles. One day when she was ill in bed a letter bearing a black seal was given her. She was at once seized by a presentiment of misfortune and her instinct was a true one. The sick girl opened the letter with a trembling hand and read there that her father, just fifty-five years of age, had died at Lourdes on the 4th March, 1871, after an illness borne with Christian fortitude.* Bernadette was once more plunged into the deepest grief. She thought she had exhausted the fountain of her tears at her mother's death but she wept afresh for the loss of her beloved father.

Sister Marie Bernard's body was bruised and crushed under the weight of physical suffering, her heart was torn by the violence of grief, only her soul remained calm and strong. And God was now going to try that with one final terrible trial.

Sister Marie Bernard had up to that time enjoyed perfect peace and certainty with regard to the subject of her salvation. During the latter years of her life she was assailed by moral and spiritual terrors a thousand times more poignant than her physical sufferings. She accused herself of imaginary faults and thought herself to be a great sinner. The innocent girl only spoke of the Appearances to say how unworthy she had been of them, and that by her want of gratitude she had deserved

"It was the thirteenth anniversary of the last day of the fortnight of Appearances. *Annales de Notre Dame de Lourdes* narrate a very touching story about this man.
* One day when he was alone in the parlour of the missioner's house he knelt down before the picture representing his daughter and began to pray fervently The missioner, who came in and interrupted his prayer, was very much touched.'

the reprobation of the Virgin of the grotto. God allowed this torture to continue until the moment when He prepared to crown His beloved child.

My readers will I think be grateful to me if I take from the *Annales de Notre Dame de Lourdes* the touching story which gives in detail the circumstances of Sister Marie Bernard's death.

* * * * *

"Bernadette has just fallen asleep in Jesus; her mission was accomplished and her soul ready for heaven. The child so innocent and simple, the religious so strictly faithful to her vows and so scrupulously careful of her rule, the gentle victim who bore the imprint of the cross upon her all her life through, Sister Marie Bernard, has gone to receive the happiness promised her by the Immaculate Virgin.

"Nobly did she fulfil the mission entrusted to her by the Mother of God. For more than eight years did she bear witness before crowds, narrating with evangelic simplicity what she had seen and heard, submitting to the inquiries of the curious and to the tortures of an inquisition sometimes hostile or treacherous, never contradicting herself and often in the end convincing even the most obstinately prejudiced opponents.

"At last she found silence and peace in the convent of Saint Gildard at Nevers. After more than twelve years of a perfect religious life, on the 22nd September 1878, she took the final vows and thus buried herself for ever in the heart of her crucified Spouse. The humble Virgin was ready for the Lamb's marriage feast.

"A few days after her final solemn consecration, Sister Marie Bernard was seized by her last illness and on the 11th December 1878, in the octave of the Immaculate Conception, she returned to her usual place in the infirmary, there to remain until the end.

"The next day and the day after, the 12th and 13th, God asked her to bear one last solemn witness to the wonders which the Immaculate Virgin had revealed to her at the grotto. Sister Marie Bernard made this final deposition before the representatives of the Bishops of Tarbes and of Nevers and in the presence of the Superior-General of the congregation of Nevers and her council. She showed on this occasion very great joy which was not usually the case ; she willingly answered a long string of questions ; she repeated once more in the quaint language of the Pyrenees the words which fell from the lips of Mary. More than twenty years after the events, in the presence of death and eternity, the religious confirmed all that she had already said as a child ; she was the ever faithful echo of the Mother of the Divine Word.

LAST ILLNESS.

" Bernadette was now free to die and she was already wasting away fast. The asthma which had poisoned her whole life tormented her in more frequent attacks, her breathing became weaker and more laboured, an enormous tumour had developed in her right knee and made it absolutely immovable and her bones were being eaten away by disease. The sick girl could no longer leave her bed and couch and she was soon lying on the open wounds which covered her fragile body ; like her Divine Spouse, the religious was on the cross.

" The severity of the pain drew from her cries which she could not restrain but she changed them at once into ardent prayer. She repeated with energy, 'My God, I offer myself to Thee. . . My God, I love Thee. . . Yes, my God, I desire it, I desire Thy cross.'

" The cross had also touched her soul. The evil one tortured her with those awful agonies of conscience which give here on earth an idea of hell to those generous souls who have offered themselves as victims for the sins of the world. Bernadette had not forgotten one of the great commands of the grotto, prayer and penitence for sinners. When her director strengthened her with the thought of heaven and with the memory of the divine beauty of that holy Virgin whom she had contemplated at the grotto, she replied : 'Yes, that thought helps me.'

" Thus did the cross break the bonds which attached Bernadette to life. When they spoke to her of making this last sacrifice she would say : 'There is no sacrifice in leaving a poor life in which I have found it so difficult to belong entirely to God.'

"As her body grew weaker her soul gathered fresh strength. Her whole life seemed to be centred in her large eyes which became more and more clear and radiant. They were lighted up with heavenly fire when she looked at the heavens, the crucifix or the statue of our Lady.

"The community chaplain, Abbé Fébvre, thinks that she had a presentiment of the near approach of death.

"'What have you asked of St. Joseph?' said he to Sister Marie Bernard after the festival of the 19th March. And the sister replied with fervour, 'I have asked for the grace of a good death.'

"It seemed that she was about to be heard. On 28th March her confessor brought her the sacraments of the dying. Before giving her the Viaticum the priest spoke a few words to her. Sister Marie Bernard replied in a voice so strong that all present were amazed.

"'My dear mother,' she said, 'I ask you to forgive me for all the sorrow I have caused you by my want of faithfulness in the religious life. I also ask my sisters to forgive me for the bad example I have set them.'

"Death did not yet come and in the rare moments of respite which her suffering allowed her, her sweet and simple nature showed something of a childlike joy. Even in speaking of her death she was bright and happy as in her earlier days. But the cruel malady soon resumed its terrible work of destruction. Bernadette's physical and moral sufferings increased, especially during the holy week of her Lord's agony. The Saviour wished to associate His courageous spouse with Him in the awful mystery of His passion.

"'What will you do at Easter?' some one asked the sufferer, and she replied, 'My passion will last until my death.'

DEATH.

"Easter arrived with all the joy of the resurrection. It found Sister Marie Bernard still on Calvary or in Gethsemane.

"Easter Tuesday was the day of her spiritual agony. The

evil one tormented her fiercely, even as he tormented Jesus Christ and His Saints. During the night of Monday she was heard to say several times: 'Depart from me, Satan.' In the morning she told her director that the demon had frightened her terribly by trying to throw himself upon her, but that she had pronounced the name of Jesus and all had become calm.

"The Christian athlete fortified herself on Tuesday morning by receiving the Viaticum and soon the fight began again. In the evening Sister Nathalie, in whom Sister Marie Bernard had great religious and spiritual confidence, was with her.

"'Dear sister, I am afraid, I am afraid!' cried the poor dying girl.

"Sister Nathalie tried to calm her.

"'Oh!' she replied, 'I have received so many favours and I am afraid because I have made so little use of them.'

"Sister Nathalie reminded her of the infinite mercy of Jesus. 'The loving Saviour,' she said, 'is rich enough to pay all your debts and we too are trying to help you with our prayers.'

"Sister Marie Bernard said, as though uttering a cry of joy: 'Now I am at peace.'

"This peace lasted to the end.

"On Wednesday, the 16th April, Sister Marie Bernard was lying on a couch, praying and waiting for death. At one o'clock in the afternoon she sent for her confessor; she wished to cleanse her soul once more in the sacrament of penance.

"'Are you suffering much?' said one of the sisters to her.

"'All my suffering is to prepare me for heaven,' answered Sister Marie Bernard.

"'I will ask our Immaculate Mother to console you.'

"'No,' replied the sufferer, 'not to console me, but to give me strength and patience.'

"She then thought of the special blessing which Pius IX. had granted her beforehand for the hour of her death. She wished to hold in her hand the papal document itself and to gain the plenary indulgence she pronounced piously the name of Jesus. A moment after she said: 'My God, I love Thee with all my heart, with all my soul and with all my strength.'

"The prayers for the dying were said. In a feeble but distinct voice she repeated the various acts after the priest. All those present noticed with emotion that her large eyes opened widely from time to time and that she cast a keen and ardent glance upon the crucifix fastened to the wall. It was placed in her failing hands. The priest reminded her of that passage in the Song of Songs where the divine Spouse invites the faithful soul to place Him, the Spouse, as a seal upon her heart. The dying sister seized the crucifix with some force and turned it quickly upon her heart, as though she wished to drive it in there. They fastened the crucifix upon her breast so that she might be able to kiss it and press it against her heart. She stretched out her arms in the form of a cross, murmuring, 'Oh, I love Him.'

"It was two o'clock; death was slow in coming. The dying sister thought it was still far distant, so she sent away the priest who left to hear confessions while the sisters departed to say the litanies of the Blessed Sacrament. Sister Marie Bernard continued to pray with some companions.

"At a quarter to three Sister Nathalie, who had just made her confession, felt herself inwardly impelled to go up to the infirmary. Putting off to another moment her thanksgiving, she hastened to the dying sister. When she entered the latter stretched out her arms to her, saying: 'Help me, help me, pray for me.' Twice, holding out her hands in supplication, she made the same request to her. The sister's prayers somewhat restored her strength. The dying woman asked Sister Nathalie to forgive her for any sorrow she might have caused her. She was indeed the Spouse of Jesus, meek and lowly of heart.

"She sought once again for strength in Jesus crucified. Taking her crucifix affectionately she slowly kissed each of the Saviour's five wounds. Then she made a sign that she wished to drink, and holding the cup herself in her failing hands she drank twice several drops. Before putting the cup to her lips Bernadette made one of those slow and solemn signs of the cross which she had learnt from the Mother of the Saviour. This sign of the cross, so characteristic of her, deeply affected the witnesses of her last agony, even as it had formerly impressed the witnesses of her ecstasies.

"The end drew near. Bernadette was in peace. The sisters

continued reciting other prayers and the dying woman joined them in heart, and even united with theirs her feeble voice. Twice did she murmur the second part of the *Ave Maria* which she had so often and so happily repeated at the grotto. A third time she said: 'Holy Mary, Mother of God,' but she could not finish it. Her sisters seeing that she was dying hastened to say: 'Jesus, Mary, Joseph, help us in our last agony.' Bernadette bowed her head and gave up her soul to God.

"It was three o'clock; the hour when Jesus died upon the cross. It was a Wednesday, the day consecrated to St. Joseph, the holy patron of whom Bernadette had asked a good death. It was Wednesday in Easter week. Twenty-one years ago on that same day Bernadette, in ecstasy at the grotto, had held her candle alight in her hands without feeling anything of the flame which passed across her fingers joined in prayer. After twenty-one years, on Wednesday in Easter week, Bernadette, that gentle pure light which the Immaculate Virgin had set upon the candlestick of the holy Church, vanished from earth but only to shine more brightly among the stars in Paradise.

"On that day the Church sang: 'This is the day which the Lord hath made, let us rejoice and tremble with joy on this glorious day. Alleluia.' The sacred liturgy recalled the splendour of the risen Saviour, and showing after many centuries the members of the mystical body of Jesus risen with their Head, spoke to them the words of the sovereign Judge: 'Come, ye blessed of my Father, possess the kingdom which has been prepared for you.' The gentle Saviour spoke also to His faithful Spouse: 'Come and arise my beloved; the winter of this mortal life has passed away with all its trials and the flowers of the eternal spring brighten with their colour the living earth. You have followed me in the humiliations and sorrows of Calvary; follow me now in the glory and delights of paradise.' The Immaculate Virgin spoke also to her humble servant: 'You have been faithful to your promise, and I will be faithful to mine. You have done me the favour of coming to the grotto during a fortnight and you have honoured me to the very last breath of your life; I also will grant you the favour that I promised you. You have not had earthly happiness; come and receive it in the other world where Jesus awaits you.' "

Sister Marie Bernard's obsequies took place with much pomp at Nevers, the 19th April, three days after her death. Monseigneur Lelong, Monseigneur Forcade's successor, officiated at them, the latter having been transferred to the archiepiscopal diocese of Aix. The dead sister's body was placed in a chapel dedicated to St. Joseph, in the centre of a large garden belonging to the mother house of Saint Gildard.

* * * * *

Many fantastic stories have been published concerning Bernadette's life in the convent of Nevers. Some of these stories related that the blessed Virgin visited her in her cell; others that she had the gift of miracles; others that she uttered prophecies on the occasion of our national defeats in 1870. All this is simple romance. Bernadette, in the convent of St. Gildard, led the life of a religious in all points faithful to her rule; that is all that can be said of her and no higher praise can be bestowed.

At the time that I am writing these lines she has doubtless found once more her who promised her happiness not in this life but in the next. God grant that she may remember her old friend at Lourdes, and obtain for him by her prayers grace that so he may himself see in heaven the IMMACULATE CONCEPTION whom he has never failed to invoke with filial confidence since that forever blessed day when he knelt so near her, under her eye and under her hand, at the Grotto of Massabieille.

APPENDIX.

I borrow from the *Annales de Notre Dame de Lourdes* a noteworthy study which Abbé Richard made in 1879 upon the spring of water in the Grotto. It confirms what I myself have said in Chapters IV. and XVIII.

The Grotto Spring.

Everyone knows Abbé Richard, the famous hydrogeologist who has devoted himself to the study of the laws by which springs and watercourses furrow the earth and make it fruitful. After having explored all the countries of Europe and part of Asia and Africa he spent a week at Lourdes examining the springs of the district. The grotto spring, which he had already observed attentively more than once, was made the object of his complete study and he has kindly communicated to us the following :

"Very Reverend Father,

"During the week that I had the happiness to pass in your house, so near the holy sanctuary of our Lady of Lourdes, in the midst of all the spiritual comforts I enjoyed I managed to make time to study afresh, thoughtfully, under God's eye, and after having asked the blessed Virgin for help, the miraculous spring of the Massabieille grotto. And although I have often answered the question so frequently addressed to me : 'What do I think of the Lourdes spring ?' I am glad to be able to let you know my whole thought as briefly as possible.

I.

"God may have called this spring into being at the time of the Appearances of the Blessed Virgin to Bernadette and especially when our Lady said to her : 'Go and drink at the fountain.'

"There is clearly nothing in this opposed to the Divine

attributes. God, Who created the world in the beginning always retains his creative power. The present question is not *could* God do it, but *did* God do it. We grant as an axiom that God modifies the exercise of His power according to the circumstances of time and place.

"When, *e.g.*, He had to bring the Jewish people, only half enlightened and under an imperfect law, into the midst of the desert where water was completely lacking, it was desirable that He should manifest His power in such a way as to terrify this uncivilised nation. He therefore ordered Moses to strike a rock and a spring gushed forth to the great amazement of the people of Israel. The rock struck by Moses was isolated from the rest of the mountain. It was a block of granite which must have been detached from the summit of Mount Horeb. Under such conditions this rock could not have contained any spring, and Moses understood that so well that he doubted and struck the rock twice. God must have created the spring at that moment to make it gush forth. I saw the rock in 1869, this being the chief object of the visit I undertook then to the Sinaitic desert. I wished to know what kind of miracle God had worked by the hand of Moses, the miracle of a spring created or of a spring discovered. The spring was created for the occasion only; it has ceased to flow and there is no more water.

"Now at Lourdes it is quite different; the circumstances are by no means the same. Lourdes is situated in a country where springs abound. One spring more would not produce here the effect which it would produce in the desert and it seems to me that God wished to touch men, not by the spring, but by the unspeakable charm and goodness of the blessed Virgin.

II.

"But if God did not create the spring entirely may He not have partially created it? When the blessed Virgin told Bernadette to go and drink at the fountain the child made a hole in the sand with her hands, and God may have then summoned from the bowels of the earth a fresh spring to supplement that which already existed. This is the case, I think, at La Salette, where I have also gone to study the miraculous source.

" At La Salette the Appearance of the blessed Virgin to Mélanie and Maximin took place near a spring which dried up every year during the months of July, August and September. Since the Appearance it has never ceased to flow; God has made it permanent; but for all that the mountain has not changed in form and the channel of the spring has remained the same. God supplements the flow of water by a mode of intervention of which He has the secret. It is like the cruse of oil of the widow of Sarepta which never failed.

" Does Lourdes come under this second method of the Divine working? I think not, as I hope to show by a third hypothesis which I have thought over for a long time and will now put before you.

III.

" Before the Appearance the soil of the Grotto of Massabieille was always damp; plants which need humidity grew there. In the lower part of the sandy floor, which was higher at the back of the grotto than at the entrance, there was always a pool. These facts have been and are attested by a large number of witnesses. Now to explain the abundance of water which the spring produces at present, is it necessary to have recourse to a *creation* of water as at Sinai or a miraculous *increase* of the flow of the spring as at La Salette? I do not think so; I prefer to admit that in this case the miracle is of a simpler character. Beneath the damp sand which lay in the grotto at the back, higher than the pool at the entrance, there was a *hidden* spring, reserved by Divine providence to be *discovered* at the moment of the Appearance. Bernadette brought this spring to light by a special and supernatural inspiration, at the express command of the blessed Virgin, who pointed out to her its exact situation with her right hand, saying to her: 'Go and drink at the spring.'

" If I examine the Massabieille rock and the little hill above it, I find them fitted by nature to contain water springs,* so much so indeed that supposing I had never heard of the Appearance nor of the spring and had come by the railway which

* The Massabieille spring is a typical spring illustrating my theory, that is to say I should quote it as one of those most characteristic of my method of discovering water springs.

passes the grotto a few hundred metres away, I should have said: 'There is a water spring there,' just as I say of other localities when I am on ground which contains hidden sources.

"To sum up, the Lourdes spring was created at the same time as the other springs but its outflow remained almost entirely hidden under the sand, as a treasure destined to reveal at the right time the bounty of Divine grace. Bernadette was the instrument of which God made use in the discovery of this spring and the miracle consists in the fact of the *discovery*, while at La Salette it consists in *ceaseless flow* of a spring which formerly dried up, and at Sinai it consisted in the *creation* of the spring which gushed forth from the rock. We take the facts just as they are in strict truth, we explain them and show the essentially supernatural character which they bear.

"And has there not been at Lourdes a series of events which prove incontestably the Divine intervention? May we not well repeat: 'What place was ever so fertile in miracles?' Cures of all sorts, the most unexpected conversions, a combination of marvels both corporal and spiritual, make Lourdes a halting-place midway between earth and heaven. God seems to say to men by all these wonders: 'You did not know what you were rejecting when you rejected heaven. Go to Lourdes and drink of the spring and when you have tasted of that water drink yet more deeply of the waters of My mercy and My grace which I there bestow so generously and you will return better.'

"I beg you to accept, very reverend Father, my thanks for your kind welcome and the expression of my deepest respect.

"ABBÉ RICHARD,
Hydrogeologist.

"Seminary of Montlieu (Charente Inf.), April, 1879."